151

9-

THE PREHISTORY OF SCOTLAND

PLATE I

CHAMFREIN, TORRS
National Museum

THE PREHISTORY
OF SCOTLAND

BY

V. GORDON CHILDE

*B.Litt., Professor of Prehistoric Archæology in
Edinburgh University, Author of The Aryans,
The Dawn of European Civilization, etc.*

LONDON

KEGAN PAUL, TRENCH, TRUBNER & CO., LTD.

BROADWAY HOUSE: 68–74 CARTER LANE, E.C.

1935

PRINTED IN GREAT BRITAIN BY
STEPHEN AUSTIN AND SONS, LTD., AT HERTFORD.

CONTENTS

CONTENTS

LIST OF TEXT FIGURES

vii

LIST OF PLATES

MAPS

PREFACE

BY her geographical position at the junction of the sea-ways along the Atlantic coasts with routes crossing the North Sea and the Channel, Scotland should be able to afford data for the solution of several most fascinating problems in British, and indeed in European, prehistory. And in fact, Scottish prehistory has found exponents who, approaching the subject with an international outlook, played a leading part in the development of the science in Europe; the works of Geikie, Munro, Abercromby, and Bryce, have exercised a guiding influence all over the world.

Moreover by 1886 Dr. Joseph Anderson had sketched the essential outlines of Scottish prehistory in a comprehensive and scientific survey such as then existed in no other country. Since his day antiquaries, field workers, and museum officials have been continually augmenting the number of relics and monuments recorded and revealing new varieties among them. But the very rapidity with which facts have accumulated has prevented the publication of a critical review of the data in their totality and in relation to the new results and fresh ideas of English and Continental prehistorians. Nor have intensive field-surveys, inspired by recent ideas, been undertaken, save in the counties explored by the Royal Commission on Ancient and Historical Monuments. No systematic campaign for the excavation of specific types of monument by the latest technical methods has been conducted. Even monographs on the classification and exact distribution of remains, compiled in accordance with contemporary ideas, are still outstanding.

This book, which must appeal to a wider public, cannot take the place of such detailed technical studies which can only appear in learned periodicals. The data it presents are accordingly incomplete, the conclusions it tentatively offers are provisional or even premature. Its aim is to stimulate interest among the mass of the Scottish people, to suggest lines for more intensive and systematic research and to reveal the significance of Scottish prehistory to students abroad. To that end it is essential to attempt a synthesis in the light of the new knowledge and new conceptions that intensive research and international co-operation have established during the last fifteen years. Only so can we present prehistory as a record of living facts of enduring significance, as a scientific discipline instead of a diversion for amateurs or a refuge for cranks.

We have to acknowledge our gratitude to the many colleagues who have so generously facilitated the preparation of this work, notably to Dr. J. Grahame Callander (Director), and Mr. A. J. Edwards (Assistant-Keeper), of the National Museum of Antiquities, to Professor J. C. Brash, Hon. Curator of the Anatomical Museum of the University of Edinburgh, Professor T. H. Bryce, Hon. Curator of the Hunterian Museum, for facilities in studying and permission to reproduce relics in the collections committed to their charge, as well as for advice and criticism, to Mr. W. Lindsay Scott for the information as to his latest results and photographs of his finds, to Mr. J. Reid, of Inverurie, for permission to illustrate the bronze dagger in his collection, to the Society of Antiquaries of Scotland for permission to reproduce, and to purchase electrotypes of, figures from their *Proceedings*, and from Dr. Anderson's *Scotland in Pagan Times* (Figs. 1, 4, 5, 6, 8, 10, 11, 16, 21, 23, 25, 26, 27, 28, 33, 34, 36, 41, 43, 44, 45, 47, 49, 54, 62, 65, 68, 75, 77, 80, 81, 82, 83), to the Society of Antiquaries of London for Fig. 67, and to the Royal Archæological Institute for Figs. 12 and 14. The material for the distribution Maps and Tables has in part been collected by Dr. M. E. Crichton Mitchell and Mr. W. Henderson, who have kindly allowed us to use in advance material which they will publish in detail in due course. Dr. Mitchell has also very kindly read the proofs.

V. Gordon Childe.

University of Edinburgh.
  October, 1934.

ABBREVIATIONS: TITLES OF PERIODICALS, ETC.

Aarbøger	. . .	Aarbøger for Nordisk Oldkyndighed og Historie, Copenhagen.
ACAG.	. . .	Archæological Collections of Ayrshire and Galloway, Edinburgh.
Amer. Anthr.	. .	American Anthropologist.
Antiquity	. .	Antiquity, Southampton.
Ant. J.	. .	Antiquaries' Journal, London.
Arch.	. .	Archæologia, London.
Arch. Camb.	. .	Archæologia Cambrensis, Cardiff.
Arch. J.	. .	Archæological Journal, London.
Arch. Scot.	. .	Archæologia Scotica, Edinburgh.
Biometrika .	. .	Biometrika, London.
BM.: Stone	. .	British Museum : Guide to Stone Age Antiquities, 1926.
Bronze	. .	Guide to Bronze Age Antiquities, 1920.
Iron	. .	Guide to Iron Age Antiquities, 1925.
Book of Arran	. .	The Book of Arran (edited by Balfour), Glasgow, 1910.
CPPS.	. .	Proceedings of the First International Congress of Prehistoric and Proto-historic Sciences, London, 1932.
ESA.	. .	Eurasia Septentrionalis Antiqua, Helsingfors.
GFF.	. .	Geologiska Föreningens Forhandlingar, Stockholm.
HBNC.	. .	History of the Berwickshire Naturalists' Club, Edinburgh.
JRAI.	. .	Journal of the Royal Anthropological Institute, London.
LAAA.	. .	Annals of Archæology and Anthropology, Liverpool.
Man	. .	Man, London.
Mat.	. .	Matériaux pour l'histoire primitive de l'homme, Paris.
Mem. Geo . Surv. .		Memoirs of the Geological Survey of Scotland.
MSAN.	. .	Mémoires de la Société des Antiquaires du Nord, Copenhagen.
Oudh. Med.	. .	Oudheidkundige Mededeelingen uit's Rijksmuseum van Oudheden te Leiden (New Series).
Oldtiden	. .	Oldtiden, Oslo.
PAASUA.	. .	Proceedings of the Anatomical and Anthropological Society of the University of Aberdeen.
PBSR.	. .	Papers of the British School at Rome.
POAS.	. .	Proceedings of the Orkney Antiquarian Society, Kirkwall.
PRAI.	. .	Proceedings of the Royal Irish Academy, Dublin.
PRSE.	. .	Proceedings of the Royal Society of Edinburgh.
PSAS.	. .	Proceedings of the Society of Antiquaries of Scotland, Edinburgh.
PSEA.	. .	Proceedings of the Prehistoric Society of East Anglia, Ipswich.
Préhistoire	. .	Préhistoire, Paris.
Proc. Soc. Ant.	. .	Proceedings of the Society of Antiquaries, London.
PZ.	. . .	Praehistorische Zeitschrift, Berlin.
RC.	. . .	Royal Commission on the Ancient and Historical Monuments of Scotland; Inventory of Monuments in the County of—

     Caithness, 1911,
     Sutherland, 1912,
     Berwick., 1915,
     Wigtown., 1912,
     Kirkcudbright., 1914,
     Dumfries., 1920,
     East Lothian, 1924,
     Mid-Lothian and West Lothian, 1929,
     Fife, Kinross, and Clackmannan, 1933,
     Skye, the Outer Hebrides, and the Small Isles, 1931,
   Edinburgh.

Real. . . . *Reallexikon der Vorgeschichte* (edited by Ebert), Berlin, 1924–9.
Rev. arch. . . . *Revue archéologique*, Paris.
Rev. celt. . . . *Revue celtique*, Paris.
SGS. . . . *Scottish Gaelic Studies*, Aberdeen.
SGM. . . . *Scottish Geographical Magazine*, Edinburgh.
TBNHS. . . . *Transactions of the Buteshire Natural History Society*, Rothesay.
TDGAS. . . . *Transactions of the Dumfries and Galloway Antiquarian and Natural History Society*, Dumfries.
TGAS. . . . *Transactions of the Glasgow Antiquarian Society.*
TRSE. . . . *Transactions of the Royal Society of Edinburgh.*
WAM. . . . *Wiltshire Archæological Magazine*, Devizes.

AUTHORS

ABERCROMBY, J. . *The Bronze Age Pottery of Great Britain and Ireland*, Oxford, 1912.
ANDERSON, JOSEPH . *Scotland in Pagan Times*—(i) *The Early Iron Age*, (ii) *The Bronze and Stone Ages*, Edinburgh, 1883, 1886.
ARMSTRONG, E. C. R. . *Catalogue of Irish Gold Ornaments in the Collection of the Royal Irish Academy*, Dublin, 1920.
BEVERIDGE, ERSKINE . *Coll and Tiree*, Edinburgh, 1903.
North Uist, Edinburgh, 1911.
BOSCH-GIMPERA, P. . *Etnologia de la Península Ibérica*, Barcelona, 1932.
BRØGGER, A. W. . *Ancient Emigrants*, Oxford, 1925.
Den norske Bosetningen på Shetland-Orknøyene, Oslo, 1930.
BULLEID and GRAY . *The Glastonbury Lake Village*, London, 1911–17.
CASTILLO, A. DEL . *La Cultura del Vaso campaniforme*, Barcelona, 1927.
CHILDE, V. G. . *The Aryans*, London, 1925.
The Bronze Age, Cambridge, 1930.
The Danube in Prehistory, Oxford, 1929.
The Dawn of European Civilization, London, 1924.
New Light on the Most Ancient East, London, 1934.
Skara Brae, London, 1931.
CLARK, J. G. D. . *The Mesolithic Age in Britain*, Cambridge, 1932.
CHRISTISON . *Early Fortification n Scotland*, Edinburgh, 1898.
COFFEY . *New Grange*, Dublin, 1912.
CORREIA, V. . " El Neolítico del Pavia " (Comisión de Investigaciones paleontólogicas y prehistóricas, *Memoria* 27), Madrid, 1921.
CUNNINGTON, E. M. . *An Early Iron Age inhabited Site at All Cannings Cross*, Devizes, 1923.
CURLE, A. O. . " Prehistoric Monuments of Scotland," Rhind Lectures, 1918 (unpublished manuscript).
CURLE, JAMES . *A Roman Frontier Post and its People*, Glasgow, 1911.
DECHELETTE, J. . *Manuel d'archéologie, préhistorique, celtique et gallo-romaine*, Paris, 1908–1914.
ELGEE, F. . *The Archæology of Yorkshire*, London, 1933.
Early Man in North-East Yorkshire, Gloucester, 1930.
ESTACIO DA VEIGA . *Antiguidades monumentaes do Algarve*, Lisbon, 1886–91.
FOX, CYRIL . *The Archæology of the Cambridge Region*, Cambridge, 1923.
The Personality of Britain, Cardiff, 1932.
GEIKIE, J. . *The Antiquity of Man in Europe*, Edinburgh, 1914.
The Great Ice Age, London, 1894.
VAN GIFFEN, A. E. . *Die Bauart der Einzelgräber* (Mannus-Bibliothek, 44), Leipzig, 1930.
HENCKEN, H. O. . *The Archæology of Cornwall and Scilly*, London, 1932.
HUBERT, H. . *The Rise of the Celts*, London, 1934.
KENDRICK and HAWKES *Archæology in England and Wales*, 1914–1931, London, 1932.
LEEDS, E. T. . *Celtic Ornament*, Oxford, 1933.

MACALISTER, R. A. S. . . *Ireland n pre-Celtic Times,* Dublin, 1921.
MACLEAN, J. P. . . *History of Mull,* Ohio, 1922.
MAHR, ADOLF . . "Archæology" in *Irish Free State Official Handbook,* Dublin, 1932 (chap. xxiii, separately paginated).
MONTELIUS, O. . . *Minnen från vår Forntid,* Stockholm, 1917.
MULLER, SOPHUS . *Ordning af Danemarkes Oldsager,* Copenhagen, 1888.
MUNRO, R. . *Ancient Scottish Lake-Dwellings,* Edinburgh, 1882. *Prehistoric Scotland,* London, 1899.
MORTIMER, J. R. . *Forty Years' Researches in Burial Mounds of East Yorkshire,* London, n.d.
OGILVIE, ALAN . *Great Britain : Essays in Regional Geography,* Cambridge, 1928.
PEAKE, H. J. E. . . *The Bronze Age and the Celtic World,* London, 1922.
PERICOT Y GARCIA . *La Civilización megalitica catalana,* Barcelona, 1925.
POKORNY, J. . *A History of Ireland,* Dublin, 1933.
REID, R. W. . Illustrated Catalogue of the Anthropological Museum, Marischal College, University of Aberdeen, 1912. Illustrated Catalogue of Specimens from Prehistoric Interments in the North-East of Scotland, Anthropological Museum, Marischal College, University of Aberdeen, 1924.
RITCHIE, J. . *Animal Life in Scotland,* Cambridge, 1920.
ROSENBERG . *Kulturströmungen in Europa zur Steinzeit,* Copenhagen, 1931.
SCHAEFFER, F. A. . *Les Tertres funéraires préhistoriques dans la Forêt de Haguenau,* Haguenau, 1926, 1929.
SMITH, J. . . *Prehistoric Man in Ayrshire,* London, 1895.
SMITH, ANGUS . *Loch Etive and the Sons of Uisnach,* London, 1885.
WATSON, W. J. . . *History of the Celtic Place-names of Scotland,* Edinburgh, 1926.

MUSEUMS

EDINBURGH . . National Museum of Antiquities (the principal collection for the whole of Scotland). Anatomical Museum of the University.
ABERDEEN . . Anthropological Museum, Marischal College (large collection from North-east Scotland).
CAMPBELTOWN . . Relics from Beacharra and other sites in Kintyre.
DUMFRIES . . . Urnfield, bronzes.
DUNROBBIN CASTLE . Private museum, important collection from Sutherland.
DUNDEE . . . City Museum.
ELGIN . . Local antiquities, some grave-groups.
FORT WILLIAM . Highland Museum (little prehistoric).
GLASGOW . . Hunterian Museum, University (large collection). City Museum and Art Gallery.
HAWICK . . .
INVERURIE . . Private collection of J. Reid, Esq.
KILMARNOCK . . Dick Museum (relics from Lochlee, etc.).
KIRKCUDBRIGHT . . Harpoon from Cree.
KIRKWALL . . Relics from cist-graves.
LANARK . . Relics from Hyndford Crannog.
PERTH . . Stone and bronze implements.
PETERHEAD . . Arbuthnot Museum
ROTHESAY . . . Relics from Dunagoil, etc.
ST. ANDREWS . . University Museum (two urnfields, scabbard).
STIRLING . . . Bronze and stone implements.

THE PREHISTORY OF SCOTLAND

I

THE PERSONALITY OF SCOTLAND

SCOTLAND is the 29,000 square miles of British soil that lies north of the Cheviots. She is essentially a part of Britain, and the prehistoric cultures to be described in this volume bear an insular, British stamp. Yet it must be insisted at the outset that Scotland is not an arbitrary political division but possesses, to use Dr. Fox's [1] happy term, a personality of her own. Though most of the cultural developments to be traced here find their closest analogies south of the Border and can best be defined in the terms current among English prehistorians, results, well grounded in Southern England, can be applied to Scotland only with reservations. The latter are largely conditioned by the geographical idiosyncrasies of the region, and these must accordingly be outlined here.

The general geographical features of Scotland will indeed be familiar to most readers. If they are not, they can easily be grasped by a study of a bathyorographical map. That will at once show that Scotland is divided—not very effectively—from the rest of Britain by the ridge of the Cheviots running north-east to south-west. Comparable physiographical features divide Scotland herself quite as effectively into well-marked regions.[2] A dissected plateau or series of ranges—the Southern Uplands—rising at points to well over 2,500 feet above sea-level, runs from the North Sea coast above Berwick to Galloway. South of the Uplands lie two Lowland plains—the Merse of the Lower Tweed and the coastal plain of Galloway, interrupted by frequent inlets and rivers and extending round the head of the Solway Firth. North of the Uplands comes the so-called Midland Valley. Bounded on the south by the abrupt edges of the Lammermuirs, Moorfoots, and Lowther Hills, and on the north by the tremendous Highland scarp, the great trough seems to extend from the coastal plains of Angus and the Lothians to Central Ayrshire. But it is itself partially interrupted not only

---

[1] Fox, *The Personality of Britain*.   [2] Ogilvie, *Great Britain,* pp. 370 ff.

by mountain chains—Sidlaws, Ochils, Pentlands, and Campsie Fells—and the long sea inlets of the Forth and Tay, parallel to its main axis, but also by transverse tracts of moorland which separate the lowland plains of Angus, Perthshire, Fife, and the Lothians from Clydesdale and the latter from the coastal plain of Ayrshire.

The Highlands, including the Islands, obviously constitute an area of their own, although separated into two sections by the Great Glen (now traversed by the Caledonian Canal). The west coast of the Highlands is broken up into islands and peninsulas by the long sea lochs, but the rocky ridges rise steeply from the water's edge leaving no continuous coastal plain but only discrete alluvial deltas or beaches at the heads of bays. On the east of the Highland massif, however, there are extensive coastal plains—the triangle of Aberdeen–Banffshire, around the Moray Firth, Caithness, and the low-lying Orkney Islands. These plains constitute a fourth region—North-east Scotland—divided and yet united by the Moray Firth.

A closer scrutiny of the map will suggest that the foregoing divisions are less complete than appeared at first sight. At either end of the Cheviots are comparatively wide valleys—those of the Till and the Eden—leading from England into the Tweed basin and the plain round the Solway respectively. The Southern Uplands are traversed by several long valleys running north and south. The Whitadder, Leader, and Gala valleys lead up to low cols beyond which lies the Lothian plain. Following the Tweed upstream, through the narrow defile between Galashiels and Peebles, it is again easy to cross from the Upper Tweed valley to the Forth by the Eddlestone and Lyne valleys or to Clydesdale through the famous Biggar Gap. From the Solway one can reach the Clyde valley via Annandale without noticing that one is climbing a hill; Nithsdale and the Ken-Doon valleys provide no less easy passages into Central Ayrshire.

The Highland massif itself is broken up by many deep glens through which one could—on paper—travel from the Crinan district on the west at least to the Tay drainage without having to surmount any high ridge. North of the Great Glen the valleys of the Bran and the Oykell offer equally inviting passages from east to west. It is true that the long sea lochs impose detours so that even now Dunoon or Campbeltown can be reached from Glasgow much more quickly by sea than by land despite the defects of the steamer services, the speed of modern cars and the excellence of the roads. Moreover the valleys are separated by jagged ridges of mountain, running north-east and south-west, which would seem to impede progress north-west —from the Lothians to the Crinan region, for instance. But in reality the high ridges are often interrupted by low saddles that a good car, following a well-planned road, can cross on top gear.

The results of such a scrutiny or of a tour based thereon are, however, thoroughly deceptive if we wish to envisage Scotland as a theatre of prehistoric migrations and settlement. We must obviously think away the fine highways along which we speed from Wooler or Carlisle to Oban in a day. The passes across the Southern Uplands are at many points narrow defiles, and the modern thoroughfares cling perilously to the sides of steep slopes that rise abruptly from torrent beds or marshy flats. And these features are still more accentuated in the Highland glens the walls of which are often frankly precipitous.

But a further effort of the imagination is required. The valleys and sheltered slopes must be reclad with forest ; the bare moors which now pasture sheep must be pictured as covered with dense scrub, interrupted by reedy lochs and quaking morasses. The treeless landscape which catches the eye of the traveller to-day is artificial and comparatively recent.[1] Save in the far north it is the result of man's handiwork accentuated by the animals he has introduced. Rabbits, probably unknown before the Norman Conquest,[2] sheep and goats introduced in prehistoric times have co-operated with the wind and rain in preventing a revival of forest growth on lands once cleared.

The historical progress of deforestation can to some extent be traced from the literary record. Before the use of coal the iron industry consumed enormous quantities of timber. To conserve supplies of oak wood for naval construction Acts were passed under Elizabeth and later prohibiting or restricting the use of English forests for iron-smelting—e.g. in Sussex and Furness. As a result the iron-masters migrated northwards and eventually settled in Scotland, where no such restrictions yet existed. Numerous bloomeries in Dumfries-Galloway, the Midland Valley, and the West Highlands are their monuments,

[1] The evidence is conveniently summarized by Ritchie, *Animal Life in Scotland,* pp. 308–322.
[2] Ritchie, op. cit., p. 248.

and the bareness of the hills, round Loch Fyne for instance, may largely be attributed to their depredations. Other forests were systematically burned or cut down to improve sheep pasture, for the extermination of wolves—still a dangerous pest in the Middle Ages—and as an incident in the pacification of districts after wars and conquests ; Tacitus mentions Agricola's activities in this direction already in A.D. 82.

Bogs too, caught the attention of the Roman strategists. If they are now no longer formidable obstacles to transit, that is only due to extensive drainage operations. Anyone who leaves his car to walk on the moors between Edinburgh and Peebles, or Edinburgh and Glasgow, will find them intersected by a network of drainage ditches. Even so they are unpleasantly boggy.

In its pristine condition, therefore, the land surface of Scotland was diversified by really formidable barriers to communication. The valley passes or defiles must have been blocked by dense forest sheltering wolves and even bears. The moorlands between the Lothians and Clydesdale and between Clydesdale and Ayrshire were unfertile tracts of swamp and forest. From this standpoint, not only are the divisions between the four areas justified, at the same time the possibilities of intercourse assume a new aspect and lead to the recognition of another division cutting across those outlined above. The early chroniclers from Adamnan on were impressed by the Highland massif—Druim Alban, Britanniæ dorsum—which divided the Picts of the north-eastern plains from the Scots of Dal Riada (Argyll).[1] Still earlier this division must have had a wider application. The boggy and forested moorlands between the Forth and the Clyde, the high watershed between the Tweed and the Solway would constitute an extension southward of Adamnan's " Spine of Britain ". The " Midland Valley " would be only a unit for physiographers, while historically it would have been effectually divided transversely. In the earlier phases of prehistory we shall find few indications of intercourse between east and west across Druim Alban.

In the Scotland now depicted, coastwise intercourse must have been at least as easy as, and in many cases easier than, communication by land. The plains fringing the eastern seaboard are really linked together by the Forth, Tay, and Moray Firths across

---

[1] Adamnan, *Vita S. Columbæ*, ii, 47 ; cf. Watson, *Celtic Place-names*, p. 74.

which the further shore (or the high hills behind it) is always visible. Coastwise voyaging would unite the lowlands fronting the North Sea from Orkney to the Tweed into an eastern province. Separated therefrom by the Spine of Britain, the glens, peninsulas, and islands of the west coast from Galloway to Cape Wrath would constitute a western province the several corners of which could always be connected more easily by coastal voyages than by any route across the wooded and mountainous interior. Despite the frequence of tempests the island-studded waters may at times be as calm as an inland sea from which the next high island or headland rises conspicuous and enticing.

The importance of this division is far-reaching. The plains of the east coast lie open to mariners coasting up from eastern England—one of the most civilized and populous regions of Britain—or the Low Countries or crossing the North Sea direct from Scandinavia. The west coasts, on the other hand, invite voyagers sailing up from Western England or Ireland. From the promontories of Galloway you can see not only the next headland but also the coasts of Cumberland, Ireland, and the Isle of Man. From Kintyre or Islay Ireland appears as close as the mainland of Scotland so that it would not be surprising if a cultural unity embraced both coasts of the North Channel as a political unity did at the dawn of history. Landings on our west coast are only likely to be made by voyagers from the south-west or by adventurers from Denmark or Norway, who, like the Vikings, round Cape Wrath. The accuracy of this forecast will be amply confirmed by our account of the principal colonizing movements that reached Scotland in the Stone, Bronze, and Iron Ages.

The recognition of the importance of maritime intercourse calls to mind the crucial position occupied by Scotland in European prehistory. Lying as she does at the very junction of the North Sea and the Atlantic, she was—particularly when there were impediments to traffic up the English Channel [1]— the natural intermediary between the vigorous culture-province of Scandinavia and precocious regions like the Iberian Peninsula, where early contact with the Ancient East had sooner kindled the spark of higher civilization. From this standpoint the peculiarly rapid development of the far north (Caithness, Orkney, and the Hebrides) will become more intelligible.

[1] Cf. Fox, op. cit., p. 23.

If the foregoing paragraphs help to explain how men might settle in Scotland, it remains to ask why they did. What resources had Scotland to offer? And were there any special inducements to colonists? If the second question be held, as it usually is, to refer to mineral resources, it must be dismissed with a negative answer. Coal and shale were of no economic interest to prehistoric man. Though lignite or cannel coal associated with the Coal Measures in Sutherlandshire (Strath Brora), Fife, Ayrshire, Bute, came to be highly valued locally, it is inferior to the jet of Yorkshire and can easily be matched on the Continent. In metallic wealth Scotland could hardly compare with Ireland or Iberia. Alluvial gold [1] was probably obtainable from several streams, and has been worked profitably in Angus, in the Lead Hills, and in the Strath of Kildonan in historical times. There are small lodes of copper ore in Galloway, Renfrewshire, Argyll, Clackmannan, Ross, Orkney, and Shetland.[2] Though there is no direct evidence of prehistoric working in any district, there are some grounds for presuming an exploitation of the lode in the Crinan district of Argyll. But in view of the superior wealth of Ireland in both metals, the gold and copper of Scotland can hardly be regarded as magnets that would attract settlers.

Game was certainly abundant in prehistoric times. The seas and rivers teemed with edible fish. Thousands of sea-fowl still nest on the capes and islands of the north, and the lochs and swamps must have been well stocked with wild fowl. The woods sheltered roe and red deer, elks, and wild cattle of the *Urus* stock at least till Roman times, and the reindeer survived in the north perhaps as late as the ninth century A.D.[3] Wild boars and bears could also be hunted. Seals still frequent the coasts, and the northern isles afford good bases for whaling. The relative abundance of wild life must not be forgotten; throughout prehistoric times the chase and fishing undoubtedly played an integral part in the economy of most European peoples. In this respect Scotland was certainly well favoured, but not better than other countries in the same latitude. Again it must be remembered that furs provided a possible export to be bartered for the products of the higher civilizations of Gaul or Roman

---

[1] *PSAS.*, xxiv, p. 90; lxiii, p. 188; Dudgeon, *Historical Notes on the Occurrence of Gold in the South of Scotland.*
[2] Wilson, " Special Report on Mineral Resources," *Mem. Geol. Surv.*, xvii (1921), pp. 124–135.
[3] Ritchie, op. cit., pp. 331 ff.

Britain, and Caledonian bears are said to have figured in the games at Rome.

As for land suitable for primitive agriculture Scotland was at a disadvantage. Like the rest of Upland Britain Scotland is mainly composed of old, metamorphic rocks or of eruptives, capped in many cases with boulder clay—the ground-up debris of such rocks left by ice-sheets. Such country is not only badly drained and heavy to till where it offers any depth of soil at all ; the soils produced by the disintegration of these old rocks are generally too acid to be good for agriculture without special treatment. The excessive acidity of the Highland soils is particularly notorious, but on the eastern plains the comparatively recent soils of glacial origin still contain, in the form of slightly weathered minerals, reserves of bases which to some extent counteract their acidity and enable them to stave off the evil effects of lime-hunger.[1] The success of Scottish agriculture is due to intensive draining and, in most areas, to the use of fertilizers of some sort. But the first settlers who tilled Scottish soils had no suitable tools for ditching and no knowledge of agricultural chemistry ; they had perforce to select patches of light, well-drained soils—gravelly alluvia, sandy tracts, or hillsides. In the Highlands the correlation between the earlier prehistoric monuments and recent alluvial gravels is surprisingly accurate. Lime being the main defect in Scottish soil, the few regions of limestone outcrops and of soils derived therefrom assume peculiar significance. The presence of limestone is at least partly responsible for conspicuous concentrations of prehistoric settlement in the Crinan region [2] and round Muirkirk in Ayrshire.

The shell in sea sand provides an alternative source of lime. Such sands not only cover extensive tracts on the eastern seaboard and on the islands, but may occur at some distance from the present coast as raised beaches formed during land sinkings to be shortly described.

Apart from the foregoing restrictions the amount of land suitable for cultivation under any circumstances is rigorously limited. Roughly two-thirds of Scotland is over 600 feet above sea-level and would to-day on that ground alone be regarded as unsuitable for the profitable cultivation of cereals. On the west coasts, save in Central Ayrshire and Clydesdale, practically the only

[1] Ogilvie, op. cit., pp. 384 and 397.
[2] " Explanation of Sheet 36," *Mem. Geol. Surv.*, p. 103.

cultivable land is afforded by narrow and discontinuous strips of raised beach platforms or alluvial deltas at the mouths of burns. These are separated by mountain ridges which, as already remarked, rise steeply from the waters' edge and were once heavily wooded. Here then there are no continuous plains to support large communities. And even in the east we have seen that much of the Lowland plains was badly drained and heavily forested. Until the introduction of iron-working made durable tools cheap, man was reluctant, and probably absolutely incompetent, to clear the dense oak woods [1] which may be expected on the heavier soils of the Merse, round the Solway and in Central Ayrshire. Under these conditions Scotland cannot have been an inviting country for agricultural settlement.

The obstacles to pastoralism were less formidable. In Galloway, the Southern Uplands, and round the Midland Valley the oak woods gave place at higher altitudes to birch woods.[2] These might perhaps be more easily cleared to provide space for grazing on well-drained slopes. In Caithness and the islands the clearing had already been done by the winds early in prehistoric times. A successful pastoralism is well attested in Orkney and Shetland before the end of the Bronze Age, and we shall find some evidence for an export of wool in Roman times. At the same time in Scottish latitudes winter grazing is a serious difficulty which, as we shall see, sternly limited the expansion of flocks and herds.

RECENT LAND MOVEMENTS AND CLIMATIC CHANGES

Hitherto we have considered Scotland as she is to-day or as she would be but for the historical activities of man. But during the human period—the Pleistocene and Holocene epochs of the geologists—both her climate and her coastline have changed enormously. During the Ice Age Scotland was entirely covered with a huge ice-sheet. There were indeed one or more warm phases or interglacials interrupting the Ice Age, during which the ice melted sufficiently to allow a temperate flora to grow in the Lowlands and even in Kincardineshire.[3] But though Scotland was at such times habitable, no unambiguous human

---

[1] On the significance of these see Fox, op. cit., p. 49; on their distribution see Tansley, *Types of British Vegetation*, p. 75; " Geology of Northern Ayrshire," *Mem. Geol. Surv.*, xxii, p. 356.

[2] Tansley, op. cit., p. 141.

[3] Geikie, *Antiquity of Man*, p. 222; Campbell, *T. Ed. Geol. Soc.*, xiii (1933), p. 180.

remains certainly derived from interglacial deposits have yet been published to demonstrate man's presence.

The disappearance, technically called the retreat, of the ice was a long process, and was in fact not continuous. It was interrupted by prolonged halts when the edges of the ice sheets remained stationary and even by readvances when glaciers again began to spread down the valleys. The halts are marked by terminal moraines—heaps of boulders carried by the ice and dropped over its edge or extruded from beneath it. At a time when the greater part of the coastline was ice free, but when in some valleys, as at the head of Loch Torriden and in Mull, the glaciers still came down to the sea front,[1] the level of the sea relative to the land stood about 100 feet higher than at present. Knapdale and Kintyre were islands, Loch Lomond an arm of the sea, and only a narrow isthmus joined the Highlands to the rest of Britain. We are not concerned with the causes of this relative land-sinking [2]; it might result from an actual depression of the parts of the earth's crust weighted with a superincumbent mass of ice or from a rise in the ocean level, produced by the release of the stupendous volume of water previously locked up in the ice sheets of Europe and America. Its reality is attested by a series of old strand lines or raised beaches visible at many points round our coasts about 100 feet above the present mean sea-level.

The climate was then still arctic. However, climatic conditions [3] improved, the ice continued to melt, and the land rose again up to, or even beyond, its present relative level. Great Britain now found herself joined to the Continent perhaps at several points. The East Coast of England and the corresponding coasts of Holland, Germany, and Denmark, lay far further out than to-day, and the Dogger Bank was certainly above the water though it is doubtful whether there was a complete land bridge along its line from Britain to the Continent.[4]

These conditions tended to make the climate of the whole of North-western Europe more continental than to-day. The summers must have been relatively hot, the winters severe.

[1] Geikie, *Great Ice Age*, p. 297.
[2] Discussed by Wright, *The Quaternary Ice Age*, who also gives the correct correlations with the movements round the Baltic.
[3] The evidence for the climatic and floristic changes described in the following paragraphs is summarized in *Science Progress*, 1931, pp. 255 ff.
[4] Cf. map in *JRAI.*, lxi, p. 330.

At the same time opportunity was given for trees to spread in from the Continent. Birch, pine, and hazel groves began to replace the tundra scrub—Arctic willows and their kin—that had previously fringed the glaciated regions. Meteorologists term this the sub-Arctic phase. When the glaciers had finally shrunk, it was succeeded by the Boreal climatic period (the Lower Forestian of Geikie). North-easterly winds prevailed during the summer, and the autumn in particular was hotter than at present, allowing a longer period for plant growth despite the severity of the winters. The peat bogs have embalmed forests dating from this period at altitudes and in regions of Northern and Western Scotland where no trees grow to-day. Indeed a full quarter of the whole of Scotland was then covered with forests. In them pine (Scots fir), alder, hazel, and birch [1] were dominant, as in the contemporary woods of Denmark and Sweden. And, as there, a few oaks may appear before the close of the period.

The decline of the Boreal dry phase and a return to moister conditions (Geikie's Lower Turbarian) coincided with, and was indeed promoted by, extensive land-sinkings along the whole coast of Southern Scandinavia and Northern Germany, which are reflected also in the British Isles. The gates of the Baltic were flung wide open permitting a great influx of warm, salt water to fill the basin to a greater extent than to-day. At the same time the Dogger Bank was finally submerged. A consequence was the establishment of a more temperate maritime climate over North-western Europe under the influence of the enlarged areas of salt water. The summers became cooler but moister, the winters milder. The phase is termed Atlantic, since Scandinavia then enjoyed a climate comparable to that ruling over the Atlantic coasts of Britain to-day. It witnessed on the Continent an intensification of forest growth with mixed oak woods replacing conifers. In Scotland on the contrary, where excess of wind and rain rather than deficiency of moisture is the main obstacle to tree growth, the Atlantic phase, ushering in a régime of westerly winds and showers, initiated the deforestation of the country. In exposed situations and on unfavourable soils the pine woods and hazel groves began to give way to peat moors becoming embalmed therein as the Lower Forest bed. Not only did the tree-line sink, but at high altitudes the increased

---

[1] Erdtmann in *J. Linnæan Soc.* (*Botany*), 46 (1922–4), pp. 457 ff., and " The Post-Arctic History of European Forests," *GFF.*, \(1928), p. 170 ff.

precipitation falling as snow may have brought about a return
to something like glacial conditions.[1]

At the same time Britain sank to between 20 and 40 feet
below her present level relative to the sea. In Scotland, as in
Sweden and Northern Denmark, this depression has been
succeeded by a re-elevation so that the sinking is marked by
a raised beach—the so-called 25 ft. beach—conspicuous nearly
all round our coast. England, Holland, and Germany were not
thus re-elevated so that the raised beaches are missing there.
Indeed these regions have continued to sink so that forests of
post-Atlantic age are to be seen below high-water mark, for
instance near Liverpool, in Cardigan Bay, and in Torbay.[2]
In Caithness and Orkney, too, the 25 ft. beach is missing ;
the submerged forest off the Bay of Skail appears to be Boreal
in age.

In Atlantic times the estuary of the Forth extended to 5 miles
west of Stirling and was deep enough for whales to swim that
far. The Firth of Tay was similarly extended inland. The flat,
fertile " carse " lands round Falkirk and Stirling and above
Dundee are composed of the silts laid down by the Carron,
the Forth, the Earn, and the Tay. Under these silts are buried
the peats that enshrine the forests that had flourished in Boreal
times, as the application of the new technique of pollen analysis
has now demonstrated. The peat from below the carse clay
near Forgandenny, for instance, showed a typically Boreal
composition, while the forests fringing the estuary while the
carse was forming, the pollen from which is included in that
clay, were Atlantic in character.[3] These results serve to correct
the view of Geikie,[4] who, in his pioneer study of post-glacial
land movements, assigned the carse to a period of depression
intermediate between that of the 100 ft. and that of the 25 ft.
beaches, represented by a " 50 ft." beach the independent status
and indeed the marine origin of which is denied by more recent
geologists.[5]

On the Continent the Atlantic phase was eventually succeeded

<hr>

[1] Lewis distinguished a " second Arctic bed " above the Lower (Boreal) Forest
in the peat moors of Shetland and Galloway, *TRSE.*, xlvii, p. 824 ; cf. *GFF.*, l,
p. 172.
[2] *GFF.*, l, pp. 133, 152.
[3] Ibid., p. 181.
[4] *Great Ice Age*, p. 296.
[5] " Report of Commission on Plio- and Pleistocene Terraces," *Union Géo-
graphique internationale*, ii, 1928, pp. 102, 117.

by a second dry spell termed the sub-Boreal period (equivalent
to Geikie's Upper Forestian). It seems to have depended upon
different meteorological conditions to those ruling in Boreal
times—the frequent establishment of belts of high pressure or
anticyclones over Central and South-western Europe. It is
a bitter experience to many that these conditions do not benefit
the Western Highlands or the north of Scotland. On the contrary
when France and England are bathed in sunshine, the gales
and rain storms in the north are apt to be intensified. Hence,
while in England and Southern Scotland the peat bogs bear
witness to a revival of forest growth and a second rise in the
tree-line—the Upper Forest of the botanists—no corresponding
renewal of vegetation is traceable in the islands. Geikie [1] and
Lewis,[2] who were the first, not only in Great Britain, but in
the whole world, to study peat moors as indicators of post-
glacial changes in climate, have indeed stated that it was the
Lower Forest that was missing in the north. This pardonable
error by pioneer workers has been corrected by the application
to Scotland of the new technique of pollen analysis, as a result
of which the geological as well as the botanical sequence here
has been brought into line with that well-established by independent investigators on the Continent.

The climatic amelioration of sub-Boreal times probably had
little effect on the habitability of Scotland even in the Lowlands.
It cannot have become dry enough to produce any reduction
in the oak woods of the valley tracts, but the upward spread
of forest (probably now mainly birch) in the Southern Uplands
must have made these ranges more formidable or less suitable
for pasture. And before Roman times the climate had changed
again and become, if anything, wetter and more stormy than
to-day.

[1] *Antiquity of Man*, p. 287.   [2] *TRSE.*, xlvi, p. 61.

II

THE FIRST COLONIZATION OF SCOTLAND

SCOTLAND was doubtless habitable long before Atlantic times, but whether she was yet inhabited is still uncertain. In a cave near Inchnadamph (Sutherland), Callander, Cree, and Ritchie [1] have explored a deposit containing the bones of reindeer and other Arctic animals, including possibly the extinct cave bear. Charcoal occurred in the layer, and some of the antlers appear to have been cut as if man had at least visited the cave. But no distinctive implement was found, the geology of the deposit has not yet been thoroughly elucidated, and dating by fauna alone so far north is unconvincing since reindeer survived into the Christian era (p. 6). The age of the reindeer-hunters of Sutherland is therefore uncertain. It is not till Atlantic times that we have unambiguous evidence of a colonization of Scotland.

Then in the period of land-sinking bands of fishers and hunters began to settle both on the west and on the east coasts. Midden-heaps along the 25 ft. beach are the memorials of their advent. They suggest that the colonists approached simultaneously by the two routes foreshadowed on p. 5—from the south-west and from the east or south-east. The south-western settlers are the better known.

An advance guard is perhaps disclosed by flints picked up during building operations on the 25 ft. beach in the town of Campbeltown in Kintyre.[2] The implements are heavily patinated and are comparable to those which further south had been current during the Magdalenian period in the closing phase of the Ice Age. The nearest analogies come perhaps from Creswell Crags in Derbyshire. In that case we need not look beyond Britain for the home of our first inhabitants; they would merely have worked up from England where they had been living during the Ice Age.

Owing presumably to the scarcity of flint—the material is of Irish origin brought over by the waves or the ice—the tools are small and rude. Knives (backed blades), scrapers (including the so-called keeled scraper), and fabricators predominate.

---

[1] *PSAS.*, lxi, pp. 171 ff.   [2] *PSAS.*, xxviii, p. 263 ; lvi, p. 261.

One core has, however, been trimmed to produce something that might conceivably have served as an adze, and to that extent suggests a rather inefficient attempt to produce a wood-working tool.   Timber had played an insignificant role in the economy of the Upper Palæolithic hunters of France and England, whose equipment was adjusted to life on treeless steppes or tundras. An axe was accordingly lacking in the Upper Palæolithic cultures of this area and in the Mesolithic cultures that are descended therefrom.

A possibly later and distinct wave is illustrated by settlements on or just above the 25 ft. beach in two caves near Oban (MacArthur Cave [1] and Druim Vargie [2]), at several points on the sandy shore of Oransay (Caisteal-nan-Gillean [3] and Cnoc Sligeach [4]), on Colonsay, and at Risga on Loch Sunart [5] as well as by stray finds from the Dee River near Kirkcudbright [6] and from Bute.[7] The MacArthur Cave opened on to the 25 ft. beach.   The refuse of human occupation lay above the beach proper, but the shingle from a secondary storm beach had been intercalated between the layers of refuse.   Hence the maximum of subsidence must have passed and re-elevation begun before the fishers settled in the cave,[8] but the sea cannot have receded far—to-day the shore is 100 yards away and 30 feet below the level of the cave floor —since in a storm the waves could still carry shingle into the cave mouth.

The settlements on the little, treeless island of Oransay were camps in the open, perhaps only occupied for a season every year.   They are marked by great heaps of shells and broken bones among the sand dunes along or above the 25 ft. beach. The refuse deposits which may be $4\frac{1}{2}$ feet thick, are interrupted by thin layers of sand.[9]   At Cnoc Sligeach the holes for six stakes, only 7 inches in diameter, were observed penetrating the midden heap.   Bishop supposes that they supported some rude cave-like shelter of drift wood, skins, and turfs.

The occupants of the caves and strand camps lived by collecting shell-fish (pecten, oysters, limpets, periwinkles, mussels, cockles,

[1] *PSAS.*, xxix, pp. 216 ff.   [2] *PSAS.*, xxxii, p. 298.
[3] Symington Grieve, *The Great Auk*, p. 47.
[4] *PSAS.*, xlviii, pp. 52 ff.   [5] Unpublished.
[6] *Arch. J.*, lxv (1908), p. 231 ; *TDGAS.*, 1927, p. 74.
[7] *PSAS.*, xxxviii, p. 37 (midden under chambered cairn).
[8] "Tertiary and post-Tertiary Geology of Mull, L. Aline, and Oban," *Mem. Geol. Surv.*, 1924, p. 414; "Report Comm. on Plio- and Pleistocene Terraces," 1928, p. 100.   [9] *PSAS.*, xlviii, pp. 80–8.

and whelks), harpooning fish, particularly wrasse and mullet, and hunting seals, red and roe deer, boar, badger, otter, and wild cat. A suspiciously fresh-looking sheep bone comes from Caisteal-nan-Gillean as also some bones described as " probably *Bos longifrons* " from MacArthur Cave, but definite evidence for domestication is totally lacking. Some bones from MacArthur Cave may have been gnawed by dogs, but the only bones of this animal found came from a superficial layer, posterior **to**

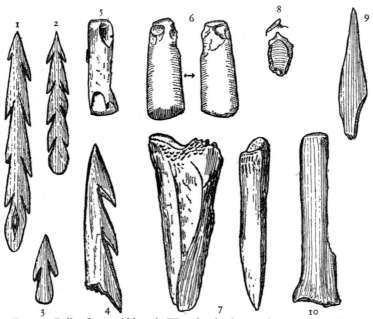

FIG. 1.—Relics from middens in West Scotland : 1–4 harpoons ; 5, 6, 10, fabricators ; 7, bone chisel ; 8, micro-graver ; 1–3, 10, MacArthur Cave ; 4, Druim Vargie ; 5–8, Caisteal-nan-Gillean. All ½.

the shell midden.[1] The first colonists of Western Scotland may accordingly be fairly designated food-gatherers.

The most distinctive implements found in the four sites excavated are flat harpoons of red deer's antler or bone. The seven from MacArthur Cave, one of seven from Cnoc Sligeach, and a stray example from the River Dee near Kirkcudbright are of antler, the rest of bone. Most are barbed alternately along both edges, but the two from Druim Vargie are barbed on one side only (Fig. 1, 5). One (Fig. 1, 1) at least was pierced with

[1] *PSAS.,* xxix, p. 423.

a slit near the butt for the attachment of the line. These flat
harpoons agree in general with those that characterize the
Azilian culture found in Southern France and Northern Spain
in early post-glacial levels, though the Continental examples
are exclusively of antler. The one antler harpoon from Cnoc
Sligeach, however, has a rounded stem from which the barbs
seem to stand out like thorns and has no parallels in the south-
west while close analogies exist on the Baltic in a very early
Atlantic context.

The remaining relics are tools for making tools. Flint being
scarce, every available pebble of that material was utilized and
used till absolutely worn out. Hence the scrapers and blades
present a sorry appearance when compared with those of the
Continental Azilian. But Breuil [1] identified a couple of gravers
and in particular a typical micro-graver from Oransay (Fig. 1, 8)
that are quite appropriate to the culture. Fabricators, used as
chisels in flaking flint, were very common at all four sites.
They are long, straight slivers of bone or antler (Fig. 1, 5),
or elongated beach pebbles (Fig. 1, 6) rounded and battered
at both ends. Hammer stones were common everywhere, but
nothing like an axe was in use. The stout polisher or wedge,
made from the leg-bone of a deer (Fig. 1, 7) from Caisteal-nan-
Gillean, and a couple of splinters of bone sharpened to serve
as piercers from MacArthur Cave (Fig. 1, 9) deserve notice.
A lump of red ochre from Oransay was presumably used in
decorating the person.

The distribution of the remains in Scotland is predominantly
western. A fabricator of antler was indeed found on the island
of Inchkeith in the Forth during building operations, but the
relation of the site to the sea being uncertain, it cannot be used
to demonstrate an extension of the south-western colonists
across the Central Valley. A harpoon from Whitburn, near
Newcastle-on-Tyne [1] does, however, seem to indicate such an
eastward extension in England, presumably by the Tyne gap.

The characteristic harpoons can hardly be regarded as local
British inventions; for they resemble the Azilian harpoons of the
Continent too closely for an independent origin to be plausible.[3]
Hence the culture found upon the 25 ft. beach of Western

[1] *PSAS.*, lvi, p. 265.
[2] Garrod, *Upper Palæolithic Age,* p. 184; Clark, *Mesolithic,* p. 14.
[3] The correct diagnosis of the Scottish relics was first made by Munro,
Arch. J., lxv, 227 ff.

Scotland may justly be termed Azilian. In other words the colonists who had settled near Oban and on Oransay in Atlantic times must have arrived by sea, ultimately from Northern Spain and South-western France. It sounds fantastic to bring primitive fishers and hunters who did not even possess an axe from so far afield, especially when intermediate finds are lacking. But we do not envisage a single voyage direct from the mouth of the Garonne to Galloway. On the contrary, the fishers would have progressed very slowly, halting at many points on the way, perhaps for several generations at each.   In South France the Azilians seem to belong to the Boreal period, so that ample time was available for them to reach Scotland in the Atlantic epoch. The apparent absence of intermediate sites may be due to land-sinking. The Azilians, not being equipped for dealing with forest, had to keep to the shore. But since England has been sinking ever since Boreal times, the sites of their settlements would by now be well under water there. Yet fabricators similar to those described above have been found in Cornwall and Wales,[1] though not in an Azilian context, and may be interpreted as evidence of the presence of Azilians on those coasts at some time.

While Azilian fishers from France were settling on the west coast along the 25 ft. beach, other food-gatherers with ancestors in the great forest that covered the North European plain were entering the Forth. Even in Boreal times the Forest-folk of North Europe had devised axe-like tools though they remained, like the Azilians, just gatherers of food and harpooners of fish. They had been reaching England already during the Boreal period and have left characteristic relics there as far north as Yorkshire.[2]   But in Scotland we have no evidence of their advent before Atlantic times. Then, during the period of land-sinking marked by the 25 ft. beach, several whales got stranded at the head of the Forth estuary, which then extended west of Stirling.[3] Humanly perforated pieces of antler were found with two whales' skeletons in the carse near Kincardine, a borer with another near Causewayhead and a perforated axe of deer's antler with a fourth in the carse at Meiklewood estate. The last implement, at least, is distinctive of the Forest Culture as we know it on the Baltic.   One end of the

[1] Clark, *Mesolithic,* p. 50.
[2] Clark, op. cit., pp. 16 f.
[3] Munro, *Prehistoric Scotland,* pp. 58 f.

section of antler (Fig. 2) has been cut off obliquely and rubbed down to an axe-like edge. The other end has been sawn through, and a hole has been bored at the point where a tine branched off. The implement stands alone in Scotland, but can easily be matched from sites occupied during Atlantic times in Denmark and North Germany, as well as in later Continental stations. The less distinctive implements found with the other whales in the carse may be attributed to the same context. (Whether the dug-out canoes from the carse are as old seems more doubtful.[1]) The axe from Meiklewood suffices to show that some adventurous fishers from North Europe did actually cross the North Sea during Atlantic times.

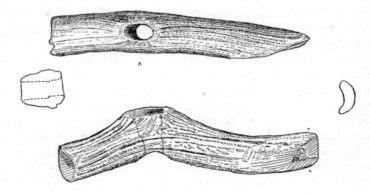

FIG. 2.—Antler axe from Meiklewood. ⅓.

Did they settle here? The flint hatchets and picks that attest such settlement in England have never been found in Scotland. But along the 25 ft. beach on the edge of the carse of Falkirk and Stirling, several middens—heaps of shells including those of oysters—have been reported.[2] Although no significant implements have been identified from them, they may possibly have been left by Forest-folk from the east. Moreover, one of the harpoons from Cnoc Sligeach on Oransay, as already remarked, agrees closely with Danish types of the Atlantic period.[3] The resemblance is almost too close to be accidental. And the use of bone instead of antler on other Azilian harpoons from Scotland

---

[1] Geikie, *Great Ice Age,* p. 292 ; cf. Callander, *PSAS.,* lxiii, p. 317.
[2] *Mem. Geol. Surv.,* Sheet 31, p. 54.
[3] *JRAI.,* lxi, p. 331, fig. 2, 9.

has been attributed by Breuil [1] to Baltic influence. It may then be that a few families from the opposite shore of the North Sea did settle round the Forth and found their way thence along the valleys to the west coast; the European Forest-folk were accustomed to living beside lochs and lagoons and to using waterways and so might more easily than other people cross the belt of swamp and forest between the Forth and the Clyde.

A third infiltration of food-gatherers at a rather indeterminate date is attested by the so-called microlithic industries from several sites in the Tweed basin,[2] from the sands round Glenluce and Stranraer in Wigtonshire, from Shewalton Moor in Ayrshire,[3] and from the banks of the Aberdeenshire Dee near Banchory.[4] All the sites are sandy, and on Shewalton Moor the relics are

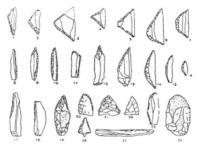

FIG. 3.—Pigmy flints from Shewalton Moor, Ayrshire, after Clark and Lacaille. ⅓.

found on an old land surface underneath dunes, generally about 50 feet above Ordnance Datum.

All sites have yielded in abundance and within relatively restricted areas " pigmies " or microliths—that is, minute flakes of flint, chert, chalcedony, jasper, or pitchstone, each very delicately and neatly retouched to form an implement or a part of a composite tool. (Small flakes without secondary working after detachment are not microliths.) The minute tools include tiny scrapers, generally more or less round or horse-shoe shaped, and many little blades, one edge of which—the back in fact— has been carefully blunted by the removal of tiny flakes (Fig. 3, 8). But a number of the implements possess a regular geometric out-line (Fig. 3, 1–7, 14)—crescents trimmed along the convex back,

[1] *PSAS.,* lvi, p. 279.
[2] *PSAS.,* l, pp. 307 ff. (Dryburgh); lxv, pp. 414 ff. (junction of Ettrick and Tweed).
[3] *PSAS.,* lxiv, pp. 34 ff.   [4] *Man,* xiii, p. 58.

triangles two sides of which are carefully flaked, and trapezes retouched on two or three edges. The micro-graver, generally associated with other pigmies in England and on the Continent, has so far only been reported from Stranraer.

In addition to the microliths themselves most of the sites, when thoroughly explored, have yielded also the cores from which the pigmy flakes were struck off, pebbles battered at the ends through use as hammer-stones and others with hollows on two faces.

The Scottish types all recur in the so-called Tardenoisian industries of the Continent and England. It is now recognized [1] that in several parts of Europe including England the Upper Palæolithic flint-workers were tending towards the production of increasingly diminutive tools as the period drew to a close. But these small native flints do not exhibit the surprisingly regular forms that distinguish the true Tardenoisian, nor yet the micro-graver. These specialized forms seem to have been evolved in North Africa, and it is usual to postulate an invasion from that quarter, connected perhaps with the desiccation which began at the close of the European Ice Age, to explain the European Tardenoisian. In England it is possible to distinguish two waves of Tardenoisian immigrants who, it is held, mingled with survivors of native Palæolithic stocks. Eventually these composite groups must have filtered into Scotland.

But they arrived here late. The micro-graver, which characterizes pure Mesolithic Tardenoisian sites elsewhere, is very rare in Scotland. Moreover, most of the sites which have yielded microliths, have also yielded polished stone axes or arrow-heads of " Neolithic " and Bronze Age types. And these are probably not intruders dropped by later visitants after the Tardenoisians had departed ; for the arrow-heads were actually imitated by the pigmy-flint makers in their own microlithic technique. A conclusive instance is the tanged and barbed arrow-head from Shewalton Moor (Fig. 3, 26). It is flaked in the microlithic style, but the form and the idea it embodies are those introduced by the so-called Beaker-folk, whose advent is generally equated with the beginning of the Bronze Age. It demonstrates, therefore, that the pigmy-flint makers survived here, carrying on their ancient industry till that period. How long they had been living here is uncertain. The infiltration

---

[1] The evidence has recently been summarized conveniently by Clark, *Mesolithic*.

represented by the finds from Stranraer may go back to Atlantic times, but the other settlements may be later.

The pigmy flints, therefore, bear witness to small bands of hunters living in open, sandy patches in the forest that covered Scotland.   Like their European ancestors, they had no tools for coping with timber, but must have lived in tiny, isolated communities in natural glades.   Eventually they must have been absorbed or exterminated by more advanced immigrants.

The groups of food-gatherers who formed the first colonists of Scotland, must have been extremely small numerically.   They can hardly have affected the subsequent population appreciably. Their contributions to the civilization of Scotland were surely negligible. In particular no grasses ever grew wild in Scotland that under cultivation might become wheat and barley.   It is extremely improbable that any wild sheep lived in the British Isles after the last Ice Age.   The plants and animals which make possible a creative, food-producing economy (as opposed to a parasitic, food-gathering one) must have been introduced from overseas. And they did not arrive as wind-borne seeds or spontaneously migrating flocks, but in the wake of fresh human colonists.

III

CHAMBERED CAIRNS

1. COLLECTIVE AND INDIVIDUAL INTERMENT

THE economic revolution which made civilization possible—
the cultivation of cereals and the domestication of cattle,
sheep, and swine—was initiated in the Ancient East. Thence
its basic ideas were slowly propagated towards North-western
Europe by three main channels—coastwise along the Mediterranean and Atlantic seaboards, up the Danube Valley and down
the Elbe and Rhine, from the Black Sea coasts across the North
European plain.[1] These three streams of cultural influence
converge upon Scotland, and colonists, inspired thereby, began
to settle on our western and eastern coasts almost simultaneously.

Our knowledge of the first colonists who brought hither
cereals and domesticated animals is derived almost exclusively
from their graves ; few remains of their settlements have survived,
whereas the tombs are often both imposing and well furnished
with grave-goods deposited with the deceased for use in a future
state. The burial rites, thus revealed, provide a convenient clue
to the recognition of the two main streams of colonization.
The settlers who arrived by the Atlantic route and occupied the
west coast and the far north were accustomed to bury their
dead in *collective tombs*—family vaults each containing the bodies
of many individuals. In the British Isles, these vaults are nearly
always chambers, built above ground and subsequently covered
with a cairn of stones or a barrow of earth—often elongated
in plan. The first people to reach the east coasts on the contrary
practised individual interment ; each body was laid to rest
singly in a simple trench or in a coffin or *short cist* of stone slabs.
Such graves might be surmounted by a cairn or barrow, always
circular in plan. The earliest individual graves of Great Britain
often contain a very distinctive pottery vessel, conventionally
designated a *Beaker*, so that the colonists practising individual
interment are often termed the *Beaker-folk*.

No metal objects have ever been found with the original

[1] Childe, *Most Ancient East,* and *Dawn.*

22

burials in collective tombs in the British Isles, and hence these structures are generally referred to a " Neolithic " period. Objects of copper or bronze do accompany Beakers, and individual interments in short cists are accordingly currently assigned to the " Bronze Age ". But this contrast may be due to a difference in economic organization or in piety rather than to a distinction in age. In Scotland few individual interments have been accompanied by metal objects, and those that have are often marked as relatively late by the character of the pottery. On the other hand, collective tombs contain stone implements that, as near as Yorkshire, have been found associated with bronze weapons in individual graves. To this extent the current use of the terms Neolithic and Bronze Age seems frankly misleading.

It has indeed been established that in Skye and the Hebrides, probably also in Arran and Caithness, the Beaker-folk only arrived after collective tombs had already been in use perhaps for several generations. But given the obstacles to intercourse between east and west indicated in Chapter I, the time relation between individualists and collectivists established for Skye need not, and probably does not, apply to the Lothians or Aberdeenshire. We are dealing with two groups of colonists who arrived independently from different quarters and may have long co-existed on opposite sides of the Spine of Britain without meeting. If the collective tombs are first considered here, that does not imply an absolute priority in time for them over the individual graves in other parts of Scotland.

The collectivists were then the first arrivals on the coasts and islands round the Solway and Clyde Firths, in Skye and the Hebrides, and on the Old Red Sandstone of Caithness and Orkney. Here they ultimately came into contact with the Beaker-folk who normally buried their dead individually. But before that perhaps they had already colonized intensively the limited land available to farmers possessed of only a rudimentary equipment and a primitive agricultural technique and had even begun to spread eastward towards the Tweed and Tay basins and coastwise to the southern shores of the Moray Firth.

It is now agreed that the collective burial chambers erected in Scotland belong to a great series of sepulchral vaults extending coastwise from the Eastern Mediterranean to the Iberian Peninsula, Brittany, Ireland, and Great Britain, and so to Denmark,

Southern Sweden, and Holland. The similarities in the plan, structure, and function of some monuments in all the foregoing areas are so close that a kinship between them all is undeniable ; the same religious ideas, the same architectural prescriptions inspired their builders everywhere. But in each region, including Scotland, local divergences from the common plan are noticeable in some of the tombs. Such divergence may be plausibly explained by the assumption that communities that had settled down and become isolated from their fellows modified the traditional rules of sepulchral architecture to suit their local needs or peculiar inclinations. From this assumption the following principle may be deduced : the oldest tombs will be those which reproduce accurately the most widely distributed architectural features ; tombs which seem to diverge from the common plan and to be restricted to specific regions are likely to be later. Nordmann's classical study of Danish burial vaults confirms this[1] assumption. And in Scotland we shall show that tombs which according to it ought to be early, are, in fact, restricted in distribution to likely points of primary settlement, while presumably late monuments have a wider dispersion.

In several areas of Europe two rather different tomb plans were current : in one group, the *passage graves,* the chamber is round or polygonal, often preceded by an antechamber, and entered by a clearly marked passage. In the other, the *long cists,* the chamber is itself long and narrow like a passage and is entered directly through a simple portal, sometimes preceded by a shallow porch. Common to both types in the West Mediterranean is a semicircular forecourt on to which the passage or portal opens. Such a forecourt may therefore rank as an early feature.

Both types of plan are represented in Scotland, but in different areas. Round or oval chambers with antechamber and entrance passage are seen in a classical form in Caithness. Long cists— long, narrow chambers with portals rather than passages—are distinctive of the Clyde and Solway coasts. Both plans are encountered in the Hebrides, while specialized derivative forms are conspicuous in Orkney and in Strath Nairn and Strath Spey. Despite the divergences in sepulchral architecture, the grave goods in all areas show a fundamental similarity. The pottery—and to some extent the stone implements—belong essentially to a

[1] *Aarbøger,* 1917, pp. 227 ff.

distinctively British family represented equally in England and Ireland, and termed, after a typical and well-excavated site near Avebury in Wiltshire, the Windmill Hill culture. This comparative homogeneity makes it practicable and convenient to treat the grave goods apart from the graves, though it will be possible to distinguish certain local divergences in the pottery that correspond to some extent to the main division in the tomb types.

2. THE LONG CISTS OF THE SOUTH-WEST

The collective tombs of South-western Scotland from Loch Etive to Galloway exhibit sufficient common features to unite them into a single main group quite easily distinguishable from that represented in Caithness. But the same features recur also in Northern Ireland,[1] the Isle of Man,[2] and sporadically as far away as Pembrokeshire [3] and Derbyshire [4] so that the whole area on both sides of the North Channel may legitimately be regarded as a single cultural province, the several regions of which were united by maritime intercourse.[5] That might indeed have been anticipated from the geographical considerations adduced in Chapter I ; it will be recalled that both Ireland and Man are visible from the Scottish coasts.

The chambered cairns of this region may be long or round, but the former are of no great length and hardly ever exceed 110 feet. All are wider at one end than at the other, and ten (three in Galloway, four in Arran, one in Kintyre, and two along Loch Fyne) still exhibit distinct *horns* at the wider end. These are constituted by stones on end grouped to form a semicircular façade, on to the centre of which the chamber normally opens. Other details as to the construction of the peristalith, if any, are lacking.

The cairns do not cluster in cemeteries, though there are cases (Blairmore, Arran, Mid-Gleniron, Kirkcudbright, and Cairn Holy, Wigtonshire), where two cairns are closely juxtaposed.

[1] *Man*, xxxiii, 117 ; xxxiv, 111 ; cf. *Arch*. xv, p. 409.
[2] *Reliquary*, 1884–5, p. 165.
[3] Notably Pentre Evan judging by model in Pitt Rivers Museum, Farnham, Dorset.
[4] *Reliquary*, 1901, p. 232 ; Borlase, *Dolmens of Ireland*, iii, fig. 739.
[5] Samson's Bratfull and other monuments in Cumberland may belong to the same family.

On the other hand the same cairn often covers several chambers, particularly in Galloway and Ayrshire, but occasionally also in Arran and Kintyre. The absence of cemeteries is presumably a corollary of the restriction on habitable land imposed by natural features. The country is divided up by sea inlets and mountain ridges, and the most suitable soils are provided by narrow and discontinuous strips of raised beach platform and the gravels at the foot of a glen. The earliest tombs, as judged by the criteria mentioned on p. 24, particularly the semicircular façade, are confined to the vicinity of such patches that are adjacent to the shore.[1] A glance at map 1 where tombs with façade are marked by solid circles will illustrate this fact.

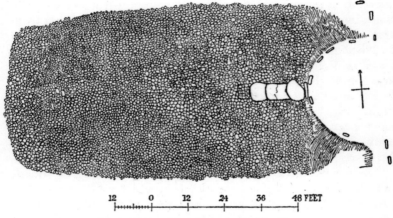

12   0   12   24   36   48 FEET

Fig. 4.—Plan of Carn Bàn, Arran, after Bryce.

The same map will justify the claim that the early tombs mark original landing-places, primary foci of colonization, from which the population subsequently spread out inland. Early tombs are restricted to suitable land close to the coast. Tombs lacking the façade and showing other signs of degeneracy have a much wider range, though they occur also on the coast and sometimes, as at Cairn Holy, in close juxtaposition to tombs with façades. It may therefore be assumed that, with the passage of time, the population grew and overflowed from the limited cultivable soil round the first landing places to settle on fresh land further away.

[1] For details see *SGM.*, l, pp. 18 ff., with map and full list of cairns.

Within South-western Scotland details in the construction of the chamber allow of the distinction of two sub-groups. The one, best represented in Arran and Bute and along Loch Fyne, may be termed the Clyde type, while the other, commonest in Galloway and Ayrshire, can be designated the Solway type.

In the Clyde type [1] the chamber or long cist opens directly on to the exterior of the cairn. There is never a passage but generally a portal formed of two tall uprights set at right-angles to the main axis of the cist and projecting so that the space

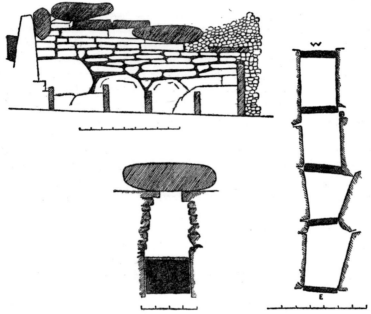

FIG. 5.—Sections and plan of Carn Bàn, Arran, after Bryce.

between them is reduced to from 10 to 18 inches in width. The walls of the chamber are composed of large slabs set on edge and arranged in pairs that are not as a rule strictly parallel, for the ends of each pair tend to overlap those of the pair in front by a couple of inches (Fig. 5). At the junction of each pair a slab, set on edge but generally lower than the lateral slabs, lies transversely athwart the chamber. Bryce terms such slabs *septal stones*. There is normally one across the entrance

[1] The general features are admirably summarized by Bryce in Balfour's *Book of Arran*, i. For references to sites frequently mentioned see p. 32 here.

just behind the portal stones to form a sort of sill. The effect
of the rest is to divide the chamber into a series of compartments
or segments. Chambers thus divided are known as *segmented cists*.
The inner end of the chamber is normally closed by a slab set
like a septal stone across the cist between the lateral slabs but
equalling or exceeding the latter in height.

The lateral slabs are themselves seldom as tall as the portal
stones and may have served merely as the foundation for a wall
of dry masonry. At Carn Bàn in Arran, such a wall was actually
found in position supporting the lintelled roof. Its horizontal
courses corbelled inwards, each course projecting inwards a little
beyond the one below so that the chamber was in fact covered
by a rudimentary barrel vault (Fig. 5). The same type of construction is seen in the chamber under a round cairn at Nether
Largie [1] near Crinan, but the evidence does not suffice to show
whether it was universally employed in early chambers. At
Kilchoan, also in the Crinan region, in the larger cist 14 ft. 8 in.
long, the roofing slabs seem to have been supported by pillars
set on end outside the basal slabs of the walls. In late and
degenerate variants at least the capstones often reposed directly
on the lateral uprights. But in all cases it must have been possible
to pass from one segment to the next by scrambling through
the gap which always existed between the septal stones and
the roof.

The earlier chambers are divided into four or five compartments and vary in length from 24 feet (Giants' Graves) to $18\frac{2}{3}$ feet
(Carn Bàn). From these imposing chambers a regular degeneration series leads through bipartite and tripartite chambers, 10 to
15 feet in length, to single cists only 4 feet long. Yet even
the last, like Glecknabae in Bute, were entered through a portal
and possessed a single septal stone forming a threshold. The
longer chambers are generally covered by long cairns and, in
Arran and on Loch Fyne, opened on to the semicircular forecourt
defined by the façade. But at Nether Largie the cist, although
20 feet long and divided into four segments, was covered by
a round cairn while at Auchoish [2] in the same region a ruinous
cist preceded by a sort of passage opened on to the long side
of a cairn, the wider end of which was " horned ". The lateness
of the smaller chambers is often attested by their irregular

[1] *PSAS.*, lxiv, p. 236.
[2] *PSAS.*, lxvi, p. 445 ; there were vague hints of an original chamber in the
wide end.

PLATE II

[face p. 28

HUT 1, SKARA BRAE

SEGMENTED CIST, KINDROCHAT

arrangement in the cairn and by the multiplication of chambers under the same cairn. Thus there was a small cist in the narrow end of the cairn that covered Giants' Graves, and two or three small cists in the cairns at Dunan Mor (Arran) and Glecknabae (Bute), as well as at Kindrochat on the Earn. Moreover, the shorter cists are found even on the fringe of the province as far away as Perthshire. Thus several lines of evidence converge to justify the typology here advanced. Yet it should be noted that the segmented cists in the horned cairns of Goward, County Down, and Cashtel yn Ard, Man, were 28 and 38 feet in length respectively, so that all the Scottish monuments might on typological grounds be regarded as secondary to the Irish and Manx. But some at least of the latter, though large, seem to diverge seriously from the common plan.

Each chamber normally contained several bodies, as many as sixteen being identified in the small tripartite cist of Clachaig in Arran. Though the bones were generally in disarray, Bryce believes that the corpses were originally deposited squatting against the walls. He found charcoal and even burnt bones in several cists, but none of these bones were definitely human, though in Giants' Graves only cremated bones were found. However, in the long cists of Kilchoan and Nether Largie burnt or cremated human bones have been expressly reported. Whether these cremations were primary is open to doubt since both tombs contained Beakers as well as Windmill Hill pottery. It may even be doubted whether the burning was intentional. Recent studies of collective burials in Greece [1] have shown that fires were often kindled in the tombs, for ritual purposes or perhaps just to purify the fetid atmosphere of the charnel house on the occasion of secondary burials. The same observations have shown that the undertakers paid scant respect to the former occupants of the tomb in making room for later burials. The disturbance of the bones observed in our chambered tombs may therefore be attributed to the irreverence of those charged with the later funerals.

Besides human skeletons, animal bones are found in the tombs, presumably the remains of food offerings to the dead. They include bones of cattle, sheep or goats, and swine as well as of wild animals and birds. The bones of domesticated species

[1] *Arch.*, lxxxii pp. 141 f. (Mycenæ); Xanthoudides, *Vaulted Tombs of the Mesara,* p. xii.

had belonged exclusively to young beasts. The slaughter of such is indicative of a rural economy which found it difficult to carry calves and lambs over the winters.

A ground stone axe-head was recovered from Clachaig (Fig. 15), a pestle-shaped mace-head from Tormore (Fig. 17), leaf-shaped arrow-heads from Giants' Graves, Sliddery Water, and Kindrochat, slug knives of flint from Giants' Graves, Torlin, Sliddery Water, and Dunan Mor (Fig. 17), flint knives ground along one edge from Torlin and fragments of pitchstone, a volcanic glass allied to obsidian that occurs at Corriegills in Arran, both at East Bennan, Dunan Mor, and Tormore in Arran, and at Michael's Grave and Glecknabae in Bute. The last-named finds are valuable as proving oversea intercourse between Arran and Bute.

Pottery allied to Windmill Hill ware was found in most of the cists of Arran and Bute, at Beacharra in Kintyre, and Kilchoan and Nether Largie near Crinan. While much of the material can be matched in any part of Scotland, baggy pots with broad, horizontal lugs from Clachaig, Torlin, and Sliddery Water, though paralleled in England, are strange to the north-eastern provinces of Scotland. And the pots of the form of Fig. 14, 2 from Clachaig (Arran), Bickers Houses (Bute), and Beacharra (Kintyre), illustrate a type peculiar to the west of Scotland, the Hebrides, and Northern Ireland. In addition to this " Neolithic " pottery, fragments of Beaker come both from the " early " tombs of Giants' Graves, Nether Largie, and Kilchoan, and from late degenerations like Dunan Beag and Glecknabae, while the tripartite southern chamber in the Dunan Mor cairn contained a piece of a Food Vessel. This Bronze Age pottery, like the fastener from a jet necklace at Dunan Beag (smaller chamber) and a buckle from Beacharra, presumably means that the collective tombs of Arran remained in use till the Beaker folk had reached the west coasts and begun to mingle with the earlier occupants. Even the pestle-shaped mace-head, and the slug and polished knives are suspected of being " Bronze Age " types. Intercourse between the families using collective tombs and the Beaker-folk must therefore have been intensive and seems to have been pacific. Indeed the Beakers from the collective tombs suggest that members of the new stock had been admitted to the older communities and so become entitled to a place in their family or communal tombs.

But the advent of the new-comers with their traditions of individual interment, eventually brought about the decay of the old funerary customs and the degeneration of the monuments they inspired. At Clachaig a short cist was intruded into the cairn originally erected over the collective tomb. And in the long cairn at Balnabraid, Kintyre,[1] there were twelve secondary short cists, one containing a Beaker and another two Food Vessels.

The Solway sub-group is distinguished from the foregoing by the smaller size of the chambers. None seem to have possessed portals, but some were entered through an antechamber or even a built passage. The cairns may be either long or round, and three of the former, all ruinous, still boast semicircular façades. In the best preserved of these, Cairn Holy,[2] the chamber is an undivided cist, $7\frac{1}{2}$ feet long, preceded by a rather narrow passage or antechamber 9 feet long, separated from the chamber by a septal stone. Under the round King's Cairn, Water of Deugh,[3] were two chambers framed by three slabs on edge measuring respectively $6\frac{1}{2}$ and 7 feet in length, but preceded by passages 22 and 17 feet long, walled with dry masonry and lintelled over. A similarly constructed passage, 2 feet wide and 2 feet high, led into a chamber $7\frac{1}{2}$ feet long, by $3\frac{2}{3}$ feet wide, by $3\frac{3}{4}$ feet high, formed of three slabs on edge and two lintels in a cairn on Cuff Hill in Beith Parish, Ayrshire.[4] Other cists seem to have been preceded by low and shallow antechambers which may have been roofed over. A multiplicity of chambers under the same cairn is very common in the Solway sub-group. There were five in the cairn, 79 feet long by 50 feet wide, at Drannandow,[5] Minnigaff Parish, one in the east end, and two on either side. The cairn on Cuff Hill seems also once to have covered five long cists, even in the cairn with frontal semicircle at Mid-Gleniron [6] there was at least one, and possibly two, chambers at the side in addition to the one opening on to the forecourt.

Most cairns in this group have been plundered for dyke-building or to clear fields. None have yielded any recorded relics. While their general distribution conforms to the rules already laid down, some are at relatively high altitudes—Drannandow is over 800 feet above sea-level—and on remote moors far away from any obviously attractive alluvial land.

[1] PSAS., liv, pp. 172 ff.   [2] RC. Kirk., No. 288.
[3] PSAS., lxiv, p. 273.   [4] PSAS., xi, pp. 278 ff.
[5] PSAS., lvii, pp. 60 ff.   [6] RC., Wig., No. 261.

It almost looks as if their builders must have been driven to a more pastoral mode of life than that attributed to the coast-dwellers. Moreover, to the same group we provisionally assign the Mutiny Stones, far away on the Lammermuirs, and two cairns recently discovered near Carter Bar on the Cheviots, although no structures are visible in either monuments.

NOTE.—The most important cairns mentioned in this section are described in the following places in *PSAS*. : Beacharra, *PSAS.*, xxxvi, pp. 103 ff. ; Bickers Houses, xxxviii, 18 ff. ; Carn Bàn, xxxvii, p. 40 ; Clachaig, xxxvi, p. 87 ; Dunan Beag, xliii, p. 342 ; Dunan Mor, xliii, p. 350 ; East Bennan, xliii, p. 338 ; Giants' Graves xxxvii, p. 48 ; Glecknabae, xxxviii, p. 37 ; Kilchoan, vi, p. 351 ; Kindrochat, lxv, p. 281 ; Nether Largie, vi, p. 340 ; Sliddery Water, xxxvi, p. 92 ; Torlin, xxxvi, p. 79 ; Tormore, xxxvi, p. 98.

3. THE CHAMBERED CAIRNS OF CAITHNESS

The group of collective sepulchres in the extreme north of Scotland is numerically larger, but geographically more compact than that in the south-west. As the result of the labours of the Royal Commission on Ancient and Historical Monuments fifty-three chambered cairns have been identified in Caithness and forty-five in the adjacent parishes of Sutherland. To these should probably be added three cairns in Orkney. In Caithness fifteen of the cairns, in Sutherland twelve, and in Orkney two are long. And here the long cairns are imposing monuments exceeding in one instance 240 feet in length.

The pioneer explorations of Joseph Anderson [1] showed as early as 1865 that the chambered cairns of the far north were not just a chaotic mass of slabs. They were, on the other hand, surrounded and outlined by a peristalith or retaining wall, or more often by two parallel walls. The Caithness flagstone of the district breaks easily along its bedding-planes into neat flat slabs that form ideal material for dry-stone building. The boundary walls are accordingly constructed of coursed masonry without the aid of uprights. The long cairns, as in the south-west, are always higher and broader at one end than at the other, but in Caithness and Orkney the boundary wall seldom encloses a mere trapeze. Normally there are horn-like projections at both ends—not at the wider end only as in the south-west

[1] *Mem. Anthrop. Soc.* (London), ii, pp. 234 ff., iii, pp. 218 ff. and 272 ff. ; *PSAS.*, vi, pp. 442 ff. ; vii, pp. 480 ff. The principal results are fully summarized in *Scotland in Pagan Times,* ii, where details as to cairns mentioned here without further reference may be found.

(Fig. 6). Similar " horns " are also appended to some short cairns. Between the tips of the horns the peristalith curves back again towards the centre of the mass so that the horns actually bound a semicircular space or forecourt at each end of the cairn. The horns accordingly fulfil the function of the semicircular façade of uprights noted in Arran and Galloway. Indeed, in Strathnaver which lies beyond the limits of the Caithness flagstone, the horns are actually marked by uprights from 3 to 8 feet in height. And even the built walls are constructed with especial care between the tips of the horns. At Yarrows they were composed of alternate large and small slabs and increased in height from 2½ feet at the tips to 5 feet at the centre of the forecourt, where the portal of the chamber opened. (Horned cairns are indicated by solid rectangles in Map 1, round cairns by squares.)

Fig. 6.—Plan of horned cairn, 240 feet long, at Yarrows, Caithness, after Anderson.

In addition to the boundary wall, Anderson found a circular wall, covered by the body of the cairn, round the chambers in the long cairn at Camster and in two short horned cairns. This inner wall was composed of heavy, square blocks as contrasted with the flat slabs of the double outer wall. But since this circular wall actually enclosed the chamber, the pioneer investigator very properly asked [1] whether it did not mark the original boundary of the cairn, the " cornute structure " being a later addition. He rejected this solution on the ground that the well-built double wall, not the single wall, should be the original finish to the monument; the inner circle would be merely structural giving support to the actual chamber walls. This does, however, raise the whole question of the chronological relation between long and round cairns. The furniture is insufficient to provide an answer, but a consideration of the distribution of the two types may clarify the issue.

[1] *PSAS.*, vii, p. 493.

D

Nearly all the chambered cairns are situated at altitudes of between 200 and 600 feet above sea-level.[1] Few are actually on hill-tops—two on Cnoc Freiceadain, and others on Warehouse Hill are among the exceptions—but none survive on the low plain of Caithness. Perhaps the latter was too swampy for ill equipped men to inhabit. The majority lie on bleak, wind-swept moors which were nonetheless cultivated even last century. To early settlers they would be attractive as they must have been free from heavy forest since Boreal times, while the slopes would provide natural drainage. Within this area the cairns cluster in groups. In Caithness there are nine or ten chambered cairns in an area of 4 square miles between Lochs Shurrery and Calder, and a similar cluster between the coast and the ridges south-east of Reay. It is only about 3 miles across the moors from Camster to the two long cairns at Yarrows, and the latter together with ten others lay within a radius of 1 mile from the summit of Warehouse Hill. There are similar clusters in Strathnaver, round the south end of Loch Shin and above Bonar Bridge.

In several places the cairns are so closely juxtaposed as to constitute actual cemeteries. At Camster a long and a round chambered cairn and an unchambered one stand side by side. There are four (round) on Warehouse Hill, three on Sordale Hill, four (now destroyed) near Loch Yarrows, two, both long, on Cnoc Freiceadain. Such must evidently mark the burying grounds of small but sedentary communities. Moreover the cemeteries on Warehouse Hill, at Camster and elsewhere comprise, besides chambered cairns, others covering no chamber but a short cist designed for an individual interment. These presumably belong to the Beaker-folk, who, as the grave goods to be cited below show, appear to have reached Caithness while the collective tombs were still in use. They might indeed be regarded as the last degeneration of the long cairn under the influence of the individualist tradition, the round-chambered cairns being intermediate forms. In any case the cemeteries imply a considerable duration for the collectivist culture in the north, though they provide no conclusive criteria for the relative age of the component structures.

From another standpoint it will be noticed that no long horned cairns survive south of the high ground (culminating in

[1] Cf. map in *PRSE.*, l, p. 63.

Morven) that separates Caithness from Sutherland, although
short horned cairns spread as far south as the Dornoch Firth.
Indeed in Caithness the monuments in question are strung out
along a natural land route from the harbours of Reay and Thurso
to Wick Bay that would cut off the dangerous passage of the
Pentland Firth. Now, it is notorious that ancient mariners
were always anxious to avoid rounding promontories so that
trade was liable to take overland routes to escape such perils.
And in the Iberian Peninsula the chambered tombs that
architecturally recall those of Caithness do cluster along, and
at the termini of, routes that would avoid Gibraltar and Cape
St. Vincent. If, therefore, the original colonization of Caithness
were connected with some sort of maritime intercourse between
the countries of the Atlantic and North Sea coasts respectively,
the long horned cairns do lie at points that would be first reached
by such traffickers ; the more widely distributed short horned
and unhorned cairns might be degenerate types erected when
population began to spread from the primary foci. To that
extent the current typology which regards the long-horned cairns
as the oldest monuments would be justified by their distribution.

Still the foregoing argument is not conclusive and derives
no additional support from the structure of the chambers covered
by the cairns. This structure is to some extent conditioned by
the geology of the district in that the walls are mainly composed
of coursed masonry appropriate to the neat, flat slabs obtainable
so easily from the Caithness flagstone.

The actual burial vault is insignificant in comparison with the
gigantic structure that may cover it, being normally a small oval
chamber some 12 feet long and 7 or 8 feet wide. Its skeleton is
usually constituted by seven upright slabs, 4 to 6 feet high, set at
right-angles to the long axis of the chamber. One slab at the rear
would form a facing and partial support to the end wall. The
rest, arranged roughly in pairs,[1] would assist to support the sides
and separate the chamber into compartments and from the
passage of entry. It should be noted that the top end of the
slab has generally been deliberately trimmed so that it slopes
down from the front edge, which projects into the chamber,
towards the side wall.[2] The wall of the chamber is built of thin,

[1] The correspondence was not always exact, e.g. at Lower Dounreay, *PSAS.*,
lxiii, p. 143.
[2] Hemp, *Ant. J.*, xiv, p. 412 notes analogies in the corbelled tombs of South
Spain.

flat slabs laid horizontally which begin to oversail inwards about
5 feet above the floor so that the whole area could be roofed
with a corbelled vault. Normally when the space between
the walls had been reduced by corbelling to 3 or 4 feet the
gap would be spanned by flat lintels as at Camster (Fig. 7).
But in the short horned cairn at Achaidh in Sutherland, the

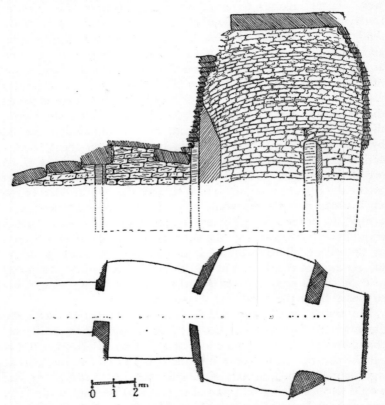

FIG. 7.—Plan and elevation of chamber in round cairn at Camster.

roof (here reposing on big slabs on edge) was corbelled, and
completed by a stone fitted in vertically like the keystone of a
true vault, between the horizontal slabs of the corbelling.[1]

The whole chamber was by no means always covered by the
corbelled vault. In one long cairn at Yarrows the space between
the rear wall and the next pair of uprights was roofed by a flat

[1] *PSAS.*, xliv, p. 104.

lintel, 3 feet above the floor, the vault covering the two front compartments only. Here we might speak of a vaulted chamber with a cell at the rear. In both the long and the round cairn at Camster (Fig. 7), in a round cairn on Warehouse Hill, and elsewhere,[1] the outermost compartment was not comprised under the dome but was lintelled over so that here we had not a tripartite chamber but at best a divided chamber preceded by an antechamber. Finally at Kenny's (round) cairn (Warehouse Hill) and in a short horned cairn at Kyleoag (Sutherland)[2] instead of the rear cell there was a lateral cell opening off the main chamber on the left. In Kenny's Cairn (Fig. 8) the portal to the cell is formed of a pair of uprights flush with the chamber wall, while the chamber itself is subdivided and separated from the passage by two pairs of uprights and backed by a fifth.

FIG. 8.—Plan of Kenny's Cairn, Caithness, after Anderson.

The division into antechamber and chamber is a recurrent feature in the collective tombs of France, the Iberian Peninsula, and even Sicily and Greece, so that it might rank as an original feature. The same is true of the addition of cells at the side or rear of the main chamber which recurs in the regions just mentioned as well as in Denmark and Ireland. Yet these features in Caithness and Sutherland are best represented in round cairns which should be late !

The chamber was always entered by a lintelled passage, the walls of which were built of coursed masonry. In the long cairn at Yarrows the passage was 10 feet long, 2½ feet high and 2 feet wide, being reduced to 1½ feet in width by the inner portal. In the round cairn at Camster the width and height of the passage were the same as at Yarrows, but its length was 20 feet. It was subdivided by three pairs of slabs set at right-angles to its axis and projecting inwards from the side walls like additional portals. The same phenomenon was noted in an oval cairn near

[1] *PSAS.*, vii, p. 495.   [2] *RC., Sutherland*, No. 83.

Loch Yarrows. There are striking parallels in Portugal and Denmark.

Normally in horned cairns the passage opened on to the centre of the forecourt, the chamber being situated in the wider end of the mound. But in the long horned cairn at Camster the chamber occupied the centre of the cairn and opened on to its southern side. Near the wider end was a tiny chamber, quite empty, entered by a very narrow passage which also opened on to the long side, not on to the forecourt.

In all chambers the remains of several individuals of all ages and of both sexes were discovered. The maximum number actually identified was thirty skeletons in the short horned cairn of Ormiegill. The bones were generally in complete disorder, broken, and trodden into the floor. But at Lower Dounreay Edwards [1] established that one body at least had been originally laid to rest in the contracted position. In the case of Yarrows I, Anderson implies that all the bones had been incinerated, while burnt human bones as well as unburnt are reported also from Yarrows II, Camster round, Kenny's Cairn, and elsewhere. The excavator, however, expressly mentions instances where the bones were only partially burnt in those sections close to the fire : " the long bones were often burned in half of their length only." [2] The cremated human remains do not therefore necessarily establish the practice of cremation. They may be the result of fires kindled in the vaults. Charcoal was actually found on the floors in most chambers and presumably came from such fires which had also scorched or incinerated the animal bones found in most chambers.

The disordered condition of the bones and their partial cremation may therefore be explained, as indicated on p. 29, as incidents to the re-use of the vault. The undertakers engaged on the later funerals would have sacrilegiously pushed aside the skeletons of former occupants of the tomb and even trodden their bones under foot. Yet it should be noted that the entrance passage to the round cairn at Camster had been deliberately blocked by a packing of stones, although two skeletons were found sitting in the passage.

In addition to skeletons the floor of most chambers was littered with the bones of animals—cattle, sheep, horses, swine, dogs, and deer—sometimes burnt. The only long horned cairn

[1] *PSAS.,* lxiii, p. 145.   [2] *PSAS.,* vii, p. 493.

to yield pottery assignable to the primary burials was that at Yarrows; the sherds described as plain black have been lost but presumably belonged to Windmill Hill ware. That pottery is certainly represented in the short horned and round cairns (Lower Dounreay, Ormiegill, Achaidh, Camster, Kenny); the sherds from the last-named tomb are decorated with stab-and-drag or finger-tip patterns, which serve to connect them with the Unstan class of the north as opposed to the Beacharra group of the south-west. In addition to pottery we have a stone axe-head from Lower Dounreay, leaf-shaped arrow-heads from Ormiegill, lopsided arrow-heads from Ormiegill and Camster round (Fig. 18), a pestle-shaped mace-head from Ormiegill (Fig. 16), narrow flint knives with ground edges from Camster and Ormiegill, a chisel-like implement of bone from Kenny's Cairn (Fig. 19), and a transversely perforated phalange of an ox from Lower Dounreay.

Nearly all the stone and bone relics recur elsewhere with Beakers or Food Vessels. They may, therefore, denote contact between the builders of collective tombs and the Beaker-folk. Such contact is more explicitly demonstrated by sherds from other chambers. A secondary short cist containing a Beaker interment had been intruded into the cairn at Lower Dunreay, but cord-ornamented sherds belonging to two Beakers were found on the floor of the chamber itself. And a short cist containing similar sherds together with a jet necklace had been erected on the very floor of the chamber in the long horned cairn at Yarrows.

These discoveries seem to mean that the chambered cairns were still in use as mausolea when Beaker-folk began to arrive in Caithness. Presumably the new-comers were admitted into the communities entitled to burial in the chambered cairns. A foreigner would hardly choose as his last resting-place a chamber, haunted by the ghosts of former inhabitants, until he had placated them by establishing at least amicable relations with their descendants. In any case the discovery of Beaker-sherds in the chambers proves that in Caithness the collective tombs remained in use for a considerable time—at least until the Beaker-folk had worked their way up to the extreme north of Scotland. On the other hand, their prestige seems to have been such that their rites of individual interment eventually superseded the older practice of collective burial. The round cairns covering short cists in the cemeteries of Camster and Warehouse Hill would be the result of this process.

On the floor of the chamber in the round cairn at Camster above the main burial deposit, Anderson found an iron knife. This can hardly denote a continued use of the chamber down to the Iron Age. It should rather be ascribed to a late violation of the tomb such as is epigraphically attested in the case of Maes Howe.

4. NORTH-WESTERN SCOTLAND

The collective tombs of the coasts and islands of Western Scotland between Loch Etive and Cape Wrath occupy, at least geographically, an intermediate position between the two main concentrations. In addition to a few on the west coast of the mainland, the Royal Commission has recorded some forty-six ruined chambers or cairns probably covering chambers in Skye and the Outer Hebrides (Mull is a blank, perhaps through lack of exploration). Of these, four in North Uist [1] and one in Skye [2] are long and still show vestiges of horns at one end. The great majority are, however, more or less circular in plan. But at least one of these possessed a semicircular forecourt on to which the chamber opened. Most of the monuments have been terribly mutilated through use as stone quarries since the Iron Age, and few have been excavated.

Surface indications suggest the existence in the area of both long cists, as on the Clyde, and passage graves, approximating somewhat in plan to the Caithness tombs. Six structures on North and South Uist [3] and some in Western Sutherland are probably long cists, not demonstrably segmented.

South Clettraval [4] in North Uist might be described as a long cist, walled with slabs on edge and divided into five compartments by septal stones in the Clyde manner. But the compartments grow wider and higher towards the inner end till the innermost is 7 feet long by 5½ wide by at least 6 feet high. And in one corner dry-stone walling filled the space between the upright blocks. The structure might therefore also be

---

[1] *RC. Hebr.,* Nos. 220, 238 (150 and 165 feet long).
[2] Ibid., Nos. 550 (187 feet long).
[3] *RC. Hebr.,* Nos. 126, 217, 231, 233, 237, 385.
[4] Information from Mr. Lindsay Scott ; a full account will appear in *PSAS.,* lxix.

described as a chamber preceded by antechamber and segmented passage. The passage opened through a wide but straight façade consisting of large uprights increasing in size towards the centre : the peristalith was composed of a dry-built wall with a kerb of tilted slabs in front and a row of uprights behind. The primary burials in the chambers and passage had been accompanied by numerous vases typical of the Beacharra class of Windmill Hill ware, but sherds of Beaker were found in an upper deposit. By this excavation and by that of Rudh' an Dunain Lindsay Scott has at last established stratigraphically the chronological relation between Beakers and Windmill Hill ware, at least in North-west Scotland.

An intermediate position might also be assigned to the chamber in the great cairn at Achnacree off the northern shore of Loch Etive. The round cairn, 75 feet in diameter, stood on a platform in a natural hollow [1] and was girt with a peristalith of tall uprights that now project through the slope of stones. The chamber,[2] entered by a passage some 20 feet long, resembles a tripartite cist in plan, the basal courses of the walls being formed of great blocks on edge. But the outer compartment, 6 feet long by 4 feet wide and 7 feet high, is roofed by a corbelled dome like the Camster chamber. The two inner compartments (lintelled) are each entered through narrow portals with septal stones between the jambs. Two typical Windmill Hill pots, one approximating rather to the Beacharra sub-group, were recovered from the chambers, as well as some white quartz pebbles.

The majority of the North-west Scottish vaults seem to have been passage graves. For geological reasons, the refractory volcanic and crystalline rocks being less suitable for dry-stone building, they diverge from the Caithness type in the greater reliance on orthostatic building and the use of huge, horizontal lintels instead of corbelled roofs.

The best known is that of Rudh' an Dunain [3] which stands on a remote and desolate isthmus at the mouth of Loch Brittle, Skye. The round cairn, 78 feet across, was encircled by a peristalith of upright blocks with panels of dry walling between them (Fig. 9). On either side of the chamber's entrance the peristalith curves inwards so as to flank a shallow semicircular

[1] According to Mitchell, *PSAS.*, lxvii, p. 323 ; Angus Smith considered the cairn to be surrounded by an artificial fosse.

[2] *PSAS.*, ix, pp. 410 ff.

[3] *PSAS.*, lxv, pp. 188 ff. ; lxviii, pp. 194 f.

forecourt. A prostrate slab in the centre of the space seems to have been an original feature with parallels in Sweden and Brittany. The façade increases in height towards the centre

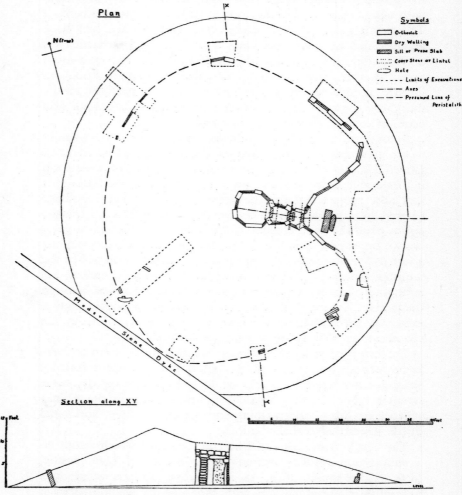

Plan

N (true)

Symbols

▭ Orthostat
▤ Dry Walling
▨ Sill or Prone Slab
⬚ Cover Stone or Lintel
⬭ Hole
- - - - Limits of Excavations
—·— Axes
— — Presumed Line of Peristalith

Modern Stone Dyke

Section along XY

FIG. 9.—Passage grave at Rudh' an Dunain, Skye, after Scott.

as in the long cairn at Yarrows. From the ruined portal a passage, only $3\frac{1}{4}$ feet long but $3\frac{3}{4}$ feet high, leads through an inner portal to a trapezoid antechamber, $4\frac{1}{4}$ feet long, $3\frac{3}{4}$ feet wide, and $5\frac{1}{3}$ feet high. Beyond another constriction

lies the polygonal chamber, $7\frac{1}{4}$ feet in diameter and about
7 feet high. The walls throughout are formed of orthostats
alternating with panels of coursed masonry, while passage,
antechamber, and chamber were once lintelled over. Exactly the
same general plan and method of construction may be seen
in a long cairn at Skelpick in Strathnaver (Sutherland) [1] save
that here the passage was over 12 feet long and the chamber
is said to have been tripartite. But at Rudh' an Dunain there
were sills or septal stones at the portals of passage, antechamber,
and chamber. Scott recognized two layers of deposit; an upper
layer, 2 feet deep, consisted of brown earth and stones and
yielded sherds of Beaker, pieces of pumice, and remains of
four individuals, one at least round-headed. The lower stratum,
1 foot thick and shiny black, comprised Windmill Hill pottery,
flint flakes, and many decayed human and animal bones, all
unburnt.

In most Hebridean cairns the chamber was probably simpler.
At Barpa Langass,[2] it was oval in plan, $9\frac{1}{4}$ feet long, 6 feet wide,
and from 6 to 7 feet high, and preceded by a passage 19 feet
long and $2\frac{3}{4}$ feet wide at the mouth. Chamber and passage alike
were roofed with long lintels resting on the large upright slabs
that formed the walls or on horizontal stones employed to bring
the shorter uprights up to the general level. This cairn had
been built on a space artificially levelled before its erection to
a depth of $2\frac{1}{2}$ feet on one side. Like other cairns in the area it
was encircled by a peristalith of orthostats, presumably once
supplemented with dry walling. A tanged and barbed arrow-head
was recovered from the chamber together with pottery.

In some cairns the stones of the peristalith seem unnecessarily
tall, and project high above the boulders of the cairn.[3] In two
or three instances the ring of uprights lies quite outside the
edge of the cairn as if the peristalith were acquiring an independent
character of its own. That seems to have happened in the famous
monument of Callernish in Lewis.[4] Here a small, circular cairn,
only 21 feet in diameter, encloses a rectangular chamber $4\frac{1}{4}$ feet
deep (on the axis of the passage) and $6\frac{2}{3}$ feet wide. It is entered
from the east by a short passage. Two slabs on edge, set transversely to the passage's axis, form, as in Caithness, the chamber's
portal, while a parallel pair at the rear of the chamber frame

[1] Anderson, ii, p. 263 ; *RC. Suth.*, No. 241.   [2] *RC. Hebr.*, No. 224.
[3] *RC. Hebr.*, p. xxx.   [4] *RC. Hebr.*, No. 89.

the door to a narrow, irregular cell or annex. Two tall uprights on the peristalith of the cairn on either side of the passage mouth belong themselves to a large circle of thirteen stones with a diameter of 37½ feet Another upright on the peristalith of the cairn and immediately behind the chamber on the line of the passage appears to stand as a tall menhir nearly at the centre of the circle. From the circle an avenue 27 feet wide extends northward for a distance of 270 feet, while alignments of uprights radiate from the circle towards the remaining points of the compass.

At Callernish we seem to see a stone circle combined with avenue and alignments growing out of the peristalith of a cairn. And other Hebridean cairns are surrounded by an outer circle of uprights in addition to a peristalith. Such complications suggest that the old traditions of collective burial persisted longer in the islands than in Caithness or Arran. Beaker-folk indeed arrived, as in Caithness, while the collective tombs were still in use and sometimes were admitted to sepulchre in the old vaults or at others built their short cists in cairns covering such.[1] Yet perhaps they did not bring about so soon as elsewhere the atrophy of the old practices, or else were absorbed by the earlier settlers.

5. COLLECTIVE TOMBS IN ORKNEY

Some twenty-one chambered cairns or mounds that may be regarded as collective burial places are known in the Orkney archipelago. Two of these, one on Rousay and one on the East Mainland, are long horned cairns, conforming at least in externals to the Caithness type. A third in Burray[2] seems to have been a short horned cairn of the same family. The rest can be regarded as late and specialized variants on the Caithness plan. Like these the chambers are constructed mainly of coursed masonry ; for the Caithness flagstone extends to Orkney. The mound, however, comprises a much greater proportion of earth than on the Mainland. Still, it is generally surrounded with a wall, of slabs even more carefully built than in Caithness cairns. The tombs often stand on the slope of a hill, and in at least three cases the chamber floor has been partially excavated

---

[1] *PSAS.*, lxii, p. 25 ; *infra*, p. 107.   [2] Anderson, ii, p. 290.

in the rock. Perhaps slabs of the soft rock had been quarried to provide material for the walls and the hollow thus formed utilized for the floor of the burial vault.

What may be regarded as a direct development of the Caithness type is illustrated by three cairns on Rousay and one on the Holm of Papa Westray. At Midhowe,[1] in Rousay, the cairn is a long oval, girt with a wall of slabs set herring-bone fashion upon a plinth with a bonding course of horizontal slabs between them. The side walls continue as horn-like projections at both ends of the mound. The chamber, opening through a short passage on the south-western end of the mound, is walled like a Caithness tomb with coursed masonry from which thin upright slabs project transversely in pairs. But it is exceedingly long—78 feet by 8 feet wide—and divided into no less than twelve compartments. The side walls are much denuded, but the surviving portions do not corbel appreciably inwards. The upright slabs increase in height from $4\frac{1}{2}$ feet at the entrance to $7\frac{1}{2}$ feet at the centre ; the rest have all been trimmed off flat about 5 feet above the floor, and there are some very ambiguous indications that over the inner half of the chamber a second story had been erected, entered by a separate passage from the north-east end of the mound.

The stall-like compartments between the divisional uprights were occupied by low stone shelves on which the bodies had originally reposed in a contracted position. The bones of at least thirty individuals were recovered, as many as four lying in a single compartment. All but one lay on the left-hand side of the chamber. The chamber also contained animal bones and a few sherds of pottery of the Unstan class of Windmill Hill ware.

The Knowe of Yarso (Rousay), also girt with a wall of tilted slabs resting on a plinth, comes still nearer the Caithness type since the chamber is divided into only three compartments. The chamber contained 29 skeletons, leaf-shaped and barbed arrow-heads and sherds of two vessels, more reminiscent of a Beaker and a Food Vessel than of Unstan vases.

In all the remaining Orkney tumuli the entrance passage leads not into the end of the chamber but into a long side. Two main variants may be detected. In one, illustrated by Unstan and Taiversoë Tuack, the chamber is subdivided by slabs projecting

[1] *PSAS.*, lxviii, pp. 320 ff. ; *Ant. J.*, xvi, p. 423.

from the side walls as at Midhowe. At Unstan [1] on the shores
of Loch Stenness near its exit, the chamber is 21 feet long and
5 feet wide near the centre (Fig. 10). The two ends are faced with
upright slabs and four pairs of uprights project from the side
walls dividing the chamber into five compartments. There were
shelves about 18 inches from the floor in the two end compartments. A corbelled cell, $3\frac{1}{2}$ feet high, opens out of the back
of the third compartment. The side walls of the chamber corbel
inwards, but the roof was probably formed of long, flat lintels.

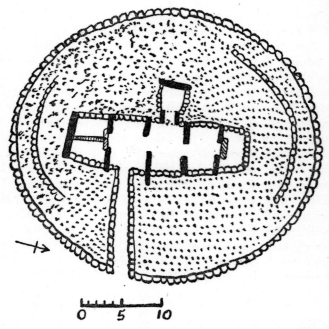

0   5   10

FIG. 10.—Plan of chamber in cairn at Unstan, Orkney. (Discoveries
of 1934 not shown.)

A narrow passage, 11 feet long, gave access to the vault. Its roof
was formed partly of flat lintels, partly of slabs set on edge.

The remains of at least eight skeletons, some of which had
been laid to rest in a contracted position, were recovered from
the chamber as well as animal bones. The grave goods included
many vessels of Windmill Hill ware illustrating the variety that

[1] *PSAS.*, xix, pp. 341 ff.; Anderson, ii, p. 293. A stepped outer wall was
found in 1934.

takes its name from this site. The disturbance due to secondary burials may be judged from the fact that parts of one bowl were found in the second compartment, the rest in the fifth! The chamber also contained three very fine lozenge-shaped arrow-heads, a fabricator, and a narrow knife with ground edge of flint—all burnt. A barbed and tanged arrow-head of " Bronze Age " type, also burnt, was recovered from the passage.

The same general plan is reproduced at Taiversoë Tuack on Rousay.[1] But here the ends of the chamber are rounded and walled with almost perpendicular dry masonry while the front (south) wall is straight and vertical. The floor was partly excavated in the living rock, the edges of the hollow forming the foundation for the concave rear wall. Three slabs that do not reach the roof, project inwards from that wall, the four stalls thus formed being provided with slab shelves a foot above the floor. The chamber, only 4⅔ feet high, was roofed with five horizontal slabs, 4 to 5 feet long and 2 to 3 feet wide. It was entered by a passage 12 feet long, which was 2⅓ feet high at the inner end, but contracts to 1 foot square at its mouth and was found blocked by a transverse slab 18 inches in. At the inner end of the passage there is a recess about 2 feet square a foot above its floor. The most curious feature of the tumulus remains to be mentioned. The lintels of the chamber just described themselves formed the floor of a second chamber, a sort of upper storey. This was probably planned much like the main chamber. But it had a separate entrance and was orientated rather differently. Unfortunately it was greatly ruined when the excavation began and seems to have yielded no relics.

The lower chamber contained five or more skeletons, some contracted, and heaps of " cremated " bone in the passage inside the barrier as well as vessels of typical Unstan pottery. Outside the barrier other sherds and the butt of an axe or mace (Fig. 16, 2) were discovered.

The vaults of Kewing Hill,[2] Wideford Hill,[3] and Quanterness,[3] in Mainland, Quoyness on Sanday[4] and on the Holm of Papa Westray[3] agree in general outline. The chamber, partly excavated in the hillside in the two first mentioned, varies in length from 10 feet on Wideford Hill to 64 feet on Holm of Papa. The walls

[1] *PSAS.*, xxxvii, pp. 77 ff.
[2] *PSAS.*, xxxvi, pp. 733 ff.
[3] *Arch.*, xxxiv, pp. 123 ff.
[4] *PSAS.*, vii, p. 398 ; plan in Anderson, ii, fig. 287.

are formed exclusively of coursed masonry and generally corbel inwards. At Quoyness the vault is 12 feet high, but only the side walls converge; the end walls are perpendicular and not bonded in to the convergent sides. From the main chamber there open off from three (Wideford Hill) to fourteen (Papa Westray) cells. These are generally corbelled and vary in area from 3 feet square to 7 by 5 feet. They are separated from

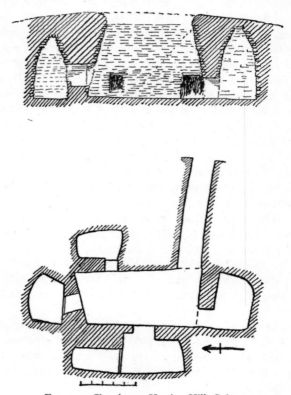

FIG. 11.—Chamber at Kewing Hill, Orkney.

the main chamber only by a flimsy wall one course deep which is pierced by a doorway not exceeding 2 feet in height. At Quoyness there were six such cells each about 6 feet high. The entrance passages are always very low and narrow and in most cases roofed with slabs on edge.

Presumably the cells were designed to contain the original burials, and skeletons were actually found in them both at

Quoyness and Kewing Hill. In each case, however, there were other bodies in the chamber proper. The remains of at least fifteen skeletons are reported from Quoyness and seven from Kewing Hill; one of the latter was definitely round-headed. No human remains were certainly obtained from the other tombs, but all yielded many animal bones generally split as if for a feast. The abundance of animal bones, suggestive of kitchen refuse, has roused doubts as to the sepulchral function of some of the chambers.[1] Secondary occupation for domestic purposes is indeed a possibility. But twenty-four dogs' skulls were found in Kewing Hill and seven in the horned cairn on Burray.[2] That sounds like ritual slaughter rather than domestic cooking.

No pottery has been found in any tomb of this class. Quoyness yielded two enigmatic implements of flagstone, and a bone pin with a lateral bulb. (A spindle whorl is also reported, but might be intrusive.) A fragment of a steatite vessel was found in Kewing Hill by Charleson, who regarded it as a Viking intrusion. But since such vessels go back to the Bronze Age, it need only illustrate the continued use of the chamber into that period. The recent discovery of Unstan pottery in fields on the slopes of Wideford Hill[3] encourages the belief that the tombs go back to the period when that ware was still current.

A plurality of cells or niches opening off the principal chamber is not uncommon in the excavated collective tombs of Greece, Sicily,[4] and Sardinia[5] and occurs sporadically even in Portugal and Ireland.[6] Ideas from these quarters may in fact have influenced the development of sepulchral architecture in Orkney. But on the whole it is not impossible to treat the tombs so far described as a spontaneous elaboration of the ideas implicit in the Caithness group. The island architects would have aimed at enlarging the family ossuary to obviate the necessity of erecting new vaults for the remains of future generations. They would have attained this object firstly by enlarging the chamber and secondly by adding to it as annexes sepulchral cells of a type already familiar from some mainland vaults. But the extravagant dimensions attained by Midhowe and Holm of Papa Westray look like the

---

[1] There are in Orkney several chambered mounds that were certainly habitations. The Howe of Midgarth and Westerleafea (*PSAS.*, xxxvii, pp. 354 ff.) illustrate what villages like Skara Brae must originally have been.
[2] Anderson, ii, p. 290.   [3] *POAS.*, xii, p. 22.
[4] In Siculan II times, Peet, *Stone and Bronze Ages*, figs. 219, 251.
[5] Childe, *Dawn*, fig. 50.   [6] *Infra*, p. 59.

E

final outcome of long brooding in isolation. Plenty of time was probably available for such aberrant development. Though a round-headed skull was found in Kewing Hill and a tanged-and-barbed arrow-head at Unstan, no cists with Beakers are known from Orkney. It may be inferred that the Beaker-folk, whose advent arrested development of sepulchral architecture in Arran and Caithness, only reached Orkney very late or in numbers too small to interrupt local burial rites.

The imposing tomb of Maes Howe [1] occupies a place apart. It is the finest chamber tomb in Great Britain internally, and the huge barrow dominating the low moorland at the head of the Loch of Harray is the most impressive monument of its kind in North Britain. The chamber is nearly 15 feet square and was perhaps originally 20 feet high. It is entered by a passage, 54 feet long with two sets of door-checks and a recess behind the inner jambs for the door. Three cells, each 3 feet high, open out of the main chamber about 3 feet above the floor. In the chamber's corners are buttresses, each faced with an upright monolith some 10 feet high, the top edge of which is sloped backward like the smaller uprights in Camster or Unstan. The corbelled roof is formed of flagstone slabs, often over 8 feet long, while the passage walls are faced with equally gigantic slabs set on edge. This truly megalithic architecture is infinitely superior to anything found elsewhere in Scotland. Yet after all it differs only in scale and finish from the stone work of Quoyness or Camster. The ideas and technique are the same down even to details like the trimming of the tops of the orthostats.

A real innovation is the gigantic fosse, 35 feet wide, that encircles the mound save for a causeway opposite the entrance. It does suggest the transplantation to Orkney of an idea more at home in Ireland. But even that need mean no more than that the chief for whom Maes Howe was designed had seen New Grange or a similar Irish monument from the outside and had been the privileged guest of the court to which the Irish tomb belonged. Unfortunately Maes Howe was violated by Norse pilgrims to Jerusalem who have left Runic records of their visit, but no relics of the earlier occupants of the princely sepulchre.

[1] Anderson, ii, p. 275; *Ant. J.*, xiv, p. 413. A more accurate plan will be published in the forthcoming volume of *RC.* on Orkney and Shetland.

6. The Stone Circles of Strath Nairn and Strath Spey

The isolated long cairns on the coastal plain of North-east Scotland [1] may be attributed to stray settlers who had crossed the Moray Firth from Caithness or Sutherland. Though none have been excavated, they resemble externally the monuments of the extreme north.

But in the valleys of the Ness, Nairn, and Upper Spey there are groups of stone circles some of which surround chambered cairns of a specialized type. The whole group may be named after the classical examples on the Nairn in the Clava estate, close to Culloden. Like so many sepulchral vaults in South-west Scotland, the monuments of the Clava type stand on, or close to, stretches of alluvial gravels. The group on Speyside round Aviemore [2] conspicuously occupies the only extensive tract of such alluvium in the Central Highlands and represents the sole indications of human habitation in that region till the forts of the Iron Age.

The circles are regularly grouped in small cemeteries of three or four, closely juxtaposed. And some structural differences are often observable between the monuments composing each group. In two monuments at Clava (Balnaruan),[3] the central cairn is bounded by a peristalith of large stones on edge, set close together and sloping slightly inwards ; the diameters are 53 and 57 feet respectively. A passage, 2 feet wide at the mouth and expanding internally to 3 feet and probably 4 feet high, leads from the south-west of the circumference to a circular chamber about 12½ feet in diameter. Its walls are founded on large blocks on edge which support courses of corbelled masonry still standing to a height of 7 feet ; they would have converged to a dome 12 feet above the floor. Each cairn is surrounded by a ring of uprights with diameters of 108 and 110 feet respectively ; the tallest orthostats stood to the south-west, while those on the north are the smallest.

A third cairn in the same group was differently planned. It was indeed surrounded by a ring of uprights, 107 feet in diameter, precisely similar to those just described, and bounded

---

[1] Longman Hill (near Macduff), Knapperty Hillock, Balnagowan, and Newhills (Aberdeenshire), Gourdon Hill (Kinc.), and possibly Easterton of Roseisle near Elgin. Cf. Callander, *PSAS.*, lviii, p. 23 ; lix, pp. 21–4 ; *Arch.*, lxxvii, p. 94.
[2] *PSAS.*, xl, 248 ff. ; xliv, p. 200 ff.
[3] *PSAS.*, xviii, pp. 343 f.

by a peristalith of 57 feet, just as in the two other monuments. But this peristalith formed a complete ring with no gap for a passage. The site of the chamber was again marked by a continuous ring of 22 feet diameter, but there was no coursed masonry on the top of the uprights and no indication that the wide central space had ever been roofed over at all. The space between the peristalith and the inner ring of boulders was completely filled with large stones; the two rings in fact bounded a ring cairn round a central hollow. A peculiarity in this monument is a set of three pebble causeways, about 7 feet in width, radiating from the base of the peristalith to three orthostats in the outer ring.

In the Clava cemetery we have a complete degeneration series from a true chambered cairn with an outer circle to a ring cairn surrounding a central hollow, presumably used for burials. The suppression of the entrance passage might be held to mark the abandonment of the practice of collective burial under the influence, perhaps, of the Beaker tradition. Exactly the same series can be seen in the cemeteries round Aviemore; at Avielochan there was a portal of stones set transversely half way up the passage of a chambered example. But in most cases the monument is now marked only by three rings of big stones; the rest of the structure has been so pillaged that recognition of an entrance passage is no longer possible. Yet traces exist of thirty such monuments in the Nairn and Ness Valleys, six or seven in Strath Spey round Aviemore, two in Black Isle,[1] one in Glen Urquhart, and six in Beauly Valley.[2] Three in Strath Nairn and four in Strath Spey were demonstrably chambered. It should be noted that the uprights, especially those of the inner ring, often bear cup-marks; in one case at Clava these must have been pecked out before the erection of the stone.

Burnt bones and fragments of urns, now lost, were found in one cairn at Clava (Balnaruan).[3] Part of a lignite armlet came to light in the entrance to the cairn at Avielochan,[4] but not on the floor. The age of all these structures is therefore doubtful; none need be very early. We shall find in the sequel that monuments directly derived from the foregoing were being erected in Aberdeenshire at the very close of the Bronze Age.

[1] *P.S.A.S.*, xviii, pp. 330 ff.
[2] *Trans. Invern. Sci. Soc.*, iii (1886), pp. 142–6.
[3] Anderson, ii, p. 301.
[4] *P.S.A.S.*, xliv, p. 203.

But whatever their age, it must be assumed that cairns of the Clava type were built by adherents of the collectivist tradition who preserved both the sepulchral practices and agricultural economy of their ancestors. It would be simplest to bring the colonists who settled on the Nairn and Spey across the Moray Firth from Eastern Sutherland. But the addition of a distinct circle outside the peristalith recalls Ireland and the Hebrides. Perhaps then the leaders in the colonization had connections on the West Coast.

THE NUMBERS AND ORIGIN OF THE TOMB-BUILDERS

We have recorded on our Map some 250 cairns, covering collective burial vaults. They are conspicuous monuments not likely to be overlooked in a careful field survey. At least in Galloway, Arran and Bute, Caithness and Eastern Sutherland the available records probably give an accurate picture of the present distribution and numbers of the tombs. The chambers in particular are troublesome to remove and have been to some degree protected by superstitions. There seem no adequate grounds for postulating any sweeping destruction of vaults, at least in the far north ; perhaps the figures might be doubled to allow for the damage done in three thousand years. It should then be possible to attempt an estimate of the density of population. Such an attempt is, however, beset with numerous pitfalls.

In the first place, how long was any given monument in use ? It has been hitherto assumed that each chamber was a family or communal vault used for several generations. But W. J. Hemp,[1] in excavating similar monuments in England and Wales, has noted indications of the complete blocking of the entrance passages—a feature also remarked by Anderson at Camster. Hemp's observations have suggested that the entrance to the chamber was completely masked by the cairn which was itself erected at no appreciable interval after the chamber. He is inclined to the conclusion that the erection of the chamber, the obsequies, and the heaping of the barrow constituted a single continuous cycle of events after which the vault was finally sealed. The majority of the corpses would then be those of wives or menials, slain to follow their lord to the future life.

[1] *Arch. Camb.*, 1927, pp. 13, 17 ; cf. *T. Bris. & Glouc. Arch. Soc.*, 1929, p. 268.

Such human sacrifice in the tomb was apparently the rule in Mesopotamia during the third millennium B.C.,[1] among the nomads of Upper Asia, and in parts of Negro Africa [2] till comparatively recent times. On this view the only function of the portals and passages would be to make the tomb more like the dwelling of the living ; each vault would, in practice, denote the burial of a single potent chief.

Though Hemp's observations are undoubtedly correct, his conclusions do not inevitably follow therefrom or at least need not apply in all cases. The entrance to the chamber would of course be hidden to prevent desecration by tomb-robbers, but the secret would be known to the initiated who could without great difficulty remove the masking stones and secure access to the vault. In Greece [3] and Denmark,[4] where a well-marked succession of ceramic styles makes possible fine chronological distinctions, the use of the same tomb for two or three centuries is amply attested. Scott's observations in Skye and North Uist would seem to justify the application of these results to the intermediate region of Scotland. We may then retain our original assumption that each chamber was in use for several generations. How many can only be guessed. The maximum number of interments recorded from any one tomb on the Scottish mainland was, it will be remembered, thirty.

Secondly, were all collective tombs in use at the same time ? In the case of the Caithness cemeteries, that include long, round, and even unchambered cairns, a negative answer was given. After the lapse of some generations a new cairn would have been erected to cover a mausoleum for the successors of those who built the first monument. In Arran or Galloway the same result might have been more often attained by constructing an additional chamber in the cairn that covered the first. If we double our numbers to allow for destruction, we shall have to halve them again to obtain the figures for tombs used concurrently.

Thirdly, what members of a society had the right to burial in a collective vault ? Was entry thereto reserved to a local

---

[1] Childe, *MAE.*, p. 172.
[2] e.g. Talbot, *Southern Nigeria,* iii, p. 478.
[3] *Arch.,* lxxxii, pp. 130–3, 231—there was here a little evidence of family likeness between the persons buried in the same tomb ; Xanthoudides, *Vaulted Tombs,* pp. vi, 7, 34.
[4] For latest evidence see *Aarbøger,* 1929, pp. 194, 200, 209.

chief and his family ? Or were all members of the community entitled to a place in the communal ossuary ? In favour of the first alternative emphasis is generally laid on the enormous labour supposedly involved in erecting the massive stones of the chambers and covering them with a huge cairn. It is thought to exceed the strength of a restricted family group unequipped with modern tackle. Yet the difficulties have probably been exaggerated. Given ample time—and simple farmers and hunters do enjoy abundant spells of leisure—two or three men really experienced in handling stone could surely have managed the quarrying, transportation, and erection of the blocks. Account must also be taken of the co-operation of neighbouring groups, particularly for ritual ends (like canoe-building in the Trobriands or the erection of a lodge on the Pacific Coast of Canada), that constitute a regular feature of many primitive societies, surviving in the modern world.

In Egypt indeed a built or rock-cut tomb was a prerogative reserved to Pharaoh and his nobles down to the end of the third millennium B.C. The same is true of Babylonia, and in parts of Africa only chiefs are buried with full ritual. On the other hand collective tombs were probably used by ordinary burghers at Mycenæ and generally throughout the East Mediterranean. In the Iberian Peninsula a cemetery comprising nearly a hundred corbelled tombs, very similar to those of Caithness, was attached to the small, fortified settlement of Los Millares in Almeria. Each tomb contained from twenty to eighty corpses. If only a nobility used these vaults, the nobility must have been very large.

Yet if we assume in Scotland that all or most members of a community were entitled to burial in collective tombs, we get a population which looks ridiculously small. In Caithness, for instance, we should have, say, sixty chambers in use simultaneously with an average content of say twenty corpses (the recorded average is much lower). That gives a total of 1,200 bodies. But these have to be distributed over three or four generations, giving a population at any one time of 400 or even 300 souls for the whole county. That figure is not really so absurd as it appears. We are dealing with the centuries of the first colonization of a not very fertile or attractive region in the remotest corner of the then civilized world. The families under consideration are the first settlers, come certainly from afar across the seas to colonize a wilderness—perhaps, indeed, boat-loads of voyagers driven against their will by the wind and currents to these remote solitudes. In estimating the density of population we have no standards to guide us; the most "primitive" modern community has been in occupation of its territories for many centuries while the cairn-builders in Caithness were perhaps the first human beings to set foot on that soil. The figures suggested are, then, not impossible. But if extraneous considerations imply that a family vault was the prerogative of a noble class within the community, the foregoing estimate would certainly not be incompatible with the consequent enlargement of the total population.

It may be safely asserted that the tomb-builders were not just the descendants of the Mesolithic hunters described in Chapter II. In fact the chambered cairn at Glecknabae in Bute was erected upon the site of an old shell-mound on the 25 ft. beach, presumably Azilian, that was already grass-grown before the cairn was piled.

The skeletal remains [1] from the tombs give only the most general indication as to the origin of their builders. All skeletons assignable to the primary interments that could be studied at all seemed to belong to a single racial type. They were slightly built people, of modest stature, males not exceeding $5\frac{1}{2}$ feet in height. Their skulls, despite a relatively high capacity, approaching or exceeding 1,500 c.c., were long and narrow—dolichocranial. A statistical study of the published measurements led Morant [2] in 1926 to conclude that their owners belonged to the same racial type as the long barrow men of England, a conclusion already reached by different methods by Bryce and Turner. They were certainly of a different breed from the Beaker-folk and are generally assigned to the "Mediterranean race".

The funerary architecture is more explicit as to the southern affinities of the colonists. The detailed agreements between the Scottish vaults and those of the Iberian Peninsula and the Mediterranean are too close and numerous to be accidental. Yet it is well to recall explicitly what such agreements actually entail. An African potentate who has visited the sky-scrapers

[1] Bryce, in *Book of Arran*, pp. 93–6; Turner, *TRSE.*, li, pp. 181 f.
[2] *Biometrika,* xviii, p. 60.

of Europe or America, is not thereby rendered competent to instruct his subjects in the technique of handling ferro-concrete nor initiated into the mysteries of the business conducted in such buildings. No more could an Azilian fisher, blown in his fragile craft from Oransay to Portugal, have learned how to erect a corbelled vault or grasped the complex plan of a beehive tomb and the ritual associations of its several parts. Nor could merchants, voyaging to Denmark for amber and calling on the way at Arran or Orkney, have inspired any unsophisticated natives inhabiting those islands with a sudden passion for monumental tombs or the skill for their erection. As W. J. Perry [1] has very properly insisted, only actual settlements of people initiated into the rites of collective sepulchre and practically trained in the technique of tomb-building could reproduce so faithfully on these distant shores monuments at home in the Mediterranean south.

The semicircular forecourt, as already stated, recurs in the sepulchral architecture of Sicily,[2] Sardinia,[3] Southern Spain,[4] and Portugal.[5] The horned cairns of Scotland reproduce this feature more faithfully than any other monuments in Great Britain. Forecourts are indeed found at one end of the chambered long barrows of England as well as in some circular tumuli in Brittany, Ireland, and Sweden. But in these the façade on either side of the portal is convex, not concave ; the forecourt is cuspidal not semicircular in plan.

The chambers opening off the forecourts in Scottish cairns reproduce no less faithfully models imported from the south. But the models for the two main types of Scottish chamber are found in different regions.

The nearest parallels to the segmented cists of the Clyde are found along both sides of the Pyrenees from the Plateau of Ger [6] (Hautes Pyrénées) to Catalonia [7] and then in Sardinia.

---

[1] *The Growth of Civilization.*
[2] Cf. *BPI.,* xxviii, p. 109 ; *Not. Scavi,* 1905, p. 194 (Siculan I) and *Ausonia,* i (1906), p. 5 (Siculan II).
[3] Peet, p. 231 ; *PBSR.,* v, pp. 119 ff. ; Leeds in *LAAA.,* ix, pl. i, n.
[4] At Los Millares, *Rev. Ques. Sci* (Bruxelles, 1893) reproduced by Leeds, *LAAA.,* ix, pl. i*e* ; and Childe, *TGAS.,* 1931–3, p. 124.
[5] Vergileio Correia, *El Neolitico del Pavia,* p. 71 ; Forde, *Amer. Anthr.,* xxxii, p. 41.
[6] La Halliade (*Mat.,* 1881, p. 525 ; the chamber was 42 feet long with seven segments).
[7] Pericot y Garcia, *Civilización megalítica Catalana,* pp. 117, 127, pls. xiv, 6–7, and iv, 2.

In South France and North Spain there are long, narrow cists, divided into several segments by transverse stones lower than the wall slabs precisely like the septal stones of Arran. Though no forecourts have been recorded in the Pyrenean tombs, the Giants' Graves of Sardinia possess semicircular forecourts flanked by elaborate horn-like façades.[1] The chambers in that island are again long, narrow cists, not apparently segmented, but walled with slabs on edge supporting a corbelled barrel vault as in Carn Bàn. The *navetas* of the Baleares are also long rectangular masses of masonry, the end through which the chamber opens being sometimes slightly concave.[2] They thus resemble a superbly constructed long cairn, and the chamber is also long and narrow like a Clyde cist. Finally, the small dolmens of Denmark,[3] the oldest collective tombs of the Baltic area, are small box-like chambers composed of two pairs of approximately parallel uprights supporting a capstone. But the upright, closing one end of the chamber, is always lower than the other three, so that access may be had to the chamber across it. It thus resembles a septal stone, and the whole structure to that extent approximates to a cist of the Clyde type reduced to a single compartment. And some such dolmens were partially covered by a long, rectangular mound enclosed in a peristalith of big blocks ; the dolmen is, however, situated near the centre of such a mound not on its edge, and the peristalith has never been observed to curve inward to form a forecourt.

Still, if the last comparison has any significance we should have a series of tombs extending from Sardinia to Denmark with the Clyde group occupying an intermediate position. In any case the Pyrenean tombs lie adjacent to a natural route from the Western Mediterranean to the Atlantic coasts.

The corbelled tombs of Caithness have even more striking parallels in Southern Spain and Portugal.[4] There we have beehive-shaped chambers, excavated in the ground or built with coursed masonry, preceded by antechambers and narrow passages and in some instances opening on to semicircular fore-courts. The chamber and antechamber in the built examples are often separated from one another and from the passage by flat slabs projecting transversely from the side walls just as in

---

[1] Peet, op. cit., fig. 88. [2] *LAAA.*, ix, pl. i, n. ; *Arch.*, lxxvi, pp. 125 f.
[3] *Aarbøger*, 1911, pp. 286–297 ; *Nord. Fort.*, i, pp. 157 f. ; *MSAN.*, 1914, p. 9.
[4] Good summary of original accounts by Forde, *Amer. Anthr.*, xxxii, pp. 40 ff. Correia, op. cit., p. 72.

Caithness; at Alcalá [1] in South Portugal, the passage is itself subdivided by pairs of such slabs precisely as at Camster—a feature which recurs in Danish passage graves. Small cells often open off the main chamber as in Kenny's Cairn, both in South Portugal and Spain.

Similarly constructed chambers occur both in Brittany [2] and Normandy [3] where stone suitable for coursed masonry was available. But in many parts of Portugal and Morbihan and in Denmark [4] the local rocks are ill adapted to dry building. Here we find chambers reproducing in detail the southern plans, but built of megalithic uprights and roofed with horizontal lintels. These look like translations into local material of the corbelled vault. Since the arrangement of the lintels differs in the three regions—in Denmark they lie parallel to the axis of the passage, in Brittany at right-angles thereto [5]—it may be inferred that the translation took place independently in the several districts.

Just as in Caithness, the beehive tombs of the Iberian Peninsula tend to cluster in cemeteries—notably at Los Millares in Almeria, Alcalá in Algarve, and Palmella, south of the Tagus.[6] Moreover the three cemeteries just named lie at terminal points on natural routes across the peninsula that would be convenient to people wishing to reach the Atlantic coasts without rounding the dangerous headlands of Gibraltar and Cape St. Vincent.

From the foregoing comparisons it must be concluded despite all seeming improbabilities that adventurous voyagers from South France and Portugal did land and settle on the western and northern coasts of Scotland respectively. The reasons which might have induced anyone to travel the treacherous roads of the sea from the sunbathed coasts of the south to our fog-enshrouded shores have been the subject of intensive speculation. Elliot Smith and Perry [7] have sought to explain their

---

[1] Estacio da Veiga, *Antiguidades monumentaes do Algarve,* iii, pl. xvii; reproduced in *Arch.,* lxx, p. 206, and *TGAS.,* l.c., p. 125.

[2] *L'Anthr.,* xliii, p. 247; *Mat.,* 1879, p. 145.

[3] Fontenoy le Marmion; the best plan is given by Coutil, " Résumé des recherches préhistoriques, Dépt. du Calvados," in *Soc. normande d'études préhistoriques.*

[4] Some of the oldest Danish passage graves have a cell annexed to the chamber (*Aarbøger,* 1917, p. 234; 1929, p. 249); in others the passage is subdivided by a series of portals precisely as at Camster and Alcalá, but these are late (ibid., 1929, p. 252).

[5] Kendrick, *Axe Age,* pp. 71, 101.

[6] Cartailhac, *Les Ages préhist. de l'Espagne,* and Åberg, *Civilisation énéolithique.*

[7] Elliot Smith, *Human History,* pp. 366 f.; Perry, *The Growth of Civilization,* pp. 65 ff.

migrations by a search for ores, precious stones, and other materials valued for supposed magical qualities as givers of life.

In Scotland there are poor copper lodes in Galloway, on both sides of Loch Fyne, in Islay, and on Rousay. Particularly at Kilfinnan on the east coast of Loch Fyne, and near Crinan, horned cairns are situated within a couple of miles of the ore deposits. But the correlation is by no means universal or exact; in particular there are no ores to attract settlers to Arran where the collective tombs were so numerous. Similarly, there is gold in the Strath of Kildonan as well as chambered cairns, but the distribution of the monuments does not point to that valley as a focus of settlement.

In the case of Denmark the connection between collective tombs and amber seems more plausible. Moreover, not only have beads of amber, possibly of Baltic origin, been found in corbelled tombs in Portugal and Spain, but a dagger of a type common in those same tombs was discovered in a settlement of the earliest builders of passage graves in Jutland.[1] There is thus a little positive evidence for some sort of trade between the Iberian and the Cimbric Peninsulas, and it would presumably follow the Atlantic route round these islands in preference to the dangers of the Straits of Dover. But such trade must not be compared to that subsisting in these days of ocean liners. We should rather do better to think of early Dutch and English trade with India involving as it did settlements both at the ultimate mart and also on the way, e.g. at Cape of Good Hope. Still better parallels are to be found in classical antiquity. Herodotus describes a Phœnician circumnavigation of Africa in the 7th century B.C. It took the explorers three years; they sailed only in " summer ", beaching their ships in " autumn " and sowed crops which they waited to harvest in the " spring ". With something of this sort in our eyes we shall be in a better position to decipher the logs of still earlier explorers, obscurely written in stone. One might imagine Caithness a sort of Cape Colony in traffic between Iberia and Denmark, a position at other times occupied by Arran and the Hebrides, on voyages from South France. In some such way we can provisionally envisage boat-loads of early mariners, bringing in their vessels seeds of grain and presumably domestic animals, landing on

[1] *De Forhistoriske Tider i Europa*, ii, p. 120; *TGAS.*, 1931–3, p. 128, fig. 5.

the coasts of Scotland. And settling here they would have perpetuated the cult of the dead that they had inherited.

How are these settlements in Scotland related to those attested by the long barrows of South-western England and the chambered cairns of Central Ireland (Northern Ireland clearly belongs to the same province as South-western Scotland)? In the English long barrows and the Irish cairns the semicircular forecourt has been replaced by a cuspidal one—which looks like a late degeneration. Though some of the Irish chambers can be compared to the Scottish and Iberian corbelled tombs, the great majority in England diverge widely from any continental model and exhibit a thoroughly insular character. On the typological principles laid down on p. 24 they should be later than the Scottish monuments. Can they be derived from the latter? Was England colonized from Scotland? A typological argument may point in that direction, but a study of the grave-goods will scarcely warrant any such conclusion.

IV

THE NEOLITHIC CIVILIZATION OF SCOTLAND

1. THE WINDMILL HILL CULTURE

THE possibility of postponing so long a detailed examination of the furniture of our collective tombs is rather surprising ; for it is due to the remarkable similarity of the grave-goods throughout Scotland. Despite the manifest duality in the traditions of sepulchral architecture, the rest of the culture associated with the tombs is fundamentally the same from Galloway to Orkney. Moreover, apart from certain types of stone implement, the distinctive elements of the same culture recur also in England and Ireland. But the culture is peculiarly British and insular ; it has only indirect or incidental analogies on the Continent.

The culture in question may conveniently be termed the Windmill Hill culture [1] after a site near Avebury, in Wiltshire. The site [2] was a sort of fortified camp surrounded by three ditches interrupted at frequent intervals by causeways. The pottery and other relics that define the culture come from the bottom of these ditches—from the primary silting. At higher levels in them so-called Peterborough ware and Beakers appear, still higher up later Bronze Age and Iron Age fabrics.

The Windmill Hill culture is best defined by its very characteristic pottery [3] which may be used to determine its distribution in Scotland,[4] thanks to Callander's masterly survey. The relevant pottery has been found in all chambered cairns that have yielded any ceramic remains at all, in domestic sites in the vicinity of the cairns—Rothesay,[5] Bute, Eilean an Tighe, North Uist, and Wideford Hill (Orkney),[6] and also at one or two sites on the east coast which will subsequently demand special explanation.

The pottery is of comparatively good quality and often quite

[1] After Leeds, *Ant. J.*, vii, p. 456.
[2] Cf. Kendrick and Hawkes, *Archæology*, pp. 56 f. ; *Arch. J.*, lxxxviii, p. 82 ; *PCPPS.*, 1932, p. 136.
[3] *Arch. J.*, lxxxviii, pp. 83 ff.
[4] *PSAS.*, lxiii, pp. 37–63 ; details will be found in this paper unless other references are given.
[5] Cf. also *TBNHS.*, 1930, p. 52.　　　　　[6] *POAS.*, xii, p. 32.

fine though white grits are frequently conspicuous in its paste. The vessels are of course all made with the free hand, unaided by the wheel. (No native Scottish pottery that falls within the purview of this book is wheel-turned.) The pots are hard fired, generally black or dark brown, but occasionally as at Rothesay, rather light reddish brown. The surface is generally smooth and sometimes slightly burnished though a slip is never employed.

The range of forms is restricted, but all may be called leathery ; they are such as could be beaten up out of a piece of soft, tensile leather.[1] Some indeed hold that Windmill Hill pots imitate

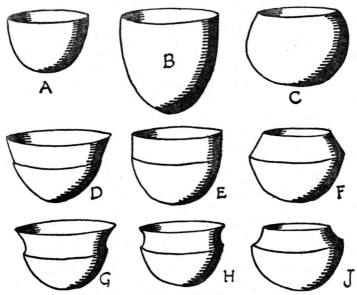

FIG. 12.—Basic forms of Windmill Hill pottery, after Piggott.

leather vessels that their makers' remote ancestors had used before they learned the potter's craft. All the vessels are round bottomed. That would be no disadvantage if they were meant to stand on soft earth or sandy floors, in the ashes of a hearth, or in a cooking hole excavated in the ground. Handles are unknown, but in England and Western Scotland the vessels are sometimes provided with two or four lugs for prehension —ledge-like projections that may be tilted downwards.

Piggott distinguishes three basic forms (Fig. 12) : A, a shallow dish ; B, a baggy pot ; and C, a bowl with slightly inturned rim.

[1] *Arch. J.,* lxxxviii, pp. 39–81.

Three variants, D, E, and F, might be supposed to arise from the foregoing by the introduction of a keel. Had the hypothetical prototype been a slightly elastic leather vessel, the variants could be produced by forcing a springy hoop down into the interior. Three further variants arise when the originally straight rims are bent out. A distinctive feature frequently recurring in Windmill Hill pottery throughout the British Isles, though not apparently in the deepest layers at Windmill Hill, is a thickening of the rim. It is effected by squashing down or rolling over the clay of the vessel's edge while still soft.

While the foregoing shapes are found throughout the British Isles their distribution in Scotland is uneven. The characteristic baggy pot B is virtually confined to Arran, Bute, Kintyre, and the Hebrides. Bicker's Houses in Bute, Unstan in Orkney, and Craig in Aberdeenshire have yielded good examples of type C. Type E occurs at Glecknabae (Bute), Largie (Crinan), Achnacree (Loch Etive), and Unstan (Orkney), but F only at Bicker's Houses, Beacharra, and South Clettraval, all in the western province. G is found at Glenluce Sands (Wigtonshire), and then at Kenny's Cairn, Unstan, and Easterton of Roseisle, near Elgin, all in the north-east. H is illustrated by almost identical specimens from Achnacree, and South Clettraval in the west and from Kenny's Cairn in the north. But groups of collared vases—forms allied to F–J—seem confined to the west, and lugs are restricted to that area save for one pot from East Finnercy, near Dunecht.[1]   On the other hand typical flattened rims are common to the whole area and almost identical sections [2] can be quoted from Glenluce, Giants' Graves, Glecknabae, and Rothesay in the south-west, Achnacree and Eilean an Tighe in the north-west, Easterton of Roseisle, Unstan, and Kenny's Cairn in the north-east, and Hedderwick, near Dunbar, in the south-east (Fig. 13).

Decoration is comparatively rare in England but commoner in Scotland. The most characteristic devices are : (1) Shallow flutings that might be produced by drawing the finger-tip with light pressure over the wet clay ; (2) shallow grooves executed with a rounded bone or wooden point (Pl. III) ; (3) punctuations, sometimes perhaps produced with a comb ; (4) finger-tip and finger-nail impressions ; (5) simple scorings with a sharp point ; (6) stab-and-drag executed with a sharp pointed implement held

---

[1] *PSAS.*, lxiii, figs. 50, 5–7.   [2] *PSAS.*, lxiii, figs. 38, 39, 44, 48.

PLATE III

NEOLITHIC VASES, SOUTH CLETTRAVAL

obliquely and jabbed into the wet clay, partially withdrawn, and then jabbed in again leaving on the surface a continuous furrow the bottom of which is interrupted by a series of undercut septa (Pl. IV, 2) ; (7) the impression of a twisted cord or a cord whipped very tightly round another or round a stiff core (Pl. IV, 3).

The first five methods of decoration are also known from England but are not quite evenly distributed in Scotland. The first device [1] is fairly common in the West (Giants' Graves, Glecknabae, Beacharra, Largie, Kilchoan, and Achnacree), but recurs in the north-east at Easterton of Roseisle and Knapperty Hillock (Aberdeenshire). Grooving, on the other hand, is

FIG. 13.—Typical rims : 1, Nether Largie ; 2, 5, Easterton of Roseisle ; 3, Achnacree ; 4, 6, Rothesay ; 7, 8, Kenny's Cairn. ½.

restricted to the west. The cord ornament seems confined to one vessel from Clachaig in Arran, but recurs at Larne in Northern Ireland.[2] Stab-and-drag [3] on the contrary, is confined to the far north—Unstan, Taiversoë Tuack, Midhowe, Kenny's Cairn, and Eilean an Tighe.

The wide distribution of peculiar forms, distinctive rim thickening, and characteristically insular decorative devices proves the underlying homogeneity of the potter's craft throughout Scotland and its essentially British character. Nevertheless, the Scottish pottery can be subdivided into two distinct classes or sub-groups. These, though merely local

[1] *PSAS.*, lxiii, p. 85.   [2] *PSEA.*, vii, p. 62.   [3] *PSAS.*, lxiii, p. 85.

F

variants on the common tradition, do correspond in general distribution to the two principal types of burial vault already distinguished.

In the area from Galloway to North Uist over which long

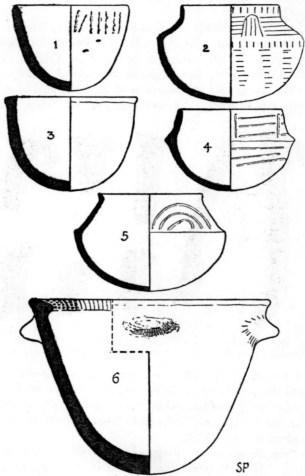

FIG. 14.—Vases from Beacharra, after Piggott. ¼.

cists allied to the Clyde type occur, we have pottery of what will be termed the Beacharra class (Fig. 14). To it is confined the manufacture of baggy pots of type B and the squat collared vases like Fig. 14, 2, the addition of lug handles to the vase, and

PLATE IV

NEOLITHIC VASES

1 CLACHAIG, ARRAN
2 UNSTAN, ORKNEY

National Museum

the employment of grooved and cord ornament. The designs are also peculiar, being frequently arranged in alternating panels particularly on collared vases like Fig. 14, 2. On the example from Clachaig, Pl. IV, 1, the panels are formed of alternating horizontal and vertical impressions of whipped cord ; on one from South Clettraval grooved lines alternate in the same way. At Beacharra and at Larne in Northern Ireland, hanging and standing semicircles occupy the panels. The whole group might be derived from the common stock by divergent specialization ; the most typical specimens come from chambers that are typologically late—Beacharra and Bicker's Houses (tripartite) and Clachaig (bipartite) ; yet it need be no later than the Unstan class.

The latter is effectively confined to areas where passage graves occur—Caithness, Orkney, and the Hebrides. It is distinguished by the popularity of large wide bowls with an overhanging rim and by the use of stab-and-drag technique in decoration (Pl. IV, 2). A distinctive pattern is the band of alternately hatched triangles. The Unstan class, too, may be treated as a specialized local variant on the Windmill Hill tradition. It is represented only in round (Kenny's Cairn) or oval (Unstan, Taiversoë Tuack, Midhowe) cairns that have been regarded as late in comparison with the long-horned variety.

The remaining elements of Windmill Hill culture detected in Scottish collective tombs or associated settlements do nothing to clarify the foregoing subdivision. Ground stone axe-heads or celts have been found in only two tombs—Clachaig in Arran (Fig. 15) and Lower Dounreay in Caithness, but occur also in the settlements at Rothesay and on Eilean an Tighe. The axe from Clachaig has been shaped by grinding as shown by the striæ reproduced in the figure, but the surface of the one from Lower Dounreay has been pecked all over. The use of such axes was, of course, by no means confined to a " Neolithic " period. There are specimens from short cists, Bronze Age villages, and Iron Age forts. Stray celts cannot then be assigned to any specific culture.

A saddle quern from Rothesay [1] is quite appropriate to the Windmill Hill complex, and is valuable as proving the cultivation of cereals by our tomb-builders. But of course such querns continued in use into the Iron Age.

[1] *TBNHS.*, 1930, p. 51.

The only arrow-heads found in the deepest layers at Windmill Hill and generally associated with that culture in England are of the leaf-shaped type, while tanged and barbed arrow-

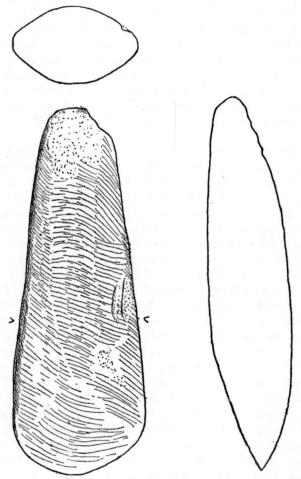

FIG. 15.—Axe from Clachaig. ½.

heads came in with the Beakers.[1]   Leaf-shaped arrow-heads were found in five collective tombs—Giants' Graves and Sliddery Water, Arran, Kindrochat on the Earn, Ormiegill in Caithness,

[1] Kendrick and Hawkes, op. cit., p. 73 ; *Arch.*, lxxvi, p. 81.

and Unstan in Orkney (the last rhomboid), as well as on the slopes
of Wideford Hill. But in England the leaf-shaped arrow-head
was by no means confined to the pre-Beaker period; an example
from Derbyshire was found in a Cinerary Urn of the developed
Bronze Age.[1] Still, the distribution of the type [2] may give
some indication of the strength of Windmill Hill influence in
several parts of Scotland. It preponderates, as might be expected,
in Galloway and the far north, where chambered cairns are
common—Wigtonshire 57 per cent, Caithness 90 per cent,
Sutherland 76 per cent, Orkney 74 per cent, Ross 52 per cent.
But it is also relatively common in parts of Eastern Scotland,
where collective burial places are rare—Banffshire 65 per cent,
Aberdeenshire 53 per cent. On the shores of the Moray Firth
(Culbin Sands), in Kincardineshire, Angus, Berwickshire, and
Ayrshire tanged and barbed specimens out-number the leaf-shaped
types. The scarcity of leaf-shaped arrow-heads in Ayrshire
proves that the surviving chambered cairns give a fairly accurate
idea of the original distribution of such monuments; the blank
in the county is not due to more intensive agriculture.

In addition to relics that can be paralleled at Windmill Hill,
both long cists and passage graves in Scotland have yielded
relics that in England are later than the Windmill Hill types,
but which yet do not specifically belong to the Beaker complex.
These may be discussed here.

Perforated mace-heads, the one approximately cushion-shaped,
the other pestle-shaped, come from the tripartite cist of Tormore
(Arran), and the short horned cairn of Ormiegill (Caithness).
In England mace-heads of this type would be assigned to the
Bronze Age; in Yorkshire a pestle-shaped specimen, very similar
to Fig. 16, 1, was found under a round barrow in a separate grave
together with a bronze knife-dagger 7½ inches long.[3] In Scotland
such mace-heads occur stray, not only in Kintyre and Orkney,
but also in the eastern counties.[4]

Narrow flint knives, finely trimmed, but polished along one
edge come from the collective tombs of Tormore (Arran),[5]

[1] Baggaley, in *Trans.* Hunter Arch. Soc., December, 1928.
[2] Worked out from collections in the National Museum by G. R. Gair.
[3] Towthorpe, C. 39; Mortimer, *Forty Years*, pl. i, 9 and p. 6.
[4] Gibson enumerates fourteen cushion-shaped mace-heads, flatter than Fig. 17,
with edges at either end. Four come from Orkney, two each from Shetland and
Lewis. One of the latter and one from Fife are made of Shetland rhyolite;
PSAS., lxviii, p. 431.
[5] *PSAS.*, xxxvi, p. 101.

Ormiegill, and Camster (round) (Caithness),[1] and Unstan (Orkney).[2]   Now Clark[3] has established the probability that other flint knives with polished edges but triangular, subrectangular or discoid in plan, belong to the Beaker complex.   And Piggott inclines to regard knives, more like the Scottish, found with Windmill Hill pottery under a round barrow and with polished flint axes under a long barrow in Yorkshire,[4] as later than the pure Windmill Hill complex.

Flint knives, finely flaked all over one face, like the slug-knives of East Anglian collectors, were found in the segmented cists

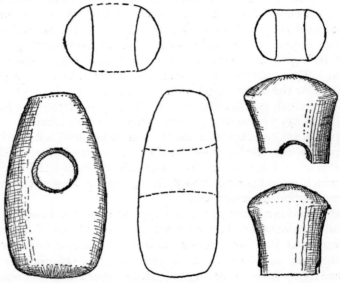

FIG. 16.—Mace-heads : Ormiegill (Caithness) and Taiversöe Tuack (Orkney). ½.

of Giants' Graves, Torlin, and Dunan Mor (Arran) (Fig. 17) and also in the long chamber at Midhowe (Orkney).   In England such knives are frequently found in individual graves, accompanied in twenty-three instances by Food Vessels.[5]   The type would, therefore, in England be definitely " Bronze Age ".

The short horned cairn of Ormiegill and the round cairn at Camster contained curious " lopsided arrow-heads ", thin, triangular flakes with oblique secondary trimming along two

[1] Anderson, ii, figs. 244, 251.   [2] Anderson, ii, fig. 282.
[3] PSEA., vi, pp. 50 f.   [4] Arch. J., lxxxviii, p. 100.
[5] Ant. J., xii, p. 160.

edges generally on both faces (Fig. 18). In Scotland Callander [1] has recorded analogous types picked up in Berwickshire (forty from

FIG. 17.—Mace-head (½) and Slug Knives (⅔). Tormore, Arran, after *PSAS*.

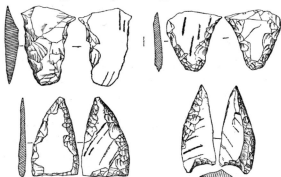

FIG. 18.—Lopsided arrow-heads: *a*, Camster round; *b–c*, Ormiegill, Caithness, after Clark. ½.

Lauderdale), Peeblesshire, Glenluce (fifteen), Angus, Aberdeen-shire, Banffshire, and Elginshire (twenty from Culbin Sands).

[1] *PSAS.*, lxii, pp. 177 f.

Clark[1] regards them all as derivatives of the *petit tranchet* or transverse arrow-head.   The latter is ultimately a Mesolithic form, but is found at Windmill Hill, though not at many other sites of that culture in England.   The English derivatives, parallel to those from Camster and Ormiegill, are associated on the other hand with Peterborough pottery or with ware contemporary with Beakers and never occur in long barrows or pure Windmill Hill sites.

A chisel-like implement, made from a splinter of a ruminant's marrow bone, was found in Kenny's Cairn (Fig. 19).   Parallels can be cited from late Mesolithic and Neolithic sites on the Baltic and in Scandinavia,[2] from Swiss lake-dwellings, and other remote regions.   But the nearest parallel was found with

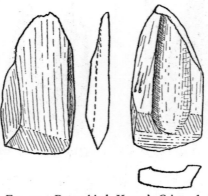

Fig. 19.—Bone chisel, Kenny's Cairn.   ½.

a Beaker in an individual grave near Cawdor Castle, Nairnshire,[3] and we shall meet the type again in the Late Bronze Age of Orkney and Shetland, and in an Iron Age broch.   Similarly the phalange of a young ox, transversely perforated, found in the chamber at Lower Dounreay,[4] has its nearest parallels in the Late Bronze Age settlement of Jarlshof, Shetland.

Any of the foregoing objects from collective tombs might be dismissed as secondary intrusions like the Beaker sherds and jet necklaces.   Still, it would be odd that types, not otherwise

[1] *Arch. J.*, xci.
[2] e.g., *PZ.*, v, p. 516, fig. 12*d*; *SMYA.*, xxviii, 2, pl. i, 3; *Stavanger Mus. Arsheft*, 1908, pl. i, 14.
[3] *Proc. Soc. Ant.*, 1861, ser. 2, i, p. 297.
[4] *PSAS.*, lxiii, p. 145.

attached to any specific cultural group in Scotland, should intrude into chambered cairns in both Caithness and Arran. Alternatively the types might have originated here and spread southward so that the English evidence for a late date would be inapplicable. The Food Vessel with which slug-knives are associated is admittedly a northern product. Polishing was applied to the faces—but not the edges—of flint knives in Egypt,[1] Portugal, and Ireland.[2] Our narrow knives might then illustrate the progress of the technique along the Atlantic route and would be the precursors of the broader knives of Beaker age. A fusion between Tardenoisians and Windmill Hill folk in Scotland might be responsible for the rise of our lopsided arrow-heads. On the whole, however, the objects in question ought to be treated as integral elements in the " Neolithic " culture of Scotland and as evidence of its late date in comparison at least with the period represented at the bottom of the Windmill Hill ditches.

It appears, then, that the " Neolithic " culture of Scotland is fundamentally homogeneous and, apart from certain elements that may be secondary accretions, is essentially identical with the Windmill Hill culture of England. At the same time it is the culture represented exclusively in the primary deposits in our chambered cairns. Conversely, in Western and Northern Scotland, at any rate, the Neolithic settlers cannot be conceived as arriving here independently of the chambered cairn builders. On geographical grounds the Windmill Hill culture ought to have been brought to Arran and Orkney by the builders of Giants' Graves and Unstan. But how is the fundamental contrast between long cist and passage grave to be reconciled with the underlying uniformity of their ceramic furniture ? How do the foreign relations, best revealed in the pottery, accord with those deduced from the funerary architecture ?

2.   The Origin of the Neolithic Culture

Windmill Hill ware, such as characterizes our collective tombs, belongs to a great family of " leathery " pottery, generally plain, that is represented in one form or another throughout Western Europe from Portugal to the Swiss lakes and down the Rhine

---

[1] Childe, *MAE.*, p. 59.
[2] *BM. Stone Age Guide,* p. 122.

into Belgium.[1]   This fabric, and tools frequently associated therewith, have significant analogies as far away as the Nile Delta [2] in North Africa. It is indeed quite likely that the cultural traditions they represent originated in the last-named quarter, which is at least near the cradle of the food-producing economy.

Did these traditions reach Great Britain first together with the idea of the monumental collective tomb ? The burying-places of the Iberian Peninsula [3] and the Pyrenees certainly contain leathery vessels of a general West European character, as well as Bell-beakers and other more elaborate products. Moreover there are specific and significant agreements between vessels of the Scottish Beacharra class and some from the Peninsula. The distinctive collared vase (Fig. 14, 2) recurs in corbelled tombs in Almeria [4] and Southern Portugal [5] and in Portuguese a passage grave [6] built with orthostats. A link with Britain may be seen in a vase of the same shape from the corbelled tomb of Fontenay-le-Marmion, Normandy.[7] A baggy pot with lugs like our type B was found at Casa da Moura, a natural cave in Portugal used as a collective sepulchre at the same time as the corbelled tombs, and there are others from Catalonia.[8]

Sherds ornamented with pendant semicircles as at Beacharra come from a settlement contemporary with the tombs, at Pavia in Central Portugal.[9] The same motive, this time arranged in panels alternating between horizontal lines, recurs on a vase from a cave, converted by megalithic walls into a collective tomb, at Conguel on the Quiberon Peninsula of Brittany.[10] Grooved decoration is found in sepulchral caves and built tombs in Southern France and in Brittany.[11] Even the stab-and-drag technique was employed in various parts of the Iberian Peninsula,[12] though it is commoner in the passage graves of Scandinavia, Holland, and North-west Germany.[13]   For cord

[1] *Arch. J.*, lxxxviii, pp. 38–42.
[2] Childe, *MAE.*, p. 60.
[3] Correia, *El Neolitico de Pavia*, figs. 40–4.
[4] In Don L. Siret's collection, *Préhistoire*, ii, p. 199, fig. 5*b*.
[5] Marcella, Algarve ; Estacio da Veiga, op. cit., i, pl. xxiii, 2 (bad drawing ; the original is at Belem).
[6] Velada, Alemtejo : Museum Belem.
[7] Coutil, *Résumé des recherches préhistoriques, Dépt. de Calvados*, p. 86.
[8] Bosch Gimpera, *Etnologia de la Península Ibérica*, fig. 114.
[9] Correia, op. cit., fig. 12.
[10] *Arch. J.*, lxxxviii, pl. v.
[11] *Antiquity*, viii, p. 36 ; *Arch J.*, lxxxviii, pl. vi, b.
[12] Castillo, *Vaso campaniforme*, p. 32 and pl. ii.
[13] *Nachrichten aus Niedersachsens Urgeschichte*, 1932, p. 35.

patterns, such as are seen at Clachaig and Larne, it is necessary to turn to the Baltic.[1]

Finally, leaf-shaped arrow-heads do occur in the tombs of Almeria and Portugal [2] though there they are in a small minority as compared with hollow-based and tanged specimens ; they are relatively commoner round the Pyrenees, but absolutely predominant only in North-east France and Belgium.[3]

There are, therefore, some explicit indications of connections between the " Neolithic " culture of Scotland and Ireland, and that illustrated in the collective tombs of Spain and Portugal. These indications refer not to Windmill Hill culture as a whole, but primarily to a subdivision thereof peculiar to Scotland and Northern Ireland. On the strength of these indications the following theory might be built up : the colonists who introduced the idea of collective burial and the architectural prescriptions and devices embodying it, would have come by sea from the Peninsula—naturally with prolonged halts on the way—bringing with them the whole apparatus of Neolithic culture, wheat and barley, sheep and cattle, and the ceramic traditions embodied in the Beacharra vases. From Scotland and Ireland they would have subsequently spread eastward across England. In the process sepulchral architecture would have been specialized to produce the aberrant structures enclosed in the long barrows while certain cultural elements would have been degraded or lost—the Beacharra style of decoration and the collared pots. At the same time a parallel spread eastward across France would have been going on with similar consequences from intermediate settlements along the Atlantic coast (Morbihan, Normandy, etc.).

Such an account is open to grave objections. Beacharra vases are found in long cists, the best parallels to which lie along the Pyrenees ; the collared pots from Iberia and France come from passage graves or corbelled tombs like those of Caithness. Secondly, serious difficulties arise if the Scottish chamber tombs be made older than the Windmill Hill culture of Southern England. We have already [4] insisted on—inconclusive—indications of the relative lateness of the furniture of these tombs. We shall in the sequel encounter insurmountable

---

[1] *Arch. J.,* lxxxviii, p. 60, pl. ixa.
[2] 9 per cent at Los Millares, 9 per cent at Palmella.
[3] *Arch. J.,* lxxxviii, p. 43, n. 1.
[4] p. 73, above.

obstacles to spreading the relics of the Bronze and Iron Ages from Scotland over a longer period of time than is occupied by the comparable material from England.

Thirdly, the pottery and other relics from the South English camps and the development in the material revealed in the ditches at Windmill Hill do not suggest that the culture in South England was a late degeneration. It looks rather like an early and unspecialized offshoot from a general, undifferentiated West European complex. It actually comprises original elements like clay ladles [1] which are widely distributed among the comparable cultures on the Continent and even in Egypt [2] but have been lost, or at least not yet found, in Scotland.

And quite recently Mrs. Hawkes [3] has described from Switzerland and South France pottery equally as primitive as the oldest from Windmill Hill. It extends well beyond the regions in which collective tombs were erected and is at some sites succeeded at higher levels by pottery of the types found locally in such structures ; the grooved ware already mentioned is among the later types. Mrs. Hawkes has in other words identified the rude and early cultural continuum from which the more familiar West European cultures—Michelsberg, Chassey, etc.—might have been subsequently differentiated. And the evidence she cites plainly indicates that the spread of the primary continuum was anterior to that of built collective tombs. The Windmill Hill culture of Great Britain would then be an early offshoot of that complex.

The causewayed camps of South England, like Windmill Hill, can be paralleled in sites of the so-called Michelsberg culture in the Rhine Valley.[4] They contain curious combs of antler which recur in a Michelsberg station in Belgium.[5] In the latter country leaf-shaped arrow-heads are absolutely predominant on Michelsberg sites. These special links between England and North-east Gaul are easily intelligible on the above view ; they would be elements inherited by the Windmill Hill and Michelsberg groups from the ancestral complex from which both are sprung, and older than the divergent specialization which separates the several groups. Finally, Piggott [6] has adduced reasons for supposing that the English long barrows containing stone-built

---

[1] *Arch J.*, lxxxviii, p. 78.
[2] Childe, *MAE.*, fig. 17.
[3] *Antiquity*, viii, pp. 25 ff.
[4] Childe, *Danube*, p. 181.
[5] *Arch. J.*, lxxxviii, pl. viii.
[6] *CPPS.*, 1932, p. 144.

chambers may be later than the unchambered long barrows. The latter would perhaps denote the burial places of the original Windmill Hill settlers ; the stone-built chambers would be secondary additions due to fresh influences from abroad.

From this standpoint a new hypothesis seems more plausible than that advanced on p. 75. Neolithic culture would have reached Western Europe from Africa through a slow spread of peasants practising semi-migratory cultivation (garden-culture).[1] Some of these would eventually have crossed the Channel to colonize the chalk downs of Sussex and Wessex. Thence the Windmill Hill culture would have been diffused northwards reaching Scotland at a comparatively late date.

On this view it would further be arguable that Neolithic men reached Scotland by landways before the builders of chamber-tombs reached our coasts. The latter would by their prestige have imposed their funerary observances, but little else, on small groups of peasants already settled in the coastal glens. The latter argument is not convincing. Wherever the first farmers to settle the north and west coast of Scotland came from, geographical considerations show that they arrived by sea, like the tomb-builders. And the distribution of their settlements follows the tombs. There are no grounds whatever for dissociating the Neolithic colonization of North and West Scotland from the introduction of the monumental tomb. But the architecture of the latter remains specifically Iberian or Pyrenean, unparalleled in South England, even if the grave-goods must now be regarded as predominantly English.

The contradiction is not insuperable. The fact of maritime intercourse all along the Atlantic and North Sea coasts from Portugal to Denmark may be accepted as established. We can then imagine that voyagers from the south would recruit companions and crews in England for further ventures. The leaders would insist upon their own traditional sepulchral architecture ; they would leave to their followers the manufacture of pots and implements. If such leaders hailed from different regions, the divergences in funerary architecture can be reconciled with the comparative uniformity of grave gear. The significance of the Portuguese and Pyrenean analogies to the tombs of Caithness and the Clyde respectively is thus preserved. The tombs in question were erected for petty chiefs whose kinsmen reposed

[1] Childe, *MAE.*, pp. 42, 300.

in Alcalá or La Halliade.   Their followers in each case were
recruited largely from the Windmill Hill stock of South England.
If we admit the presence also of Portuguese and Pyrenean families,
the peculiar foreign parallels to some Beacharra pottery will
also be explained.   We could add some folk brought back on
return voyages from the Baltic to account for the decoration
of the vases from Clachaig and Larne, and the stab-and-drag
of Unstan.

Our initial account therefore holds good in all essentials.
Neolithic culture—domestic animals, cereals, pottery, ground
stone axes, pressure-worked flint implements—was in fact
introduced by small boat-loads of adventurers coasting along
the Atlantic.   These established primary settlements near suitable
landing places in Galloway, around the mouth of the Clyde and
Loch Fyne, on Skye and the Hebrides, in Caithness and Orkney.
The bulk of the settlers were, in a sense, of English extraction, but
they were captained by chiefs endowed with the magical attributes
of the Divine Kings whom Fraser [1] has described so brilliantly.
These were foreigners and by their prestige secured, even in
that barbaric milieu, the funerary honours of a more southern
clime.   To receive their mortal remains and those of their families
monumental tombs were reared in accordance with prescriptions
brought from Southern Spain or Sardinia.

From the primary landing-places colonies were sent out to
the next convenient bay or glen as the population grew.   But
while this expansion was in progress, other invaders, coming
directly or ultimately from Holland and the Rhine Valley, were
landing on the eastern coasts.   Some, crossing the island, followed,
as we shall see, the earlier colonists.   In Arran and Skye they
may have replaced the old Iberian or Sardinian chiefs, and the
same may have happened in Caithness.   In South-west Scotland
the Beaker invasion eventually caused the atrophy of the old
funerary customs and " Neolithic " culture.   In the Hebrides and
Orkneys, in Strath Nairn and Strath Spey, the latter maintained
its individuality longer.   A comparison between Maps I and II
will show that here the distribution of chambered cairns and
Early Bronze Age burials is virtually exclusive.

At the same time it is quite likely that some Windmill Hill
people followed Beaker-folk from England into Scotland.   That
is the simplest explanation of the Windmill Hill pottery from

---

[1] *Lectures on the Early History of the Kingship.*

PLATE V

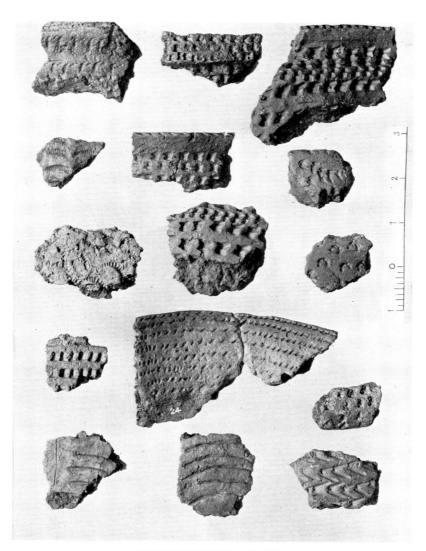

PETERBOROUGH WARE

East Coast sites, remote from any collective tombs, notably at Hedderwick, near Dunbar.   Contact between Windmill Hill and Beaker-folk is well established in Yorkshire.   And Beaker sherds are found as well as those of Windmill Hill ware at Hedderwick.   Perhaps then people of the older stock attached themselves to the new conquerors in Yorkshire and followed them northward.

3. Peterborough Ware in Scotland

The same explanation may be advanced to account for the presence at several sites of another class of pottery which in England is always regarded as Neolithic and may be pre-Beaker. The fabric in question is termed Peterborough ware,[1] after a classical site in the Fenland capital.   It is generally very coarse, the paste comprising large grits.   The vessels have been built up out of successive rings, each pressed down and over the one below ;   the vases are liable to break along the join thus revealing the method of construction.   They are generally imperfectly fired and consequently soft ;   the surface may be dirty brown or red.   The leading shape seems to have been a round-bottomed bowl with a thick, heavily moulded rim, and often a concave neck.

Peterborough vases are generally richly decorated along the rim and neck and over the greater part of the body.   The ornamentation is arranged exclusively in horizontal bands encircling the vessels continuously, and consists of little more than zones in which the same simple stamped element is repeated again and again.   The components are, however, very varied. They are produced by the following techniques :   simple strokes or jabs with a sharp-pointed implement ;   grooves, made with a square-ended tool (wood ?) and consequently flat-bottomed ; cord-impressions including semicircles and loops pressed in with the thumb (Plate V, 9) ;   impressions of two cords whipped together, especially the casts of short lengths producing what is graphically termed the " *maggot pattern* " (Plate V, 7) ;   the imprint of the joint of the leg bone of a bird or small mammal[2] (Plate V, 2, 3, 5) ;   comb impressions ;   the imprint of the edge of a cockle shell (*Cardium*) ;   finger-nail and finger-tip impressions ; round pits formed with the finger or the top of a shell.

---

[1] *Arch. J.,* lxxxviii, pp. 110–119.   [2] *Antiquity*, iii, p. 282.

Pottery of this kind has been reported from Hedderwick near Dunbar,[1] a cist grave at Drumelzier near the head of the Tweed,[2] a hut circle at Muirkirk (Ayrshire),[3] Old Kilpatrick (Dumbartonshire),[4] Glenluce Sands [5] and Shewalton Moor.[6]   Beaker sherds have been picked up at all sites, and the association of Beaker and Peterborough wares at Drumelzier and Muirkirk is unambiguous.

The affinities of Peterborough ware are admitted to lie in the great forest of North Europe.[7]   The nearest analogues to the British vases come from dwelling places on Bornholm, in Sweden, and round the Baltic. Its makers are supposed to have come from that quarter. In England they displayed a marked preference for the edges of marshes and rivers in choosing sites for settlement—a choice which again shows their Baltic affinities. And the settlements seem most dense in Eastern England—the Thames and the Fens. Yet Peterborough ware is found as far west as Somerset and even Anglesey. At Windmill Hill its makers occupied the site only after the original occupants who take their name from the site had departed and little, if at all, before the advent of Beaker-folk. Elsewhere in Western England such associations as exist point at least to an overlap between Beaker and Peterborough ware as in Scotland.

Quite possibly the Peterborough folk reached Eastern England from some now submerged tract of the North German or Dutch coast. But they seem to have spread across England in the wake of the Beaker-folk who had come from the same quarter. And very likely they reached Scotland under the same leadership. Peterborough ware in Scotland may accordingly be provisionally regarded rather as an incident of the Beaker invasion than as evidence of a distinct period.

[1] *PSAS.*, lxiii, pp. 67 f., figs. 51–2.
[2] *PSAS.*, lxv, p. 367.
[3] *PSAS.*, lxi, p. 272 ; lxiii, p. 95.
[4] *PSAS.*, lxiii, p. 95.
[5] *PSAS.*, lxiii, figs. 54–5.
[6] In Dick Museum, Kilmarnock.
[7] *Arch J.*, lxxxviii, pp. 60 ff.

V

THE ROUND-HEADED INVADERS

1. BEAKERS

THE first farmers to settle on the plains of East Scotland differed from the colonists just described not only in burial customs, but also in physical type.[1] The leaders in whose graves Beakers have been found were of very modest stature, five out of nine measurable males standing less than 5 ft. 4 in. high, and only one (from Shetland) exceeding 5 ft. 6 in., but all were markedly round-headed. The population of Eastern Scotland formed of them perhaps differs in some respects from the contemporary average of England,[2] presumably owing to the inclusion of different non-Beaker elements.

The immediate origin of the round-headed invaders has been determined once and for all by Abercromby from a masterly study of the characteristic pottery—the Beakers—deposited in their graves. His paper,[3] published in 1902, really marks the beginning of a new era in British archæology, and his general account still holds good. Nevertheless thirty years researches have inevitably entailed certain modifications in the results of such pioneer studies. Abercromby[4] envisaged a single group of invaders, landing at one point in South-East England and thence overrunning the whole country. To-day it is generally admitted that independent landings may have taken place at several points along the east coast of Scotland as well as of England.

It is, moreover, now clear that the term Beaker covers two distinct, though cognate, varieties of vase, two slightly different traditions in fact. Abercromby himself was conscious of the

---

[1] Low, *PAASUA.,* 1904–6, p. 147 ; Bryce, *PSAS.,* xxxix, p. 438 ; cf. also lxiii, p. 150 ; lxvii, pp. 36, 231.

[2] Turner, *TRSE.,* li, pp. 90 ff. ; *Biometrika,* xviii, p. 66 ; xx, 380. In these accounts all skulls found in short cists are included ; nineteen from Orkney are of uncertain age and affinities.

[3] *JRAI.,* xxxii (1902), pp. 391 ff.

[4] The final statement is in *Bronze Age Pottery,* 1912, subsequently cited here as " Abercromby ".

distinction, but failed to give it due prominence owing to his adoption of the terminology and typology of the English antiquary, Thurnam.[1]   In 1871 the latter had divided British Beakers according to their shapes into three classes, denoted by the letters A, B, and C.   These were regarded as marking three stages in the evolution, or rather degeneration, of a single type of pot. In the first class the neck would be straight and relatively tall in comparison with the globular body, and separated therefrom by a well-marked shoulder (Plate VI, *a*).   In B Beakers neck and body are of approximately equal length, but there is really no sharp division between the two parts (Plate VI, *b*) ; the vase's walls contract gradually towards the neck, but widen out again at the brim so that the profile is a continuous " S " curve from the base to the rim.   In C Beakers finally the neck is definitely short in comparison with the body and is generally separated therefrom by a marked shoulder.

To-day the B Beaker can no longer be regarded as derived from form A ; both represent separate types, decorated in different styles, associated with different grave-goods, and, in England, distributed over distinct areas.[2]   Most Beakers classed as C may, however, be treated as degenerations of class A, but, at least in Scotland, there are similarly shaped vessels which must be regarded rather as derivatives of type B.   We thus have Cb Beakers as well as Ca Beakers.

Beaker ware is generally comparatively fine in texture, well fired, and reddish to brown in colour. Some Beakers have been coated with a red slip which is often burnished. The most distinctive device, employed for the decoration of Beakers, was a narrow comb with very short square teeth, or a notched slip of wood, the edge being often not straight but slightly convex. This, when pressed on to the soft clay, produced an almost continuous line subdivided at its bottom by tiny ridges of clay into minute rectangles. This style of decoration, like simple incision and finger-nail impressions, is found on both A and B Beakers. But decoration by means of a continuous cord impression is confined to B Beakers.   There are further divergences in the arrangement of the designs. This is always in horizontal zones. But in the A group the zones are divided into panels and the

---

[1] *Arch.,* lxiii, p. 391.

[2] This was pointed out by the author in his Inaugural Lecture in 1927 and repeated in *The Bronze Age* (1930), p. 155.   Detailed proof has been given by Clark, *Antiquity,* v (1931), pp. 415 ff., and by Grimes, *PSEA.,* vi (1931), pp. 347 ff.

zones are so wide that the vertical division catches the eye rather than the horizontal. In the B family the zones are narrower and the range of motives poorer.

Secondly, A and Ca Beakers in England are frequently accompanied by round-heeled bronze knife-daggers with rivet-holes,[1] flint daggers, perforated axe-hammers of stone, " pulley-rings ", and buttons with " V " perforation. Types B and Cb, on the contrary, are associated with flat-tanged metal daggers without rivets (called the West European type),[2] and bowman's wristguards of stone. Finally, in Southern Britain B Beakers are common only on the Suffolk and Essex coasts, in Kent, in the Thames Valley, and on the Downs from Sussex to Dorset. A Beakers, on the other hand, predominate round the borders of the Fens, in South-west England and in South Wales. It follows, therefore, that A and B Beakers stand for different cultures introduced by distinct bodies of invaders.

None the less all the vessels comprised under the term Beaker may be regarded as indirectly related and descended from the Bell-beakers of the Continent.[3] These constitute a surprisingly homogeneous group, though found in places as far apart as the Iberian Peninsula, Brittany, Sicily, South France, Upper Italy, and Central Europe, from the Vistula and the Theiss to the Rhine and the Alps. Like British Beakers the Bell-beakers often accompany round-headed (brachycranial) skeletons and are associated with flat-tanged West European daggers of copper, bowmen's wristguards, and buttons with " V "-perforation.

Detailed peculiarities in the decoration show that British Beakers, especially of type A, are most closely allied to the Bell-beakers and Zoned-beakers (a hybrid between the Bell-beaker and beakers associated with the battle-axe wielders who made corded ware) of the Rhine Valley and Central Holland (Veluwe). Some Scottish B Beakers, particularly those decorated with continuous cord impressions, have closer analogues in the S Beakers (another hybrid of the Bell-beaker with battle-axe elements) of Northern Holland. It may, however, be taken as virtually established that all Beaker-folk reached Britain immediately from the coasts of the Low Countries and the Rhine. Yet it must be borne in mind that the tanged-and-barbed

[1] Childe, *Bronze Age,* fig. 7, 3.
[2] Childe, *Bronze Age,* fig. 7, 2. Fig. 23, 2, here.
[3] Childe, *Danube in Prehistory,* chap. x ; Castillo, *Cultura del Vaso campaniforme* ; Ebert, *Real.,* s.v. " Glockenbecher ".

arrow-heads, exclusively associated with Beakers in Great Britain, are hardly ever [1] found with their Dutch and Rhenish relatives where hollow-based forms predominate. Moreover there are analogies between certain British Beakers and those of France that have recently raised doubts whether some Beaker-folk did not reach this island from that quarter.

Only one Scottish Beaker can possibly be assigned to Abercromby's form A (Pl. VI, *a*) ; it comes from a cist in the disc-barrow at Ballymeanoch, Crinan (Argyll).[2] And many of the Ca Beakers are extraordinarily clumsy and degenerate-looking. The thick coarse Beakers of the Western Isles and extreme north (Pl. VI, *c*), with their grooved decoration, look particularly

FIG. 20.—Beaker from Ellon, Aberdeenshire. $\frac{1}{3}$.

late. In several examples from Mull, Skye,[3] Banffshire, and Aberdeenshire the walls are so thick that the rim itself has become a medium for decoration. In two Beakers from Aberdeenshire (Fig. 20), and others from Angus and Lanarkshire [4] the rim is internally bevelled. Both these peculiarities may be attributed to the influence of Food Vessels [5] or their " Neolithic "

<hr/>

[1] Once at Ede (Gelderland) ; van Giffen, *Bauart*, fig. 112 ; and at Hilversum with a West European dagger though no Beaker, *Oudh. Med.*, ix, p. 71.

[2] Abercromby, No. 185 ; *PSAS.*, vi, p. 348.

[3] *PSAS.*, lxvi, p. 209.

[4] Abercromby, Nos. 230, 231, 213.

[5] Abercromby, i, p. 40.

PLATE VI

a

d

b

c

BEAKERS

a	BALLYMEANOCH	*c*	KILMAGIE
b	DRUMELZIER	*d*	CAWDOR

a, d British Museum   *b, c* National Museum

[face p. 84

ancestors. It must not, however, be inferred from this apparent lateness that all Scottish Beakers are degenerate descendants of English ancestors. Two Beakers, from Fife and Aberdeenshire respectively,[1] preserve white filling in the incisions, a device for enhancing the effect of the decoration that was popular on the Continent but seldom employed in England. Some Dutch Beakers are as squat as the Scottish and exhibit similar designs or decorative devices.

Moreover, in contrast to the A–C family, several Scottish B Beakers are of exceptionally fine quality and graceful profile. Some, like those from Bathgate and Tentsmuir, with their polished, red-slipped surface come as close as any in the British Isles to Continental models both in form and technique. Those from the eastern plains, from Drumelzier near the head of the Tweed (Pl. VI, *b*) [2] and from Glenluce, bear the imprint of a single length of cord wrapped spirally round the vessel. The same device was employed for the decoration of Beakers both in the Rhineland and Northern Holland and in France.[3] One of the latter examples comes from the long segmented cist of La Halliade, already quoted as a parallel to the collective tombs of the Clyde. On the other hand, both in Banffshire and at Glenluce, the spiral cord ornament is combined with horizontal ribs or mouldings, a device very common on North Dutch S-beakers with cord ornament.[4]

Only two handled Beakers have been found in Scotland,[5] one from a cist at Balmuick near Comrie on the Earn, and the other from Cairnhill (Monquhitter), Aberdeenshire ; the Comrie specimen is pushed further into the Highlands than any other Scottish Beaker and probably accompanied a cremated interment. Fox [6] has recorded sixteen handled Beakers from England and Wales. But they occur also on the Continent,[7] so that the idea must be attributed to the Beaker complex as a whole.

Map II shows conspicuous concentrations of Beakers in the Lower Tweed basin round the edge of the Merse, on the shores of the Forth, along the river valleys of Aberdeenshire, and on

---

[1] Abercromby, Nos. 190, 239.
[2] *PSAS.*, lxv, p. 366.
[3] Abercromby, Nos. *9, *17 ; cf. *Oudh. Med.,* xiv, pl. i, 7, 14.
[4] *Oudh. Med.,* xiv, pl. i, 1–2.
[5] *PSAS.,* xviii, p. 307 ; xxxvi, p. 683.
[6] *Arch. Camb.,* 1925, p. 16.
[7] van Giffen, *Bauart,* p. 93, fig. 112, iiie ; Childe, *Danube,* fig. 105.

the lowlands fringing the Moray Firth, but only sporadic settlements along the west coast and no appreciable penetration of the Highlands. The groups round Dunbar, round Muirkirk in Central Ayrshire, and in the Crinan region, may be correlated with the presence of limestone soils, those along the Lothian and Fife coasts with sandy soils. But if that indicate a preference for light and not too acid soils, it would be rash to infer that gaps in Galloway, Clydesdale, and Angus imply a deliberate avoidance of other types of country. The Map shows that these areas were, in fact, well settled about the same time by makers of Food Vessels. The distribution of Beakers is not obviously conditioned by soil-values but rather by orographical relief and by historical conditions—the routes taken by the invaders and the absence of other occupants.

The coastal concentrations of Beakers and particularly the discovery of Beaker settlements near sandy beaches and landing places at Hedderwick near Dunbar, Gullane (East Lothian), Tentsmuir (Fife), and elsewhere emphasize the part played by maritime intercourse in the invasion. But the details of the colonizing process can only be established by minute comparisons between the decoration of Beakers in various parts of Scotland, in England, and on the opposite side of the North Sea. Mitchell has undertaken such a survey and the results of her recently published paper [1] can be summarized here.

The makers of Ca Beakers in the Tweed basin would have come from Northumberland, where there was a large colony on the limestone between the Cheviots and the coast. And colonists from the same quarter also spread into the Lothians either across the Lammermuirs by the Whitadder or more probably by sea. On the Forth they may have been reinforced by fresh arrivals from the Rhine or England since several Beakers are decorated with horizontally hatched triangles—a motive not at home in the Tweed area. But in the Lothians there are also B Beakers decorated with continuous cord impressions—a device unknown in North-east England. It is, however, found in North Holland, and may therefore have been introduced directly from that quarter. Since, however, the same device is employed on B Beakers from Glenluce on the west coast (as also in West Yorkshire) and then at intermediate sites like Drumelzier on the Upper Tweed and Bathgate (West Lothian), a derivation

[1] *PSAS.*, lxviii, pp. 132 ff., with map and full catalogue.

from France by the Atlantic Coast route (p. 84 above) is not absolutely excluded.

The Fifeshire Beakers might have come by sea across the Forth, and in this county the B types are also conspicuous. Between the Tay and the Dee there are no indications of landings so that the settlers in this corner of the Midland Valley presumably came by land from south of the Forth. Some may have advanced into Aberdeenshire.

But there must have been landings on the Aberdeenshire coasts of settlers come from further south and perhaps also of fresh arrivals from Holland. An extension of settlement from Aberdeenshire would account for most of the Beakers on the coasts of the Moray Firth. But here we have also a cluster of Beakers showing patterns exceptional north of the Southern Uplands, but with exact parallels in Holland—e.g. the broad band of close-set chevrons (Pl. VI, d). These may then betoken direct settlement from the Low Countries. The B Beakers with cord ornament from the collective tombs of Caithness too may have been brought by voyagers coming direct across the North Sea, or sailing up from South-Eastern Scotland.

On the west coast the position is different. There are a few hints of intercourse with the east coast such as the cord-ornamented B sherds from Glenluce. But most Beakers from the west find closer parallels in ornament in Wales than in Eastern Scotland. It would then seem likely that the bulk of the colonists on this side came up by sea along tracks already traced out by the builders of chambered cairns. And a Beaker recently found in Strathnaver belongs by its decoration to the Western group, so that the track in question must have rounded Cape Wrath.

Scottish Beakers were seldom accompanied by the objects characteristically associated with the English specimens. Tanged and barbed flint arrow-heads accompanied Beakers in eight burials.[1] Bowman's wristguards were found in only three graves,[2] one in Mull. The West European dagger that accompanies English B Beakers and Continental Bell-beakers is represented by only one stray specimen, and the round-heeled bronze knife-dagger associated with type A in England accompanied only three Beakers in Scotland (one from Mull), all very late looking.[3] The

---

[1] Abercromby, Nos. 190, 228–9, 230–1, 248, 277.

[2] Abercromby, Nos. 217, 228–9, 269 ; the one from Mull has only one hole at each end, the others two.

[3] Abercromby, Nos. 217, 262, and perhaps one from Kirkcaldy of doubtful type.

flint imitations of metal daggers found with several A–C Beakers in England have never been found in a Scottish grave at all; the National Museum possesses stray specimens from Berwick-shire, Roxburghshire, Peebleshire, the Lothians (two), and Angus.

No hammer-axes of the English Beaker type accompanied those vessels in Scotland, but one was found under a tumulus between two cists, each containing Food Vessels.[1] A conical button with " V " perforation may have accompanied a Beaker at Keith Marischal, East Lothian, but the records [2] are contradictory. Bone rings with two small loops projecting from the exterior surface were twice found with Beakers in Aberdeenshire (Fig. 21).[3] They may be compared to the " pulley rings " of shale or jet that accompany A–C Beakers in England. In seven cases portions of " jet " necklaces were associated with Beakers, but they are far more frequently associated with Food Vessels. A pair of massive bronze armlets, penannular, but with the ends

Fig. 21.—Bone ring from Clinterty, Aberdeenshire, after Reid. ¼.

tightly joined, accompanied a Ca Beaker near Crawford (Lan.), but similar armlets were found with a Food Vessel in a grave near Kinneff Castle (Kinc.).[4] Finally a polished stone axe probably accompanied a Beaker interment at Cruden Bay (Aber.). A curious find was a spoon-like object of horn accompanying a Beaker at Broomend of Crichie, Inverurie.

The foregoing list completes the inventory of contributions made by the Beaker-folk to the culture of Scotland, as far as the grave-finds go. Neither associations nor distributions serve to connect the flat, metal axe with the Beaker-folk. Fox [5] has suggested that most English specimens were imported from

---

[1] *PSAS.*, xlviii, p. 318.
[2] *PSAS.*, xxxiii, p. 68, and xxxv, p. 274.
[3] *PSAS.*, vii, p. 112 ; xxxix, p. 434 ; lvii, p. 156, fig. 15, i. Reid, *Prehistoric Interments*, p. 18.
[4] *PSAS.*, xvii, pp. 450–1.
[5] *PSEA.*, vii, p. 155.

Ireland, and their range in Scotland accords with that view
The same author contends [1] that the round-heeled daggers were
imports in Great Britain, and there is no evidence to the contrary in Scotland; the Beakers accompanying them here are
extraordinarily degenerate specimens. The advent of the
round-headed invaders doubtless profoundly modified the
human geography and economy of Scotland, but it cannot be
contended that they introduced metal implements, nor the
knowledge of metallurgy. Yet in Aberdeenshire they must
have constituted the chief users of metal tools and weapons.

2. FOOD VESSELS

Partly at least contemporary with interments accompanied
by Beakers, are graves containing what are termed Food Vessels.
Only in two instances [2] were the two types found together in
the same grave, and the circumstances of these discoveries do
not guarantee contemporary deposition. The English evidence,[3]
however, fully establishes an overlap between Food Vessels
and Beakers even of form A, and Food Vessels are believed to
have originated in North Britain or Ireland and spread
southwards. The distribution of Food Vessels as compared with
that of Beakers in Scotland points the same way. While the
distributions overlap at several points they are in other regions
virtually exclusive. The differences are not such as would
result from the natural expansion of a population that began
by making Beakers and later adopted the Food Vessel. Food
Vessels, that is, do not only spread on to inferior lands on the
edge of Beaker colonies, as they do in Yorkshire,[4] but also
occupy, e.g. in Angus, good lands to the exclusion of Beakers.

All Food Vessels are coarser and heavier than the better
Beakers; the walls are thick, and the surface colour tends to
dark or muddy brown hues. The firing is generally rather
imperfect. The shapes are excessively varied.

It has long been believed that one parent at least of the Food
Vessel was " the " round-bottomed " Neolithic " bowl. On
this assumption vessels with more or less round bases may be
termed type A. Such are very common in Ireland, and in

[1] *Arch. Camb.*, 1928, p. 150.
[2] Eddington Mill (Berw.), R.C. Berwick, p. xxxii, and Clashfarquhar, Deeside.
[3] Abercromby, i, pp. 97–107.
[4] Elgee, *Archæology of Yorkshire*, p. 78.

Scotland are most numerous in the Crinan district. Most are relatively shallow and approximate to form C of Fig. 12 (Fig. 22, 1). But some (Pl. VII, *a*) are deeper, resembling shape B on the same figure, and may be denoted by the letter A′. More often Food Vessels stand on a good flat base. When the body is shaped like an inverted cone and surmounted by a concave neck, we may speak of form B. Those lacking a well-defined neck and shoulder will then be form C.

An undoubtedly early feature in Food Vessels is a groove

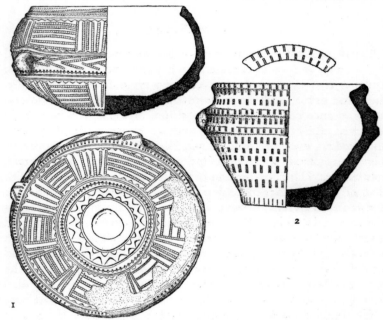

FIG. 22.—Food Vessels : Kilmartin (A1a) and East Lothian (B1a). ⅓.

encircling the body, below the maximum diameter in form A and at the shoulder in form B. It presumably served to take a cord either for the suspension of the vessel or for securing a cover of cloth or hide. To keep the cord in position the groove is generally spanned by perforated lugs (Fig. 22). In one Scottish specimen there are horizontally pierced lugs [1] projecting from the wall, but no groove. The presence of the groove may be indicated by adding the numeral " 1 ", that of perforated

[1] *PSAS.,* lxvii, p. 165 (Kelso, Roxburgh.).

lugs by the addition of an " a ". So we could have A1a, B1a, and Ba. There is no evidence for any chronological relation between such variants.

However, in many examples of form B1 the groove is interrupted by lugs that are not pierced (Pl. VII, *d*). Such lugs have no function ; indeed they prevent the groove from taking the string it was designed to accommodate. Such vessels are clearly degenerations, and there is actually some evidence that they are later than types with perforated lugs. They may be termed B1b. The groove may now be widened so as to become the vehicle for decoration and finally the lugs may be suppressed (giving, of course, B10 (Pl. VII, *c*)). And the groove may itself be suppressed giving a form that may be termed Bo, but is sometimes indistinguishable from C. Or else the grooves may be multiplied as in an example from Stirlingshire where there are three grooves. It could be termed B3 (Pl. VIII, 2).

The same result might, however, be obtained by a different process—by the addition of ribs or mouldings to the upper parts of the vessel instead of grooving a shoulder. And this seems actually to have happened. The early type A1a vessel, of Fig. 22, 1, was found in an eccentric cist under the south cairn on Kilmartin Glebe [1] near Crinan ; the central cist under the same cairn, presumably contemporary with, if not earlier than, the foregoing, contained a Food Vessel with a moulding on the shoulder and another midway between shoulder and rim (like Pl. VII, *b*). The wide, concave spaces between the two mouldings and the moulding and rim were richly decorated. Such a type, considering the circumstances of its discovery, cannot be treated as a degeneration of form B1. Again, a Food Vessel bearing six mouldings lay on the floor of a corbelled collective tomb on Carrowkeel Mountain, County Sligo.[2] It will therefore be well to distinguish such vessels from variants on B1 and to term them C2 or C6 according to the number of the mouldings. Yet of course they are formally indistinguishable from B10 or B2.

The miscellaneous forms denoted by the letter C are equally puzzling. They might be derived from A' or from series B by a complete suppression of the shoulder. What is certain is that double-grooved types, B2 with a definite neck, are later than the similar single-grooved forms with lugs B1 ; at Drannandow [3] in the Cree Valley (Kirkcudbright) a vessel of form B2 was found

[1] *PSAS.*, vi, p. 340.   [2] *PRAI.*, xxix, C, pl. xxv.   [3] *PSAS.*, lvii, p. 70.

in a secondary cist intruded into a cairn built over a burial with B1.

Food Vessels of form A are common only in Ireland and in Scotland, particularly round Crinan. But there are isolated examples in the Lothians and Aberdeenshire.[1] Series C2–4 again has a western distribution. It extends as far south as Galloway and is represented in East Lothian, Stirlingshire, Western Perthshire, and Kincardineshire. The most widely distributed forms belong to group B.

All Food Vessels are richly ornamented. The wide, often bevelled, rim is made a vehicle of decoration as well as the walls. In Argyll, Arran, and Bute, as in Ireland, vessels of forms A, B1a, and C are often decorated also on the base with radial patterns.

For decorating Food Vessels the finger-nail, a notched slip of wood, and a twisted cord as with Beakers, a wider straight-edged comb or a shell edge, whipped cord, the joints of birds' leg-bones, and other stamps, as in Peterborough ware, and a triangular point may be employed. The whipped cord is often used to produce maggot-like impressions, as on Peterborough sherds, but also (Pl. VII, *a*) to produce parallel lines, as on the Windmill Hill pot from Clachaig; the maggots are generally arranged herring-bone fashion. Both motives may be imitated with a coarse short-toothed comb (Fig. 22, 1).

Sometimes two cords are braided together to give what Abercromby terms the chain-looped cord effect. It may be reproduced by twisting two lengths of string together not too tightly and impressing the braid on plastocene. Then twist them together in the reverse direction and impress the new braid parallel to the first. The triangular point was impressed obliquely on the clay so as to yield triangular impressions. These are generally so arranged as to leave a zig-zag band in relief between alternating triangular depressions. Abercromby terms the result " false relief " (Fig. 22, 1). The device was also employed on the Continent from Spain to Greece[2]; there it is expressively termed fretwork decoration (Kerbschnitt). The effect is certainly one appropriate to wood carving, as a glance at any ethnographical collection will show. Indeed, the form of Food Vessels too, is often suggestive of wooden models.

[1] Abercromby, i, 303*a*, 303, 304.
[2] Childe, *Danube*, pp. 211, 281, 308 ; Frankfort, *Studies in the Early Pottery of the Near East,* ii, p. 50 ; Goldman, *Eutresis,* fig. 124.

PLATE VII

a

b

c   *d*

FOOD VESSELS

a	DOUNE	*b*	ARRAN
c	LEITH	*d*	BRIDGENESS
a, b	National Museum	*c, d*	University Museum

That is seen even in the heavy bevelled rims, but most strikingly in the structure of the feet of two Yorkshire specimens [1]; a wooden vessel of similar form was actually found in a grave with Corded ware in Thuringia.[2] As stamps, in addition to ready-made natural objects, specially prepared dies of baked clay in the form of hexagons or rhombs were sometimes employed; one such die has actually been found in Ireland.[3]

Many elements in the form and decoration of Food Vessels have doubtless been taken over from Beaker or older ceramic schools. The cogged stamp must, and the cord might, be derived from the Beaker. Pit, leg-bone, and maggot ornament are presumably due to the Peterborough tradition. These motives were most freely employed in Eastern Scotland,[4] and nothing proves that they are specially early; maggot ornament for instance is well illustrated on an unmistakably late B1 Food Vessel from Milton of Pitreavie, and recurs on Cinerary Urns. Whipped cord could be derived from the Beacharra group of Windmill Hill ware. But both the form and ornament of the Food Vessel from Doune (Pl. VII, a) can be matched among the very earliest vases from Danish passage graves.[5] Since Beakers appear as intruders in such tombs at a considerably later date, the coincidence just noted could be used as an argument for regarding some Food Vessels as at least as old as any Beakers.

In any case there are elements in Food Vessels, especially those from the West of Scotland, and their Irish relatives, that cannot be derived from native traditions but point to the influence of the old Atlantic sea-route, as Scott [6] has very rightly insisted. False relief represents an absolute innovation in British ceramic decoration. But it is illustrated on Bell-beakers both from the Iberian Peninsula and from Central Europe,[7] though it is foreign to Dutch and Rhenish as to British Beakers.

The radial ornament on the base of Irish and West Scottish Food Vessels is strikingly similar to that on Beakers from

[1] Abercromby, 222, 223 bis.
[2] JST., i, pl. xxiii, 248.
[3] Rosenberg, *Kulturströmungen in Europa*, p. 160.
[4] Kenny's Hillock, Elgin (C.), Rothienorman, Aberdeenshire (C.), Pitreavie, Balmerino, and Crail, Fife (C.); Hagg Wood, Berw.; Kelso; Rachan near Biggar.
[5] *Real.*, ix, pl. 81, C.; Rosenberg, p. 156; chain-looped cord was also used for decorating pottery from Danish dolmens, ibid., fig. 143.
[6] CPPS., 1932, p. 134.
[7] Castillo, *Vaso campaniforme*, pls. lxxiii, 1 (Catalonia); cxxxi, 1 (Bavaria); clxxi (Thuringia).

Thuringia and the Iberian Peninsula.[1]   And both in Portugal
and on the Spanish slopes of the Pyrenees it reappears also on
shallow hemispherical bowls with thick, decorated rims that are
associated with Bell-beakers.[2]   Such bowls might serve as prototypes for the Food Vessel.   Moreover, on the French side of the
Pyrenees, bowls of similar form but provided with little lug
feet are encircled by a groove spanned by pierced lugs precisely
as in our Fig. 22, 1.   And one such bowl came from the segmented
cist of La Halliade,[3] previously quoted as a parallel to the Clyde
collective tombs.   It really looks as if not only decorative elements
but the fundamental form of the Food Vessel itself might be
brought from the Iberian Peninsula via Ireland.

Other cultural elements, associated with Food Vessels, point
in the same direction.   Food Vessels, though normally found
in short cists, more often accompany cremated bones than do
Beakers ;   even the type A' vessel from Doune with its early
Danish parallels was associated with a cremation.[4]   As a result
the physical character of the people buried with Food Vessels
is very uncertain ;   one such individual stood 5 ft. 5 in. high [5]
and another from Bridgeness stood 5 ft. 7 in. with a cranial index
of 75·9.   A stature of 6 ft. 2 in. is assigned to a male from Glenlyon
but a man from Fyrie (Aberdeenshire) stood only 5 ft. 4 in. and
was markedly round-headed.

The relics associated in Scotland with Food Vessels, in contradistinction to Beakers, are few, though this need not indicate
greater poverty among their makers.   The most important are
the necklaces of lignite beads which, although found in seven
cases with Beakers, accompanied Food Vessels in no less than
fifteen graves.   The distribution of such ornaments confirms
the association.   In addition, a cylindrical mace-head transversely
perforated was found with a Food Vessel of type B1a at Doune
(Perthshire),[6] and a pair of bronze armlets (identical with those
accompanying the Beaker from Crawford, Lan.) with one of
type C2 at Kinneff Castle (Kinc.).

But apart from relics certain other traits may be attributed
to a " Food Vessel complex ".   In regions as far apart as Arran,

[1] Abercromby, i, 30* ;   Castillo, pl. xi (Central Spain) ;   lix (Almeria).
[2] Castillo, *Vaso campaniforme*, pls. xiii (Toledo) ;   xli (Portugal) ;   lxxvi (Pyrenees) ;
cf. cxviii (Sardinia).
[3] Childe, *Dawn*, fig. 135.
[4] *PSAS.*, xxxvi, p. 685.
[5] *PSAS.*, lxv, p. 421 ;   cf. *PAASUA*, 1904–6, p. 147.
[6] *PSAS.*, xvii, p. 452.

Clackmannan, and Easter Ross [1] Food Vessels occupied cists at the true centres of megalithic stone circles. In other words, one type of stone circle may be attributed to the Food Vessel complex. Such monuments are, of course, common in the megalithic province of the Atlantic coasts. In the Crinan district again a Food Vessel was the only relic found in any of the group of nine curious grooved cists described on p. 106. The nearest parallels to such graves come from the Scilly Isles.

The coverstone of a cist containing a Food Vessel of form B1a at Tillicoultry (Clackmannan) [2] was marked with those artificial hollows surrounded by concentric grooves that are termed *cup-and-ring marks*. There is thus some evidence for connecting this widely distributed group of rock-sculpturings with the Food Vessel complex. Their closest foreign analogies lie in Spain and Ireland.

The Food Vessel may thus be regarded as the hall-mark of a distinct complex which even possessed a distribution of its own. Was this complex introduced by new immigrants, fresh colonists landing on the West Coast like the tomb-builders and spreading eastward but burying their dead individually ? Did these absorb or drive out the Beaker invaders and Peterborough folk ? Only in Aberdeenshire did the Beaker complex retain its purity for a long period, and Peterborough elements were incorporated in the decoration of Food Vessels mainly in East Scotland. Or is the Food Vessel merely a product of " aboriginal " stocks— Windmill Hill and Peterborough folk, Tardenoisians and Azilians —subjugated by the Beaker folk but retaining ancestral connections with the west or east ?

In any case the two groups, if they had any separate identity, must have mingled freely ; that is proved by the types common to both. And there are many cultural phenomena, assignable to the period when Beakers and Food Vessels were the current funerary wares, that cannot be attributed to one group rather than to the other.

3. RELICS OF THE EARLY BRONZE AGE

In addition to burials accompanied by Beakers or Food Vessels short cists containing contracted skeletons but no pottery have been found all over Scotland. Such cannot, of course, be assigned

[1] *PSAS.*, iv, p. 499 ; xxix, p. 191 ; lxv, p. 258 ; *infra*, p. 112.
[2] *PSAS.*, xxix, p. 192 ; *infra*, p. 117.

definitely to either complex.   But they often contain objects identical with those associated with Beakers or Food Vessels (wrist-guards,[1] bronze knife-daggers, jet necklaces, etc.), or are juxtaposed in the same cemetery or under the same cairn to cists containing such ceramic furniture.   It is therefore likely that all or most such cists belong to the period when Beakers and Food Vessels were current and before these were replaced by Cinerary Urns.   The relics contained in such cists may therefore be used to supplement our knowledge of the culture of the period in question.

Again, the weapons and ornaments found in short cists reappear, sometimes with other associates, in what are termed *hoards*.[2] These are groups of objects deposited or hidden by their owners and not recovered ; in the hoards which concern us the presumption is that all the objects were current simultaneously. By combining these sources of information we obtain a clearer picture of the material culture of the inhabitants of Caledonia in what may be termed the Early Bronze Age than could be derived from grave-goods alone.   Dr. Callander [3] has enumerated and analysed the Scottish hoards.   We shall consider here those that he assigns to Periods I and II.   If we combine these two periods to form an Early Bronze Age, that must not be taken to mean that the period thus named was at all strictly parallel to the Early Bronze Age of England.   In reality twelve out of the thirteen hoards in question come from sites north of the Southern Uplands, while six out of seven hoards assignable to Callander's Period III come from south of those ranges. We shall subsequently show that the Early Bronze Age over the greater part of Caledonia covers also the Middle Bronze Age distinguished by English archæologists.   With that reservation it may be said that the following metal implements were in use in Scotland during the Early Bronze Age : flat axes, knife-daggers, and halberds.

Flat axe-heads are represented in nine hoards and by stray examples all over the country ;   the number with exact provenances recorded to date is 131, and the absolute total 193. The material of their manufacture has not been determined by analysis.   But one from Sluie, Morayshire, certainly contained tin ;   the surface coating was indeed so rich in that element as

---

[1] e.g. Alness, Ross., *PSAS.*, xiii, 255.   [2] Childe, *Bronze Age*, pp. 43 f.
[3] *PSAS.*, lvii, pp. 125 ff.

to give the impression that the object had been tinned.[1] It may be assumed that the great majority are actually composed of bronze and not unalloyed copper.

It has been suggested that flat axes were imported from Ireland. In Southern Scotland the distribution confirms this impression. And some bear hammered decoration on the face or edge quite in the Irish manner. On the other hand more than half the total come from North-eastern Scotland between the Tay and the Pentland Firth. And in this region moulds for their manufacture have been found.[2] (Flat axes can be cast very simply by pouring the molten metal into a hollow receptacle of the desired shape. This can be covered with a flat stone while the metal cools. The casting will then have to be finished off by hammering; sometimes the sides have been beaten up to form low flanges.) In this area, therefore, the implements in question were being produced locally.

The technique must have been introduced into the country by actual immigrant smiths, though the natives could eventually acquire it by apprenticeship. The smiths in question might have been mere captives or perambulating craftsmen. But if they were immigrant families who settled down to live and die in Scotland, they might be identified with some group using Food Vessels—probably those of the Irish types A or C2. It may be remarked that in the Crinan district, where such Food Vessels are most common, representations of flat axes have been found on the walls of two short cists.[3] It will be remembered that copper ore was available in the district which would accordingly be an appropriate locality for an early settlement of metal-workers.

Flat axes were the only metal tools in use during the Early Bronze Age, and even they may have served chiefly as weapons. Most everyday implements were still made of stone and bone. The majority of stone axes may thus be assigned to this period; they are in fact commoner in regions, like the Lothians and Aberdeenshire, where collective tombs are rare, than in centres of such " Neolithic " monuments. A few only are made of flint.[4] All belong to the West European type with

---

[1] *PSAS.*, ix, p. 432.   [2] *PSAS.*, xxxviii, p. 488. Fig. 23, 1 here.
[3] *PSAS.*, lxiv, p. 133 ; lxv, p. 271.
[4] The National Museum possesses examples from Orkney (2), Banffshire (4), Aberdeenshire (9), Kincardineshire (2), Angus (2), East Lothian, Berwickshire, Peebles, Wigtonshire (2), Islay, Lewis.

an oval or pointed-oval cross-section; though in one or two examples the small sides are slightly flattened, I know from Scotland no axe with the rectangular cross-section distinctive

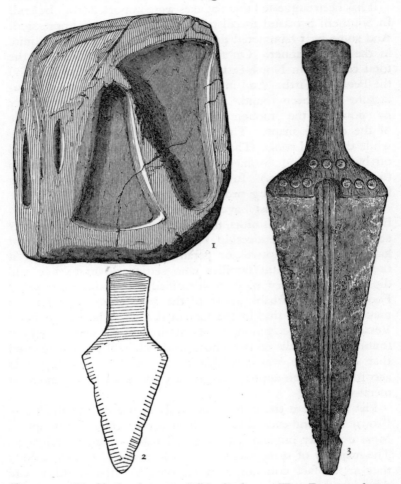

FIG. 23.—1. Moulds for flat axes, Culbin Sands; 2. West European dagger, North-east Scotland; 3. Dagger in horn hilt, Wester Mains of Auchterhouse (after *PSAS.*). ½.

of the Nordic province from the Zuider Zee to the Oder.[1] Half a dozen axes, beautifully polished and made of choice stones, preferably green in colour, are very flat with pointed butts.[2]

[1] Childe, *Dawn*, fig. 97.   [2] *PSAS.*, xxxii, p. 130.

The type seems to be at home in Brittany, and the Scottish specimens bear further testimony to the continuance of intercourse along the Atlantic coast route mentioned in the last section. But such axes have been found in East Scotland—Fife, Perthshire, and Roxburghshire—as well as in the western counties—Wigtonshire, Kirkcudbright, and Stirlingshire. Adzes are common only in Orkney and Shetland, and diverge substantially from the Danubian form.

Scrapers and knives—including the polished and slug types already mentioned—were abundant in the Beaker-Food Vessel phase. In addition to a bone chisel, like Fig. 19, a pricker made from the longitudinally split marrow-bone of a sheep was found in a grave with a Beaker at Cawdor Castle, Nairnshire.[1]

The daggers found in Early Bronze Age graves or hoards were fitted with horn or wooden hilts, attached to the blade by rivets. The imprint of the hilt can often be seen upon the blade and exhibits a curious semicircular indent—a feature traceable throughout Western and Central Europe to extremely early Egyptian weapons.[2] Such a hilt of solid ox-horn was actually found in position attached to a dagger in a grave in Angus [3]; though it has now shrunk terribly, the excavator was able to make an accurate drawing of it which is reproduced here as Fig. 23, 3. The end of the hilt must sometimes have been bound with a corrugated band of thin gold, and a gold cap might form a pommel.

Two types of blade should, as Callander has pointed out, be distinguished. Those actually found in cists with skeletons (and sometimes Beakers) are all quite flat, seldom exceed 6 inches in length, and are generally rounded at the point. There are, however, a few rather longer blades that have sharper points. Several are strengthened with some sort of *mid-rib*—that is a cast ridge down the centre of the blade on both faces. In two, both found with burnt bones, at Blackwater Foot (Arran) and Auchterhouse, the mid-rib is represented by three distinct ridges converging upon the point. Yet the gold mountings on the specimen from Blackwater Foot, Arran, were identical with those accompanying a short, flat dagger in a grave contemporary with a Beaker at Collessie, Fife.[4] Nonetheless the longer class

[1] *Proc. Soc. Ant.,* 2nd ser., i, p. 397.
[2] Childe, *Bronze Age,* p. 78 ; *Most Ancient East,* fig. 39.
[3] *PSAS.,* xxxii, p. 205 ; cf. that from Orkney, *PSAS.,* xxi, p. 340.
[4] *PSAS.,* lvii, p. 129, fig. 2, 6–7.

of triangular daggers may be the later and should correspond in time to the ogival daggers of England.

A halberd is really a dagger mounted at right angles to its shaft; a very early flint dagger from Egypt [1] was perhaps thus mounted, and the collective tombs of the Iberian Peninsula [2] certainly contain flint halberds. The metal blades are, however, generally recognizable owing to their *asymmetrical* form—in plan they are scalene, not isosceles, triangles. The Scottish specimens all possess broad, stout mid-ribs and were attached to the hilts by large rivets. It is generally agreed that the idea of the halberd was transmitted from the Iberian Peninsula to Ireland and developed there. Many believe that the device was transplanted from Ireland to North Germany. In that case the Scottish

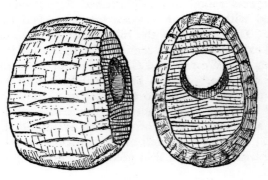

FIG. 24.—Facetted mace-head, Bonar Bridge. $\frac{2}{3}$.

examples would mark stages on the way thither. All may in any case be regarded as of Irish manufacture. Their age is, however, not well established; they certainly illustrate a superior metallurgical technique to that exemplified in the flat axes and flat daggers. One was actually found in a cist grave at Bishop Mill near Elgin.[3] The rest occur stray or in hoards with no dateable associates. A halberd was indeed accompanied by a Late Bronze Age socketed axe in a hoard from Islay, but this was a collection of scrap metal destined to be remelted so that its contents may be of disparate ages. The association of a flat axe with halberds at Sluie, Morayshire,[4] is in any case doubtful. The weapons have been found in Galloway, Ayrshire, Bute, and Islay on the

---

[1] Childe, *MAE.*, p. 59.   [2] Childe, *Dawn*, p. 117.
[3] In Elgin Museum unrecognized and now badly corroded.
[4] *PSAS.*, iv, p. 187; ix, p. 432.

west, in Sutherland, Inverness-shire, Elginshire, and Aberdeen-shire in the north-east, and also in Fife.

The armoury of the Early Bronze Age comprised also the flint daggers, mentioned on p. 88, the numerous tanged and barbed arrow-heads and a few perforated hammer-axes and mace-heads of stone. Battle-axes are surprisingly rare. Only one stray from East Lothian might conceivably be Scandinavian, but another, said to have been found in a cist on the Pentlands, Midlothian, might have been influenced by Nordic models. As battle-axes, allied to the Scandinavian family, are very widespread, occurring not only in Holland, but even in the Paris basin and Brittany, their absence from Scotland is surprising ; no fore-

FIG. 25.—Bronze Armlet from Melfort, Argyll, after *PSAS*. ¼.

runners of the Vikings were landing here in sub-Boreal times. Perhaps to this period may be assigned two mace-heads, oval in plan and rectangular in cross-section, the sides of which have been polished so as to produce facets (Fig. 24).[1] Specimens come from the vicinity of Bonar Bridge (Sutherland), and Kenny's Hillock (Morayshire), while there are examples from Staffordshire and Merionethshire in Wales. R. A. Smith compares these to maces made from the basal portion of a stag's antler which have been carved in a similar fashion.

The women of the Early Bronze Age wore metal bracelets and ear-rings and necklaces of amber or lignite beads. In addition

[1] *PSAS.*, xliii, pp. 380 ff. ; *Arch.*, lxix, p. 6.

to the massive bracelets mentioned already,[1] a wide type like a metal cuff was in use. The most interesting (Fig. 25), found in a cist with a jet necklace at Melfort, Argyll,[2] is made of very thin bronze plate or ribbon, 1¾ inches wide. It is decorated with grooved lines and ridges and rhomboid bosses, hammered up from the inside. Sets from a cist grave at Williamston, St. Martin's Parish, Perthshire, and from a hoard at Migdale, in Sutherland, were made of narrower but stouter plate, and decorated with cast horizontal ridges.[3] Cuff-like armlets are quite common all over Europe and may be imitations in metal of leather wristlets.

Two curious basket-shaped ear-rings of gold (Fig. 26) were found in a cist grave at Orton, Morayshire,[4] and a pair in bronze

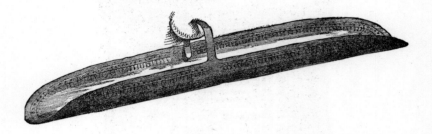

FIG. 26.—Basket-shaped gold ear-ring from Orton, Elginshire, after Anderson. ¼.

in the Migdale hoard. Similar ear-rings were worn by a woman interred unburnt under a round barrow in Yorkshire, and recur in Ireland. The type must be derived from far more elaborate ear-rings of the same shape discovered by Schliemann in the ruins of the second city at Hissarlik, the site of Homer's Troy.[5] Whether the type reached Scotland by the Atlantic route is uncertain since the same idea, executed, however, in coiled wire, had reached Central Europe by the Danube thoroughfare.[6]

The most interesting ornaments of the Early Bronze Age

---

[1] The matrix for such a ring was carved on the same stone as that for a flat axe ; *PSAS.*, lvii, p. 130.

[2] Anderson, ii, fig. 57.   [3] *PSAS.*, lvii, p. 132.

[4] Anderson, ii, p. 65 ; the type recurs in Ireland, Armstrong, *Catalogue Gold Ornaments*, p. 38, pl. xviii, 423-4.

[5] Childe, *Dawn*, fig. 29, 1. Cf. Blegen, *Zygrouries*, pl. xx, 11, for a closer parallel from Early Helladic Greece.

[6] Childe, *Dawn*, fig. 89, 5.

in Scotland are undoubtedly the so-called " jet necklaces ". The material is not true jet but rather lignite such as is available locally in the coal measures of Sutherland, Fife, Ayrshire, Bute, and Skye. It was, as Callander [1] has noted, doubtless valued, like amber, for its electrical properties ; when rubbed, pieces of lignite and amber will attract light objects. To unsophisticated men that would appear a manifestation of some potent magic or *mana* resident in the material. The inhabitants of Denmark had come to value amber, presumably for this reason, at a very remote period even in Atlantic times, and affection for the substance had been communicated to the mixed Beaker people of Holland.[2]   Quite possibly, then, jet was adopted by the Beaker-folk as a substitute for amber when they reached Scotland, where the latter material would be hard to get. Beads of amber are actually combined with others of jet in necklaces from Cruden Bay (found with a Beaker) and Blinmill, Rothienorman (with a Food Vessel) in Aberdeenshire, and from Lanarkshire.[3]

The valuation of amber may, however, have reached Scotland direct from Denmark, apart from the Beaker invasion, as a result of the maritime intercourse with Scandinavia attested in the parallelism of sepulchral architecture on both sides of the North Sea. In any case the substitution of jet for amber was apparently effected in Scotland earlier than in England.

Two classes of jet necklace may be distinguished. One is composed of a single strand of beads (generally flat discs), strung together with a triangular plate at one end to serve as a clasp. Such have been found in thirteen graves, four times with Food Vessels and thrice with Beakers.

The second type consists of several strings of beads, mostly barrel-shaped, held together by trapeze-shaped plates or spacers ; the fastener is again a small, triangular plate and the terminals are also triangular. The spacers and terminals are embellished with punctured rectilinear patterns—crosses, lozenges, triangles —similar to those engraved or incised on Early Bronze Age ornaments and vessels, including British Beakers, all over Europe. The precise arrangement of the beads to form a crescentic collar has only been settled by the late J. H. Craw's precise observation

---

[1] *PSAS.*, l, p. 206.

[2] For amber with Dutch Beakers, see van Giffen, *Bauart,* p. 167 (Drenthe) ; *Oudh. Med.,* ix, p. 65 (Utrecht) ; xiv, p. 73 (Gelderland), etc.

[3] See lists given by Callander, *PSAS.,* l, pp. 238, supplemented by lxiii, p. 171, and *HBNS.,* xxvii, p. 96.

of their position in a grave he excavated in the Crinan plain [1] (Pl. VIII).

The same brilliant archæologist has established the probability that the special form of necklace under discussion was devised in Scotland and most probably among the Food-vessel makers of Angus and Fife. The idea of a multiple string necklace was indeed very old in the Orient; necklaces with semicircular terminals were worn from the Indus to the Nile early in the third millennium B.C.[2] It was early introduced into Denmark,[3] and our jet necklaces may be immediately inspired by the Danish ones of amber. But in Scotland they were given a special form.

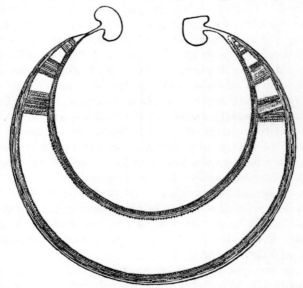

FIG. 27.—Gold lunula from Auchentaggert, after Anderson. ⅔.

Over fifty examples have been found in the country (sixteen from the north-eastern counties from the Dee to Orkney, fifteen from the east coast between the Forth and the Dee, and thirteen from Argyll, Arran, and Bute). In eleven graves they were definitely associated with Food Vessels, only twice with Beakers. From Scotland they seem to have spread across the Border, probably in company with the Food Vessel. There are only a dozen from England and a few from Ireland with similar associates. The crescentic jet necklace is an essentially Scottish contribution to the Bronze Age culture of Great Britain.

[1] *PSAS.*, lxiii, pp. 164 ff.   [2] e.g. Childe, *Most Ancient East*, pl. xxiv.
[3] Childe, *Danube*, p. 114.

PLATE VIII

1 JET NECKLACE, POLTALLOCH

2 FOOD VESSEL, BIRKHILL, STIRLINGSHIRE

Craw has gone further and drawn attention to certain connections between the jet necklaces and the crescentic collars or
gorgets of thin gold that are termed *lunulæ* (Fig. 27). Only five
or six such ornaments have been found in Scotland, whereas over
sixty are known from Ireland, four from Cornwall, one from
Wales, and isolated specimens from Brittany, Belgium, North
Germany, and Denmark, and related forms from Portugal and
North-west Spain.[1] All show narrow bands of finely engraved
ornament parallel to the edges. The body is plain near the
centre, but the two horns of the crescent are engraved with
rectilinear patterns. These not only agree with the motives
on the jet necklaces' plates, but are often arranged across the
horns in panels, which themselves resemble the spacers of our
necklaces. Craw accordingly suggests that the lunula type of
gorget is just a translation into gold of the plate and bead
necklace of jet.

The earliest lunulæ would then be those in which the arrangement of the engraved patterns corresponds most closely to that
of the decorated plates in the necklaces. Now three out of the
five surviving Scottish lunulæ comply with this condition as
against only nine out of fifty-two from Ireland. Craw accordingly
boldly suggests that the translation was effected and the lunula
created in Scotland. Gold was certainly obtainable locally and
was actually employed during the Early Bronze Age in Scotland
also for dagger mounts and ear-rings. Furthermore, the Breton
and Belgian specimens approximate more closely to the early
" Scottish " type than to the derivative Irish patterns. If this
argument be accepted, the lunula will be another Scottish contribution to the Bronze Age culture, not only of the British Isles
but of North-western Europe as a whole.

Another class of " jet " ornament, assignable to the Early
Bronze Age, is a ring with thin, perforated walls. A specimen
was found in one of eight cist graves (one containing a Food
Vessel) on the Yarrow Water, Selkirkshire.[2] It is $1\frac{7}{8}$ inches in
diameter at one edge, only $1\frac{1}{2}$ inches at the other, concave on the
outside, and pierced with four holes. Callander[3] mentions
stray examples from Midlothian, Lanarkshire, and Glenluce.
The type may be a poor copy of the English " pulley rings "
which have thicker walls perforated with convergent holes
(" V "-borings).

[1] *Préhistoire,* ii, p. 229, figs. 40, 42. [2] *PSAS.,* ii, p. 484. [3] *PSAS.,* l, p. 221.

VI

EARLY BRONZE AGE MONUMENTS

1. CISTS AND CAIRNS

THE makers of both Beakers and Food Vessels were buried individually in graves finally closed after the funeral. Occasionally the remains and funerary offerings were placed in simple trench-graves or pits. More often they were enclosed in a coffin of thin stone slabs, termed a short cist. The cists are generally from 3 to 4 feet long, by 2 feet wide. The sides are normally formed of four slabs while a fifth, often unnecessarily large, covers the cist. The bottom is often roughly paved with pebbles, but a slab pavement is quite exceptional. It has several times been observed that the joints of the cist were carefully luted with clay. In one or two cases [1] two cists were juxtaposed so as to have an end-slab in common.

A special type, restricted in Scotland to the Crinan district, must be mentioned here since one example contained a Food Vessel and a jet necklace. The peculiarity of these Crinan cists is that in each side-slab a pair of grooves has been neatly hammered out to accommodate the end-slabs. In one instance, [2] however, the end-slabs stood outside the grooves. The latter, Craw believes, contained wooden planks lining the cist. A total of nine grooved cists has now been identified in the Crinan district. [3] They are unknown elsewhere in Scotland, and the nearest parallels come from the Scilly Isles. [4] These cists once more emphasize the privileged position of the Crinan region and its exceptional foreign relations.

To the same period may, on English analogies, be assigned burials in coffins roughly hollowed out of oak trunks. Two such burials are reported as having been found under cairns in Aberdeenshire. [5] An oak trunk coffin, 7 feet long and 1 foot wide, was more recently discovered under a cairn on Dunglow

---

[1] *PSAS.*, xxxvi, p. 671 (Edinburgh); xxxii, p. 214 (Wester Mains of Auchterhouse, Angus).
[2] *PSAS.*, lxiii, p. 161.   [3] *PSAS.*, lxiv, p. 146.   [4] *Antiquity*, ii, p. 419.
[5] *New Statistical Account*, xii, pp. 354, 733.

on the borders of Kinross and Fife.[1] Others have been mentioned
from Castle Hill, Edinburgh, and from a peat moss near Oban.[2]
Similar oak-tree coffins are not uncommon in England and one
at least contained a Beaker though another contained an Incense
Cup.[3] The same sort of coffin was regularly employed in Den-
mark, North Germany, and Holland [4] during the Middle Bronze
Age, but tree-trunk burials in Britain need not be ascribed to
Nordic immigrants.

The cist normally contains a single skeleton buried crouched
in the so-called contracted attitude with the knees hunched up
towards the chin. Exceptionally two skeletons lay in the same
cist.[5] In one instance both skeletons were men, but in two
other cases one skeleton belonged to an infant. Charcoal is
often reported in cists with skeletons.

More rarely cists contain cremated remains. There are
three or four well authenticated instances of cremated bones
being accompanied by a Beaker.[6] More often cremations are
accompanied by or contained in Food Vessels.[7] In one instance
both unburnt and burnt bodies lay in the same cist, accompanied
by a Food Vessel.[8] Cremation deposits with Food Vessels may
also lie in simple pockets in the soil as at Balmerino, Fife.
While it is generally believed that cremations are, as a whole,
later than inhumations, cases are reported where the primary
burial was after cremation, and secondaries were unburnt.[9]

Short cists are often found without any superficial indication
of their presence. Indeed more than half the recorded examples
appear to have been such " flat graves ". Commonly, of course,
cist graves are covered by a barrow—an artificial mound of
earth or stones. Cases are on record of individual graves or
short cists having been dug into long or round chambered cairns.[10]
Such are, of course, intrusive in a different sense to the Beaker
sherds found in the collective burial vaults. But even in these
themselves short cists were sometimes erected to contain secondary burials.[11]

The mounds actually erected over short cists are generally

[1] *PSAS.*, xxxix, p. 179. [2] *PSAS.*, xiii, p. 337.
[3] *WAM.*, xliv, pp. 103 ff. ; Kendrick and Hawkes, p. 109 ; Elgee, *Yorkshire,*
p. 64.
[4] van Giffen, *Bauart,* p. 28. [5] *PSAS.*, xxxii, p. 49, xl, p. 33.
[6] Abercromby, pp. 41–2, Nos. 261, 267 ; *PSAS.*, lxii, p. 26.
[7] *PSAS.*, xxxvi, p. 685 ; xxxviii, p. 38 ; li, p. 28 ; lviii, p. 318 ; lix, p. 210, etc.
[8] *PSAS.*, lvii, pp. 245–7. [9] *PSAS.*, vii, p. 519.
[10] Above, p. 39, and *PSAS.*, lxii, p. 22. [11] Above, pp. 30, 39.

round.   Scotland being a stony country, the majority are cairns
of stones.   Earthen barrows are, however, not uncommon in
Angus, Fife, and the Lothians.   The same round cairn or tumulus
may cover a plurality of interments.   Some of these may be
secondary, lying high up in the mound or near its edge.   Such
secondary graves might evidently have been inserted into the
monument at a considerable time after its original erection ; they
are in fact not seldom accompanied by Cinerary Urns or other
indications of a relatively later date than the period denoted by
Beakers and Food Vessels.   But there are instances of Food Vessels
or even Beakers [1] accompanying obviously secondary interments.

In many instances, however, several interments have been
noted on virgin soil beneath the same barrow.   In a famous
cairn at Collessie, Fife,[2] there was a cist with a Beaker and a
skeleton on the ground at the centre, but cremated bones with
a bronze knife-dagger in a pit to one side.   Again at Balmerino [3]
in the same county a single cairn covered an empty central cist
and four distinct deposits of cremated bones on the ground,
together with Food Vessels of types B1, B2 (C2), and C, and
parts of a jet necklace.

The cairn or tumulus is seldom a mere heap of stones or earth.
When adequate observations have been made during excavation
it is seen to have been constructed with great care.   At Collessie
the ground had first been carefully levelled and even covered
with a layer of fine clay.[4]   Here too, and in several other instances
the whole area beneath the cairn was mottled by fires presumably
kindled for some ritual before the erection of the mound.

Many cairns covering short cists, like those containing
chambers, are encircled by a kerb or peristalith of boulders.
Such a kerb might be regarded as a purely practical device,
needed to keep the mound in shape, but often the boulders
seem unnecessarily large.

Moreover, there are often structural features within the cairn
the practical function of which is harder to admit.   In the cairn
at Drannandow on the Cree (Kirkcudbrightshire) [5] a double
wall of boulders, 2¾ feet wide, extended for 11 feet inside the
cairn to the west of the central cist, which contained a Food

---

[1] *PSAS.*, xl, p. 281 (Foreglen, Banff.).
[2] *PSAS.*, xii, p. 441.   [3] *PSAS.*, xxxii, pp. 635 ff.
[4] As in the chambered cairn of Bryn Celli Ddu in Anglesey, *Arch.*, lxxx,
pp. 180 ff. ; Kendrick and Hawkes, p. 116.
[5] *PSAS.*, lvii, p. 65.

Vessel. From either end of the wall double rows of boulders extended westward so as to form a " D "-shaped enclosure, open on the west, about the cist. The cairn was composed largely of flat slabs all lying tilted with their points towards the centre of the pile. Similar " D "-shaped enclosures have been reported under two cairns in Ross. And at Hagg Wood, Foulden, Berwickshire,[1] a crescentic setting, open to the west, touched at either end the peristalith of inward tilted slabs and itself enclosed an inner ring of similarly placed slabs. Two cists, containing cremated bones and Food Vessels, were enclosed by the inner ring. There was another crescent of slabs on edge also open to the west under the cairn at Collessie. ORiordain[2] has recently recognized a similar crescent of stones under a cairn in southern Ireland and has drawn attention to analogies in Holland.

In the Law Cairn, Urquhart, Elgin, which was 62 feet in diameter, the central cist was completely encircled by an inner wall of big boulders standing 2½ feet high. Again at Westermains of Auchterhouse, Angus, on the Sidlaws,[3] the double central cist, containing Fig. 23, 3, was covered by a mound of fine, black earth, 20 feet across. This core was delimited by a ring of boulders some 3½ feet long and had been covered by a pyramidal cairn, bounded in its turn by a kerb, 62 feet in diameter. Conversely, in the Scalpsie Bay cairn, Bute,[4] the cist was covered with a core of tightly packed stones, upon which rose the tumulus of big stones and earth.

Canon Greenwell[5] excavated a great cairn, 110 feet in diameter, on Kilmartin glebe. Entirely buried under the mass of the cairn he found, to the south-west of the centre, two concentric rings of uprights standing 2 to 3 feet high, and placed at intervals of 3 to 5 feet. At the centre of these circles with diameters of 27 and 37 feet was a cist containing an unburnt body and a type A1 Food Vessel (Fig. 22, 1). At the centre of the cairn was a larger cist containing a type C2 Food Vessel.

In the same district two remarkable cairns have been recently excavated by Craw.[6] Each covered a central cist to the north-east of which was a crescentic setting of slabs on edge standing 3 to 5⅔ feet high. The concave side of the setting was directed in each case to the periphery of the cairn and away from the central

[1] *PSAS.*, lviii, p. 318.
[2] *J. Cork Hist. Arch. Soc.*, xxxviii, p. 81.
[3] *PSAS.*, xxxii, p. 215.
[4] *PSAS.*, xxxviii, p. 53.
[5] *PSAS.*, vi, p. 337.
[6] *PSAS.*, lxiv, pp. 139–141.

cist. The settings, though entirely buried in the mass of the cairn, are thus reminiscent of the crescentic façade round the entrance to a chambered cairn.

The phenomenon just described is clearly an instance of a fusion between the so-called megalithic tradition of the collective tombs and the individual traditions of the short-cist people. A similar fusion might be invoked to explain other structures under round cairns. But it must be remembered that even in Holland graves containing Beakers were often surrounded with palisades or rings of posts.[1]   Hence the uprights and walls might be translations, appropriate to a stony country, of the Dutch wooden structures. The idea need not be derived from the builders of collective tombs but might have been brought over by the round-headed invaders. Still, Bursch and van Giffen hold that the wooden posts and palisades of Holland are substitutes for megalithic circles.

A special type of burial mound, very common in Southern England, is known as a bell barrow.[2]   In such the mound is surrounded by a continuous fosse. Between the inner lip of the latter and the base of the mound intervenes a level space or *berm*. There may be a bank outside the fosse. Such barrows may cover primary interments accompanied by Beakers or Cinerary Urns. In Scotland isolated monuments from East Lothian, West Lothian, and Fife have been described as bell cairns.[3]   There is a fine example on the summit of Cairnpapple Hill, near Linlithgow. It is surrounded by a bank enclosing an octagonal space, 200 feet across, with a fosse inside the bank. The central mound is bordered by a peristalith 90 feet in diameter. Such monuments are exceptional, and none have been excavated.

The term bell cairn has sometimes been applied to monuments which approximate rather to the English *disc barrows*.[4]   The latter may be regarded as a development of the bell barrow. But now the central mound has practically vanished. A monument at Ballymeanoch,[5] in the Crinan district (Fig. 28), approximates to this type. A low, stony mound, 72 feet in diameter, is here encircled by a fosse, from 7 to 12 feet wide, with a broad bank on the outside. There are two cists in the central area, one of which, to the side,

[1] van Giffen, *Bauart* ; Bursch, *Oudh. Med.,* xiv.
[2] *PSEA.,* vii, pp. 204 ff.
[3] RC. *East Lothian,* No. 232 ; *Midl.,* No. 386 ; *Fife,* No. 114 ; *Suth.,* No. 164 is doubtful.
[4] *Antiquity,* i, p. 425.   [5] *PSAS.,* lxv, p. 278.

contained the Beaker of Plate VI, *a*. This monument differs, however, from the English types in that the ditch is traversed by causeways on the north-east and south-west. If, as is widely held, the continuous ditch[1] of the bell and disc barrows was designed magically to cut off the dead from the living in a manner consonant with the tradition of individual burial, the causeways at Ballymeanoch offer to the living a means of approach as do

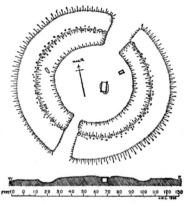

FIG. 28.—Plan of cairn at Ballymeanoch (Crinan), after *PSAS*.

the passage and portal of a collective tomb. After all, Maes Howe and New Grange are gigantic bell barrows, but for the causeways opposite the passage entries. Ballymeanoch might then be inspired as much by the collectivist tradition as by that of the Beaker folk. And formally it approximates to fossed circles of the type of Crichie.

2. STONE CIRCLES AND ALIGNMENTS

A circle of upright stones surrounding a central burial is patently related to cairns such as those just described. Stone circles are exceedingly numerous in Scotland and, some at least have been erected round primary burials of " Early Bronze Age " character. Sometimes the grave was marked by a barrow as in the cairns of Clava type. Two concentric rings, of which only three stones survive, may have encircled a barrow at Newbridge,

[1] Ditches surrounding barrows are widespread in Europe, e.g. continuous round barrows with Corded ware (*Księga Pamiętkowa k. U. Prof. W. Demetrykiewicza*, Poznan, 1930, p. 149) and penannular containing Middle Bronze Age interments in Rheinhessen (*Mainzer Zeitschr.*, 1927, p. 44).

near Edinburgh, on the Glasgow Road.[1]   A knife-dagger is supposed to have been found in a cist under the central mound.

More often there is a cist undistinguished by any barrow at the circle's true centre. A representative group of five such monuments was excavated by J. Bryce[2] on Mauchrie Moor, Arran. One was 45 feet in diameter, the tallest stone, on the west, standing 16 feet high. The central cist contained a Food Vessel of class C2 (Pl. VII, *b*) together with a skeleton. Another circle on the same moor comprised two concentric rings of uprights 36 and 45 feet in diameter. Other Arran circles may be smaller with diameters as low as 17 feet.

Similar sepulchral circles are known from many parts of Scotland. One, round an empty cist at Ri Cruin,[3] on the Crinan plain, measured 43 by 40 feet across. At Edderton, Ross,[4] the central interment was accompanied by a Food Vessel with cord ornament. The whole area between the ten uprights, 35 feet across, is stated to have been paved.

It cannot, however, be assumed that all, or even most, sepulchral circles were erected in the Early Bronze Age. In many cases cremated remains or Cinerary Urns have been found within them. These may sometimes be due to secondary burials, as at Tillicoultry, but we shall subsequently describe circles which apparently date from the very end of the local Bronze Age.

Another type of circle, girt with a fosse, may be assigned to the period when inhumation was still practised on the evidence obtained from a famous monument at Broomend of Crichie, close to Inverurie, Aberdeenshire.[5] Here a fosse, 20 feet wide with an external bank, encloses an area 50 feet in diameter. Six uprights stood within this area to form a circle. The fosse is traversed by causeways on the north and south, and there are traces of an avenue of uprights leading to the circle from the south. It is said that the avenue once extended northward to another circle consisting of three concentric rings round a central barrow. At the centre of the existing monument, a small cairn, 15 feet in diameter and entirely hidden under the turf, covered a cist containing a skeleton. An upright now stands on the site of the cist, but its original position is uncertain.

[1] RC. *Midlothian*, No. 131.
[2] *PSAS.*, iv, pp. 499 ff. ; *Book of Arran*, pp. 113 ff.
[3] *PSAS.*, lxiv, p. 130.
[4] *PSAS.*, lxv, p. 258.
[5] *PSAS.*, liv, pp. 155 ff., Anderson, ii, pp. 105.

The interrupted fosse and cist burial at Crichie suggest comparison with the sepulchral monument at Ballymeanoch.   But the ring of uprights and the avenue are reminiscent of larger and more famous monuments, like Avebury, that are not demonstrably sepulchral in function.   Closer approximations can be cited from Orkney.

The impressive Ring of Brodgar,[1] standing on a ridge between the Lochs of Stennis and Harray is encircled by a fosse, 29 feet wide and still 6 feet deep.   There is a bank outside the fosse which is traversed by two causeways.   Thirteen feet inside the brim of the fosse is a circle composed of flat slabs attaining a height of 14 feet and perhaps originally sixty in number.   The diameter of the circle is 340 feet.   As at Stonehenge, many large tumuli stand all round the great circle.   To the south of it are several tall uprights, perhaps the last remnants of some sort of avenue leading from the Ring of Brodgar to the Ring of Stennis. The latter stood apparently on a flat-topped mound, 3 feet high and 104 feet in diameter with an external fosse.   On the next hill north of the Brodgar Ring is the Ring of Bookan.   A causewayed ditch, 44 feet wide, here encloses an area 136 feet across, on which no stones are now standing.

These fossed circles may be assigned to the earlier part of the Bronze Age at latest on account of their striking similarity to those of Avebury (Wiltshire), Arbor Low (Derbyshire), and Stripple Stones (Cornwall).   The function of all these monuments is still uncertain, and the relation of the Orkney examples to the English and Cornish is unexplained.   The deliberate use of enormous stones in these and other circles may be regarded as in general a western idea that also infected the architecture of the collective tombs.

Indeed, it may be that all sepulchral circles are due to a survival of that tradition.   Callander [2] has recently suggested an evolution of the Stone Circle from the peristalith of the chambered cairn. We have already seen how this acquired an individuality of its own in the Hebrides.   It only wanted the abandonment of communal interment and the suppression of the cairn to produce a circle of the Arran type.   Even so, fresh foreign impulses would have to be admitted to explain such features as the causewayed fosse and its analogy to monuments of Ireland and Anglesey.

At the same time the timber circles and palisades under

---

[1] *Arch.,* xxxiv (1851), pp. 96 f.   [2] *Arch.,* lxxvii, p. 97.

Dutch barrows must again be recalled. These surround the graves of corded and bell beaker-folk, the ancestors or first cousins of our round-headed invaders. The latter might therefore have introduced the circle idea quite independently of the builders of collective tombs.[1]   Moreover, Crawford[2] has suggested that the stone circle might be a substitute for the ring fosse of the English disc barrow appropriate to a stony country where ditch digging was impeded by the native rock. At least a blending of two traditions is likely to be exemplified in our monuments. But, on the whole, Atlantic elements seem to preponderate and suggest a maintenance of intercourse with the coastal countries of Western Europe such as is also attested by the stone axes of Breton type from Scotland or the gold lunulæ from Brittany.

The same conclusion can be drawn from other monuments of still less certain age or import. Stone avenues have already been mentioned in connection with certain circles.[3]   And a single outlying stone or pointer not seldom stands a hundred feet or so from the circumference of a stone circle ; one such is attached to the Newbridge circle for instance. But in addition to such accompaniments of circles, there are in Scotland rows of stones unconnected with any such monument.

A remarkable series of stone rows has been recorded from Caithness and the Strath of Kildonan, just across the border of Sutherland. They are composed of quite small stones, set on end and only standing 1 to 3 feet above the ground. They are often arranged on a fan-like plan, the rows seeming to converge upon a cairn. Thus at Garrywhin, in Wick Parish, Anderson found six rows extending for some 200 feet, and all pointing to a cairn on the hilltop ; the cairn covered a cist burial with a Beaker.[4]   There are similar rows converging upon cairns near the Loch of Watenan. And at Allt Breac, Sutherland,[5] fourteen rows appear to point to a cairn near the summit of the hill, though they stop short over 100 feet from it. The finest assembly of stone rows, also convergent, runs up a hill close to Mid Clyth Station, Caithness.[6] It comprises no less than twenty-two rows that extend for 150 feet up hill, the group being 118 feet

---

[1] The "timber circle" at Bleasdale, Lancs., which most closely recalls the Dutch barrows surrounded a primary cremation with Cinerary Urns. *LAAA.,* xx, p. 188.

[2] *Antiquity,* i, p. 428.   [3] Above, pp. 44, 112.

[4] Anderson, ii, p. 126, fig. 133.   [5] RC. *Sutherland,* No. 379, fig. 53.

[6] RC. *Caithness,* No. 292 ; Anderson, ii, p. 131.

wide at the north end and 188 feet at the south end. The stones are set in all cases with their broad faces on the line of the row.

These remarkable monuments bear a general resemblance to the celebrated alignments of Carnac in Brittany. And Curle[1] reminds us of Aristotle's statement that the Iberians were wont to erect round a deceased warrior's tomb obelisks, equal in number to the enemies he had slain.

Shorter alignments of larger stones occur elsewhere, for instance, in Mull and on the Crinan plain.[2] There at Ballymeanoch four stones stand in line, all over 9 feet high and one adorned with cup and ring markings.

3. EARLY BRONZE AGE ART

The northernmost of the cairns on Kilmartin glebe at the head of the Crinan plain covered a single cist, the lid and an end slab of which were carved. The cover-stone bore the representations of ten axes as well as forty-one cup marks; two more axe figures had been carved on the inner face of the end-slab. The figures are shallow depressions formed by *pecking*, i.e. hammering the rock surface with a chisel-like tool of flint or hard stone but are too shallow to be moulds. Similar representations were noted many years ago on the end-slab of a cist at Ri Cruin[3] less than a mile south of the last-named cairn. A rake-like figure was carved on a narrow, upright slab, which formed part of the end-wall of the same cist; it has been interpreted as a conventionalized representation of a high-prowed boat containing nine banks of rowers (Pl. XI).

The axe and boat figures from Crinan are, as Craw has remarked, the only indubitably Bronze Age representations of real objects from Great Britain, save for an axe representation from a barrow in Dorset. But axes, this time hafted, are represented on the stones of Breton collective tombs[4] and of Portuguese[5] cist graves, as well as in South Russian barrows,[6] and on the rocks of the Maritime Alps[7] and of Sweden.[8] The conventionalized boat recurs in the collective tombs at New Grange (Ireland) and in Armorica. Our Scottish examples are therefore fresh witnesses

---

[1] Rhind Lectures, 1918.   [2] *PSAS.*, lxv, p. 271.
[3] *PSAS.*, lxiv, p. 133.   [4] Le Rouzic, *Corpus des signes gravés*, pls. 25, 37.
[5] *Préhistoire*, ii, p. 238, fig. 43.   [6] *ESA.*, ii, p. 238, fig. 43.
[7] *Antiquity*, iii, p. 158.   [8] *Real.*, iii, pl. 51, 56.

to the intercourse between Scotland, and especially the Crinan district, and countries further to the south-west.

But in the caves along the coasts of Fife there are carvings, technically or stylistically allied to the foregoing, which may be equally old. On the walls of the Wemyss Cave [1] has been pecked out a boat, very similar to that from Ri Cruin. A much more startling representation has recently been discovered by Edwards [2] in a cave now filled with the concrete foundations for a boiler-house by the Michael Colliery, Wemyss. The walls of this cave were ornamented not only with normal "Bronze Age" cup-and-rings, but also with more irregular pecked lines. Among these Edwards has very ingeniously recognized the outlines of an elk's head (Pl. IX). This rather conventionalized representation is apparently unique in the British Isles. The theme at least recalls the engravings of the so-called Arctic culture in Norway, though the style and technique may point rather to the supposedly later Bronze Age carvings of Scandinavia which are often associated with cup markings.[3] It will be remembered that the elk survived in Scotland down to Roman times, but the Wemyss pecking may still be the memorial of a visit from Scandinavian fishers during our Bronze Age, similar perhaps to that attested very much earlier by the antler axe from Meiklewood.

Curvilinear geometrical carvings are far commoner than representations and occur, as in the northern counties of England, also on natural rock surfaces. The cover-stone of a cist containing a Beaker near Carnwath, Lanarkshire,[4] was covered with con-centric rings, an imperfect spiral, and a lozenge, pecked all over. Pecked spirals also adorned the cover of a cist containing a Beaker at Catterline, Kincardine,[5] and another spiral was found on a stone in a cairn covering a Food Vessel or Cinerary Urn at Coilsfield, Ayrshire.[6] On rock surfaces spirals are exceptional, but there are fine examples in Ayrshire, Galloway, and Wigtonshire.[7] The design also occurs in Northern England, on a stone at the centre of the chambered tumulus of Bryn Celli Ddu, Anglesey,[8] and classically at New Grange, in Ireland.[9] The stones of the latter tumulus also

---

[1] Cast in National Museum.   [2] *PSAS.*, lxvii, p. 172.
[3] e.g., *Real.,* iii, pl. 50.
[4] Childe, *Bronze Age,* fig. 21, 2 ; *PSAS.,* x, p. 62.
[5] *PSAS.,* lviii, pp. 30 f.   [6] Munro, *Preh. Scotland,* p. 138.
[7] *PSAS.,* lvi, p. 45 ; lxi, p. 121.
[8] *Arch.,* lxxx, p. 197 ; Kendrick and Hawkes, fig. 48.
[9] Coffey, *New Grange* ; *PRIA.,* xxxvi, C, pp. 1 ff.

PLATE IX

[face p. 116

2 CARVING IN A CAVE IN FIFE

1 CUP AND RING MARKINGS NEAR CRINAN

bear lozenge patterns comparable to those on the Carnwath cist-cover. A quasi-synchronism between the Irish corbelled tombs and the British separate graves with Beakers is thereby established. The origin of the British spiral ornament is still unsettled; connections through Sicily and Malta with the Ægean seem probable.

The so-called cup-and-ring marks are much more common. These consist in essence of a central depression surrounded by from one to eight grooves (Pl. IX). Sometimes the rings are incomplete, at others a gutter runs from the cup across the rings. Or the cup may be suppressed so that the centre appears like a boss in relief. Both the cups and the grooves and gutters have been formed by the pecking process. Marks of this class decorated the cover-stone of a cist at Tillicoultry, Clackmannan,[1] which, as already noted, contained a Food Vessel.

On natural rock-surfaces or isolated stones they are found all over Scotland. But their conservation and recognition clearly depend to an exceptional degree on geological and climatic factors —the weathering qualities of the rock, the rapidity with which it becomes covered with protective vegetation. On soft rocks, easily disintegrated by frost or rain, survival for any length of time would be impossible unless the rock were covered with moss or turf soon after the execution of the designs. And then only accident or climatic change would lead to their rediscovery. A distribution map of recorded examples would therefore have little value without a long geological preface. Still, the exceptionally large number of elaborate cup-and-ring marks in Galloway and Ayrshire and the remarkable concentration of them in the Crinan district must be regarded as significant. In the eastern counties, on the other hand, they are relatively rare, though they are again abundant in Northumberland.

Quite apart from distributions the south-western connections of cup-and-ring marks are apparent. Simple cup-marks [2] indeed occur on stones associated with burials even in the Old Stone Age in France. And they appear in Denmark on the capstones of the dolmens that precede the passage-graves. But the more elaborate patterns with rings and gutters seem to be restricted to the Atlantic coasts. The nearest foreign parallels to the British designs may be found in the tin-bearing region of Galicia (north-western Spain).[3] The cup-and-ring mark is thus perhaps another Iberian idea introduced into Britain during the Early Bronze Age. It may,

---

[1] *PSAS.*, xxix, p. 193.   [2] *CPPS.*, 1932, p. 122.   [3] *Préhistoire*, ii, p. 227.

however, be noted that in Palestine the " Natufians ", a people so ancient as to be termed Mesolithic, carved basin-like hollows surrounded by grooves or ridges on the rock floor of their sepulchral cave.[1]

4. Early Bronze Age Settlement

Dwelling sites, certainly referable to the first phase of the metal age, are scarcely known. No Food Vessels have ever been found on domestic sites. Fragments of Beakers have, however, been picked up in shell heaps or kitchen middens at Gullane, East Lothian, Tentsmuir, Fife, and in the Hebrides. The sites all lie on sandy soil close to the shore and are generally exposed by the shifting of sand dunes. Near Gullane the middens lie close to old strand lines about 100 yards from the present shore. The sites appear as conspicuous white patches of shell that may cover an area of from 30 by 30 to 150 by 40 square feet.[2] Actually the middens are low heaps with a central depth of about 12 inches composed of shells of whelk, limpet, and oyster, crabs' claws, bones of domestic animals, deer, and fish, mixed with black soil, stones fractured by heat (pot-boilers), hammer-stones, flints, and a few sherds. Of the actual dwellings nothing survives, and they must have been of a very flimsy character.

The middens have then been left by a poor population still relying to some extent on hunting, fishing, and collecting shellfish and nuts. But they possessed cattle and sheep, and a grain adhering to the base of a Beaker[3] proves that they cultivated some cereal, probably wheat.

On the limestone hills round Muirkirk, Ayrshire,[4] once covered with birch scrub, but now bare moors, are not only numerous sepulchral cairns, but also several hut circles. Fragments of Beaker pottery together with sherds rather in the Peterborough tradition were found on the floors of two of these—in one case below a mediæval layer. The circles are low banks of stone and earth, now about 2 feet high and 3 feet wide at the base. A gap in the bank on the south or south-west marks the doorway. One circle was 18 feet, the other 34–8 feet in diameter.

The smaller circle was roughly paved and possessed a hearth of flat stones with stones on edge at one side as a kerb. In the

---

[1] *JRAI.*, lxii, p. 266.   [2] *PSAS.*, xlii, pp. 308 ff.
[3] *PSAS.*, xlii, p. 289.   [4] *PSAS.*, xlviii, pp. 374 f. ; liv, pp. 210 ff.

larger circle a hole at the centre, 4 feet in diameter and 3 to 6 feet deep, is believed to have been the socket for a central post. A hearth of flat slabs was situated 12 feet to the west of the central pit, and a cooking-hole, 22 inches wide and 12 inches deep, had been dug about the same distance from the centre to the east. It is difficult to imagine so large an area having been spanned by a single roof. Possibly a large skin tent stood within the bank.

The rare and poor habitation sites provide no adequate basis for a reconstruction of Early Bronze Age economy. For that we must have recourse once more to the graves. Now burial under an imposing cairn or in a circle may well have been the prerogative of " chiefs ". A cemetery of burial cairns or circles might therefore be taken as denoting the occupation of the same territory by a single community over several generations ; for each cairn would represent one generation of the chiefly family. But such clusters of unmistakably Early Bronze Age funerary monuments are not common, save perhaps in regions where the collectivist tradition had been strong. The Crinan plain furnishes classical examples (Fig. 29).

Four great cairns are aligned on the flat alluvium beside the Kilmartin Burn. The southernmost covers a collective tomb— the segmented cist of Nether Largie ; there were Beaker burials both in the chamber and in a cist near the edge of the cairn. Next, on Kilmartin glebe, stands the cairn which yielded Food Vessels of types C_2 and A_{1a}, then that covering grooved cists. Finally, the northernmost covered the cist with axes carved on its lid. These monuments may mark the graves of a line of chieftains ; the oldest would repose in the segmented cist, their successors, possibly of different lineage, in the short cists in the same and the more northerly cairns.

In any case, Craw[1] has pointed out that these monuments lie along an old valley route from Lochgilphead on Loch Fyne. South of the chambered cairn of Nether Largie the same line would pass the alignment of Ballymeanoch, cross the decorated cist at Ri Cruin, and pass three more sepulchral monuments before reaching the ford over the Add. And it will be noted that all these monuments lie in the plain below the 100 ft. contour. Other cairns and circles lie on the plain's edge, but north of Kilmartin a large cairn covering a C_2 Food Vessel crowns an eminence.

[1] *PSAS.*, lxiii, p. 155.

F ig. 29.—Monuments in the Crinan region : **O** cairn ;   + cist grave ; • standing stone ;
squares = forts ; ✕ = rock-carving ; other symbols as on Maps I, II and IV.

The numerous and richly furnished burials thus attest the presence of one or more prosperous communities occupying the area for a considerable period. They would be attracted and kept to the district by the extent and fertility of the alluvial soil derived from the limestone hills and perhaps also by the copper ores. At the same time the convergence of several routes upon Kilmartin would bring diverse currents to the plain. The road from Lochgilphead, already mentioned, would be taken by anyone travelling northward from the Clyde Firth to avoid the exposed coasts of Kintyre. From Kilmartin you may proceed either to the more sheltered waters of Loch Melfort and the Firth of Lorne or turn inland beside Loch Awe, the easiest crossing from Argyll to the Tay basin.

The seven circles on Mauchrie Moor in Arran would again seem to denote a community occupying an area of suitable alluvial soil for several generations. But in the east, where the collectivist tradition had never been implanted, unambiguously Early Bronze Age cemeteries are harder to cite. Groups of tumuli situated on alluvial flats, as at Kilmartin, near St. Mary's Loch, on the Upper Tweed, and on Biggar Water might belong here. Moreover, multiple interments under a single cairn, particularly common in Fife, constitute a sort of cemetery though the issue is here complicated by the apparent contemporaneity of the burials. And we shall have subsequently to ask whether the " secondary " interments with Cinerary Urns in Early Bronze Age barrows, do not represent the graves of the direct descendants of the chief in whose honour the cairn was first erected.

Short cists frequently cluster in small cemeteries even in the east of Scotland. Generally any funerary vases in such cists are Food Vessels. Thus at Aycliffe House, Ayton, Berwickshire,[1] a group of twelve cists, one containing a Food Vessel, was un-covered. Six, three containing Food Vessels, are reported from Pitreavie, near Dunfermline.[2] Groups of three cists are quite common. In Aberdeenshire even Beakers occur in such flat cemeteries.[3] Three cists recently explored by Marshall in Bute all contained the unburnt bodies of children.

But interment in a simple cist can hardly have been denied to any member of a community. Such graves may perfectly well belong to commoners. Near Yarrows Kirk, Selkirkshire,[4]

[1] RC. *Berwick*, p. xxxii.   [2] RC. *Fife*, p. xxix.
[3] e.g., at Crichie, *PSAS.*, liv, p. 155.   [4] *PSAS.*, ii, p. 484.

for instance, besides eight cists there was a cairn covering several interments and a group of standing stones. Burial in a flat cemetery was not then necessarily restricted to members of a single family, and so some graves in them may be contemporary. We shall see, however, that they provide the prototypes, and sometimes the nuclei, for the later urnfields.

On the whole, then, the Early Bronze Age communities seem to have been exceedingly small and far from rooted in the soil. The impression of semi-nomadism is enhanced by the few glimpses of habitation available—a few middens near the coast and isolated hut-circles on a hillside. Tillage was undoubtedly practised, but it need have been no more than the cultivation with a digging stick or foot-plough of a small plot which was abandoned after a few seasons. Life would have been to some extent nomadic and largely dependent on pastoralism and hunting for which Scotland was so well fitted. If this be correct, the total population, considering the restrictions imposed by mountains, forests, and swamps, may have been quite small.

The records are too imperfect and the unknown factors too numerous for estimates of the population based on grave finds to have anything but a limiting value. The number of recorded burials in short cists or accompanied by Beakers or Food Vessels [1] does not exceed 1,000. And these must be distributed, judging by the cases of Kilmartin and Mauchrie Moor, over four or more generations. Assuming, then, that the numbers recorded represent one-tenth of the actual total, we should have 2,500 as an average population for the Scottish Mainland. That number is not advanced as an estimate, but figures of that order may be considered possible.

Maritime adventure towards the beginning of the second, or even as early as the close of the third, millennium B.C. had brought to the coasts of Scotland chiefs and colonists. These formed relatively settled communities which, despite continued inter-course with relatives overseas, retained their economic self-sufficiency ; they did not need to import any essential article of use, being content with home-made stone, wood, and bone implements. The advent of the Beaker-folk altered this economy in two respects. If the analysis of the preceding para-graphs be correct, a bias was given to pastoralism as against

[1] In round figures, only 275 Beakers and 250 Food Vessels have been recorded in Scotland.

sedentary agriculture in primary production.   And secondly the Beaker-folk were prepared to make some sacrifice of economic independence to secure metal for weapons and ornaments. Though we can no longer regard them as the bringers of metal, they appreciated its value and to secure it had to admit some sort of trade.

Internally, intercourse was established across the mountain spine, as the distribution of jet necklaces shows.   And they illustrate also communication beyond the borders as much as do the imported bronzes.   The Beaker-folk may have established some sort of connections with Holland whence they came. But the satisfaction of their demand for metal did not come from that quarter.   The long-established nexus binding Scotland to Ireland, Brittany, and the Iberian Peninsula had not been interrupted by the invasion.   On the contrary, it was from the Atlantic countries that metal and metal objects were obtained. And in their wake came new ideas in art, religious symbolism, and funerary ritual.   Metal workers eventually immigrated or were captured and brought over from Ireland.   Whether an infiltration on a larger scale should be invoked to explain the rise and spread of the Food Vessel complex remains undecided.

At the same time, save in isolated enclaves, the Early Bronze Age witnessed the absorption of the old collectivist communities and the formation of a composite stock.   This, however much dominated by the Beaker-folk, eventually tended to adopt the "Atlantic" Food Vessel as its distinctive sepulchral vase, and may have spread southward therewith. In Aberdeenshire the round-headed invaders preserved their individuality almost as successfully as in South-western England ;   here the Beaker culture was imposed, elsewhere it was absorbed or transformed. No less than eighty-seven Beakers, or nearly one-third of the total found in Scotland, come from Aberdeenshire and Banffshire !

VII

CINERARY URNS

THE duality of traditions symbolized by the contrast between Beakers and Food Vessels is finally transcended when those vessels were replaced in the graves by the so-called Cinerary Urns. At the same time cremation finally ousted inhumation.

Cinerary Urns are generally larger than the sepulchral vases hitherto considered. But in Scotland they never attain such a great size as some English specimens and hardly ever exceed 21 inches in height; some stand only 10 inches high. As compared with Food Vessels, Cinerary Urns are taller and narrower. But there are many points of agreement between the two classes of sepulchral pottery. The walls of the urns are coarse and thick, the body has been built up of successive superimposed rings, the lip is thick and generally bevelled on the inside.

Two series of Cinerary Urns may be distinguished. The classical group to which the majority even in Scotland belong, may be held to begin with the Overhanging Rim Urn. The body is an inverted truncated cone. Separated from this by a sharp shoulder is a concave neck surmounted by a very wide everted brim or collar (Fig. 30, 2). Decoration is concentrated on the collar and on the internal bevel of the lip, but often spreads over the shoulder. Several variants may be derived from the foregoing by a process of degeneration. The concavity of the neck may be filled out and the shoulder rounded off and eventually suppressed altogether. We thus reach the Collared Urn in which the original rim alone survives as a broad, flat moulding or collar below the lip (Pl. X, b).

In the Cordoned Urn the collar too has disappeared as a distinct member of the pot. But horizontal mouldings, encircling the vase like hoops, mark the points where on an Overhanging Rim Urn the shoulder and the base of the collar would project (Fig. 30, 3). The decoration is confined to a zone above the top cordon that simulates the base of the collar. In some late Cordoned Urns a third moulding is added, which is purely decorative. In some urns from the West of Scotland, Shetland,

PLATE X

a

b

c

d

CINERARY URNS

a	MOUNTBLAIRY	*b*	KINGSKETTLE
c	GLENBALLOCH	*d*	FLEMINGTON

National Museum

and Ireland, though the collar is suppressed, the vase walls
begin to converge again a few inches below the lip. Such an
urn may be termed Biconical (Pl. X, *d*). The decoration is confined to the short, truncated, upper cone which reproduces the
collar of the earlier urns.

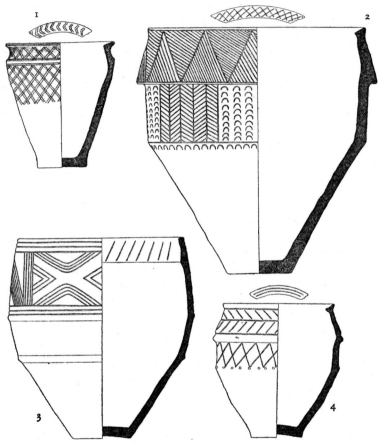

FIG. 30.—Enlarged Food Vessel, Crichie ; Overhanging Rim Urn, Largs ;
Cordoned Urns, Magdalene Bridge. ⅛.

Urns of this family are decorated with the same devices as
were employed for the ornamentation of Food Vessels in Eastern
Scotland—with a twisted cord, with whipped cord (Fig. 30, 2),
with a chain-looped cord, and even with the joint of a bird's leg-
bone. The horse-shoe impression of a loop of cord and the

maggot pattern are found,[1] but not the false relief or stamp patterns of the "Western" series of Food Vessels. Horizontal corrugations are, however, observable on the collars of some urns [2] (Pl. X, b), and these might be derived from the ribs on B3 or B5 Food Vessels.

The patterns are poor and simple—zig-zags, criss-cross lines, horizontal or vertical rows of alternately hatched triangles, or triangles arranged with their apices touching. Most of the patterns can be paralleled on Food Vessels.[3] But a tendency to panelling is conspicuous and the similarity of the band of alternating triangles to the typical Unstan ornament is striking.

It is generally admitted that the Overhanging Rim Urn can be derived from the Food Vessel. But precisely where the type was evolved is uncertain. Overhanging Rim and Collared Urns are found throughout Great Britain from Dorset to Sutherland, in Ireland, and even in Western Holland.[4] Examples with well-marked shoulders and concave necks are certainly commonest in the south and, in Scotland, can hardly be found north of the Dee. In the north and on the west coasts degenerate Collared, Cordoned, and Biconical Urns probably predominate. Yet it must be insisted that Cordoned Urns and Collared Urns occur side by side in the same cemeteries. Abercromby thought that the Overhanging Rim Urn was created in South-western England and spread northwards. Elgee [5] has recently argued for North-eastern Yorkshire as the cradle of the type. Cordoned Urns in any case are virtually confined to the more mountainous western and northern parts of Great Britain. They are thus shown to be late by their distribution. They may indeed have been influenced by the contemporary Deverel and Rimbury Urns that were introduced by Continental invaders who occupied lowland England. But the whole series is essentially British and derivable from the Food Vessel.

That is even more obviously the case with the second family of urns which are indeed termed Enlarged Food Vessels. In form these are, in fact, just Food Vessels that are relatively tall. Not only do they possess the inverted-conical body, concave neck, and bevelled rim of the type B Food Vessel, but sometimes

---

[1] Magdalene Bridge, Largs, Leuchars (Fife).
[2] Kingskettle, Fife (*PSAS.*, lv, p. 39), Thankerton, Lan.
[3] e.g., cf. Abercromby, ii, 180*b*, and i, 160 ; ii, 199, and i, 272, 387 ; ii, 188, 193, and i, 266, 343, 361 ; ii, 180*a*, 203, and i, 267.
[4] *Oudh. Med.* xiv p. 81.   [5] *North East Yorkshire*, p. 88.

even the groove on the shoulder.[1] One example at least (Pl. X, *c*) shows stop-ridges between the rim and the shoulder, quite like those on some degenerate Food Vessels. The decoration is that appropriate to Food Vessels, always very simple and never panelled as on Collared Urns.

A local derivative from the last-mentioned group is what is known as the Encrusted Urn. These vessels resemble in shape the Enlarged Food Vessel, some even preserving the grooved shoulder,[2] but are distinguished by the use of plastic decoration. Strips of comparatively fine clay are applied, principally to the neck, to produce designs in true relief. The strips may be arranged to form zig-zags between horizontal ridges or may even simulate the stop-ridges of the Food Vessel. They are sometimes combined with pellets that appear as bosses or with small rings (Pl. X, *c*). After the strips or pellets had been stuck on, the neck and upper part of the urn was washed over with a slip of clay, finer than that used for the body, which served to affix the applied material more firmly. Patterns may be executed on this slip by incision or by the impression of a cord, as in other types of urn.

The Enlarged Food Vessel and the Encrusted Urn are commonest in Upland Britain. The former is obviously native. Dr. Fox[3] has suggested that the Encrusted Urn is derived from it under the influence of the foreign types of Lowland Britain. He believes that the Encrusted Urn arose thus in North Britain and spread thence south-westward to Wales and Ireland. It must be insisted that the technique employed on these urns is not the same as that adopted on the foreign urns of England. Moreover, Encrusted Urns and Enlarged Food Vessels are found in the same cemeteries as Collared and Cordoned Urns.

Cinerary Urns are often accompanied by, and sometimes even contain, diminutive vessels, standing only 2 or 3 inches high, that are termed Pigmy Vessels or Incense Cups. In England such vessels exhibit a great variety both in form and ornament, but the Scottish types are less varied. A common feature everywhere is a pair of small holes pierced through the walls side by side. In one Scottish specimen (from Galloway)[4] and in many

[1] Abercromby, ii, Nos. 504, 512, 516, 517, 518. (St. Andrews, East Lothian, Angus, Lanarkshire, and Aberdeenshire.)
[2] *Ant. J.,* vii, pls. xxiii, 1, 4; xxv, 2; xx, 3.
[3] *Ant. J.,* vii, p. 126–7.
[4] Abercromby, ii, No. 331 (Kirkcudbright).

English and Irish examples, however, the walls are pierced with two rows of relatively large triangular apertures producing a decorative lattice effect. Most Scottish Pigmy Vessels are bowl-shaped or biconical in form, but one or two are just miniature Food Vessels [1] (Pl. XI, *c*).

Pigmy Vessels in Scotland are decorated with rectilinear patterns simply incised or impressed with a cord. Some English specimens are, however, ornamented with finely engraved lines and punctures or with knobs. These techniques as well as the open-work ornament all have parallels in the " late Neolithic " Chassey pottery of North-western France and have probably been derived from that quarter.[2] The Pigmy Vessel to this extent seems to denote a foreign element in Britain.

With the Overhanging Rim Urn and the Pigmy Vessel the funerary pottery of Great Britain attains a degree of uniformity achieved at no other moment in our period. Is this the result of fresh movements of people or merely cultural spreads through a homogeneous population ? The rise of the Overhanging Rim Urn and the Pigmy Vessel cannot be traced in Scotland. Yet neither burial rites, associated relics, nor distribution give any hint of a change in the population.

Cinerary Urns were designed to contain cremated bones, but cremations had accompanied both Beakers and Food Vessels. Exceptionally, Urns have been placed in regular cist graves of slabs.[3] More often they are set in a shallow depression. In most cases the Urn is inverted over the ashes. Presumably the mouth of the urn had been covered over with a skin or cloth, tied on by a cord that was fixed in the concave neck. In that case it would have been easy to invert the urn full of ashes leaving the vessel inverted over the heap. In some instances the mouth of the urn was closed with a flat stone that might be trimmed to form a disc.[4] Less commonly the urns stand mouth upright.

Extremely few instances can be cited from Scotland that attest the persistence of the practice of erecting a cairn over the grave. Cinerary Urns were found at the centres of cairns in Aberdeenshire and Inverness and presumably denote the

---

[1] Abercromby, ii, No. 330 (Angus) ; Anderson, ii, fig. 45 (Fife).
[2] *Arch. J.*, lxxxviii, p. 52.
[3] Longcroft, Lauderdale (RC. *Berw.*, p. xxxvi) ; Meikelrigg, E. Lothian (*PSAS.*, xiv, p. 221) ; Denbeath (Fife, RC. *Fife*, p. xxix) ; Magdalene Bridge, Abercromby, ii, p. 20, etc.   [4] *PSAS.*, xiii, p. 256.

PLATE XI

1 PIGMY CUPS

MUSSELBURGH ; SOUTH RONALDSHAY ; NORTH QUEENSFERRY

National Museum

2 CARVED SLABS FROM CIST NEAR CRINAN

primary interments.[1] At Ardeer on the Stevenston sands, Ayrshire, a curious " cairn ", 15 feet long by 10 feet wide, but only a few inches deep, comprised seventeen Cinerary Urns, together with two deposits of ashes in bare earth.[2]

On the other hand, Cinerary Urns are very commonly found in cairns originally erected over short cists containing Beakers or Food Vessels. Six Cordoned Urns, as well as small cists filled with ashes, were deposited round the northern edge of the cairn over a B Beaker at Drumelzier on the Upper Tweed.[3] On Great Cumbrae a cairn covered a short cist with a Food Vessel at the centre and four late collared Urns near the edge.[4] Six Cinerary Urns had been inserted into the body of a barrow on Calais Muir, Fife, while a Food Vessel lay in a cist at the centre.[5] Fragments of a Cinerary Urn have been reported even from the long cairn termed Longman's Hill, near Macduff, Banffshire.[6]

It seems obvious from the last-named instance that interments in Cinerary Urns may be separated by a very long interval from the erection of the cairn into which they are intruded. And usually it is assumed that a comparable, though shorter, interval must have elapsed between the erection of the cairns over Beakers or Food Vessels and the deposition of the secondary Cinerary Urns therein. The latter would be due to new-comers who, arriving after the cairn had already stood for generations, used it as a receptacle for their urns to avoid the trouble of erecting a cairn of their own. Yet another possibility must be borne in mind : the secondary interments may be due to the direct descendants of the person buried in the central cist who had lived on in the locality and used the ancestor's cairn as a family burial place. In that event no long interval need be interpolated between the primary and the secondary interments. In the case of the cemeteries unmarked by any external monument we shall see that an uninterrupted use from the period of Food Vessel interments to that of Cinerary Urns must be admitted.

Similar uncertainties apply to Cinerary Urns found near the periphery of Stone Circles. In the moated circle of Crichie, Aberdeenshire, there was a central inhumation in a cist presumably

[1] Abercromby, ii, pp. 55, 56 (Pittodrie, Aberdeens., and Glen Urquhart).
[2] PSAS., xl, pp. 378 ff. Such a cairn may be compared to that of Knockast (PRIA., xli, c, p. 254) and other monuments that are supposed to show influence from " Urnfield invaders ".
[3] PSAS., lxv, p. 366. [4] Abercromby, ii, p. 22.
[5] RC. Fife, p. xxix. [6] PSAS., lix, p. 26.

K

contemporary with the erection of the monument. An Enlarged
Food Vessel stood near one upright, a Collared Urn near another,
while small pockets of cremated bones were also found.[1] At
Tuack in the same district there was a circle of six uprights
surrounded by a continuous fosse. Cordoned Urns stood inverted
over cremated bones near the northern uprights while the primary
interments seem represented by four pits filled with cremated
bones grouped round the centre.[2] A Collared Urn was again
found near the edge of the stone circle at Tillicoultry.[3] Others
have been reported from within stone circles at Glenballoch,[4] near
Rattray (Perthshire), Balbirnie House (Fife), Newton of Mount-
blairy, on the Upper Deveron,[5] and elsewhere, but in no case
do the data suffice to prove that the urns were connected with
the primary interment.

A very large number of urns, especially south of the Tay,
come from flat cemeteries or urnfields. Such have generally
come to light incidentally in the course of sand-digging, road-
making, or building ; few have been accurately examined and
none systematically explored, so that data as to the number
or arrangement of the urns are generally inadequate. No less
than thirty urns are mentioned from the urnfield on Scotstarvit
Hill, Fife,[6] twenty-two at Alloa [7] and at Carphin House,
Fife,[8] twenty at Lawpark, St. Andrews [9] and at Magdalene
Bridge [10] between Edinburgh and Musselburgh. These are the
largest aggregations yet recorded in Scotland.

At Carphin House fourteen out of the twenty-two urns stood
in a row. At Scotstarvit Hill, at Westwood, near Newport, Fife,
and Gilchorn between Arbroath and Brechin, Angus, the urns
are stated to have been arranged in circles and a semicircle of
urns was recently noted at Maxwelltown, Dumfries. Such
arrangements recall the situation of the urns in the stone circles
of Crichie and Tuack and prompt the question whether a wood
circle, comparable to those now familiar in England, may not
have once marked these sites.

It is quite likely that urnfields were used over several generations ;
all types of urn from presumably early Collared and Enlarged
Food Vessel forms to Encrusted and degenerate Cordoned Urns

---

[1] Anderson, ii, p. 104   [2] Anderson, ii, p. 102.   [3] *PSAS.*, xxix, p. 190.
[4] Anderson, ii, p. 111 (Encrusted Urn, Pl. X, *c* here).
[5] Anderson, ii, p. 115 (Enlarged Food Vessel, Pl. X, *a* here).
[6] RC. *Fife,* No. 130.   [7] Anderson, ii, p. 62.   [8] RC. *Fife,* No. 146.
[9] Abercromby, ii, p. 54, No. 504.   [10] Abercromby, ii, p. 21, No. 180.

were included in the urnfield at St. Andrews. In Continental urnfields the interments are often found to be arranged in a chronological order, the later ones lying nearer the edge or one side than the earlier. Exact observation of the disposition of the urns in a Scottish urnfield might, therefore, give a valuable indication of the relative ages of the several types of urn represented in the same cemetery.

On the Continent the urnfields are generally attributed to cremationists who spread from East Central Europe. An extension of the same movement provides the best explanation both for the urnfields and the foreign urns found in them in Southern England. But no foreign influence of this sort need be invoked to account for the phenomena observed in Scotland. Flat cemeteries of cist graves containing Food Vessels have already been described; the urnfields may be just a continuation of the same practice with Cinerary Urns instead of Food Vessels and ashes instead of skeletons. Actually, short cists containing contracted skeletons were juxtaposed to the cremations in several cemeteries—Magdalene Bridge, Alloa, Dalmore (Alness, Ross), etc.

It really looks in such cases as if the ground selected as a cemetery by the inhumationists remained in use for the same purpose after cremation and the Cinerary Urn had replaced inhumation and the Food Vessel. If that be true, it constitutes a cogent argument in favour of continuity in the population. The flat cemeteries being distinguished by no external monument, only those who had already been using the plot would be cognizant of the hallowed ground.

The distribution of Cinerary Urns is again favourable to the hypothesis of a continuity of settlement. Clearly, the urns have a poorer chance of surviving than Beakers or Food Vessels, being clumsier and more unsightly, softer and more fragile, and less often protected by cists. Maps of their distribution are liable to be even less complete than those of Beakers and Food Vessels. A comparison of Maps II and III, however, shows that the distribution of Cinerary Urns coincides in its main lines with that of Food Vessels.

One very striking discrepancy will be observed. The Crinan plain, which had been such a centre of settlement in the phases covered by Maps I and II, has yielded no Cinerary Urns. For this gap a historical explanation might be suggested: perhaps the poor copper lodes which may have been valuable to earlier settlers ceased to be profitable when improved trade had made the products of better lodes more generally accessible. An alternative explanation that the Food Vessel complex maintained its independence in this corner would involve a truly alarming reduction of the dates assigned to the other monuments and relics of the district. It must, however, be kept in mind as a possible means of establishing the continuity of culture in Argyll. The absence of Cinerary Urns of our series from the western and northern isles is in harmony with the general isolation of those districts after the Beaker period. One Biconical Urn that might be treated as a last degeneration of the Overhanging Rim Urn is known from Shetland (Pl. X, *d*) and a Pigmy Vessel from Orkney. But the normal Cinerary Urns from the islands seem to belong to a quite different series and will be described separately in Section 2.   The failure of the Cinerary Urn to reach the western isles is important from two aspects. It reinforces the agreement in distribution between Cinerary Urns and Food Vessels. On the other hand, it emphasizes the lack of connection between the Urns and the new types of tool and weapon that characterize the Late Bronze Age ; these are relatively well represented in the isles.

Such relics as accompany Cinerary Urns are by no means incompatible with the theory of continuity advanced above. But, as in the rest of Europe, the grave furniture becomes much poorer after the practice of cremation was generally adopted, so that relatively few types of implements and ornaments can be associated with Cinerary Urns in Scotland.

Perforated mace-heads of stone were more or less definitely associated with Cinerary Urns in eight instances. At Low Glengyre (Glenluce) an axe-hammer was discovered 30 feet away from a degenerate Collared Urn [1] ; the weapon in plan resembles the simple axe-hammers associated with Beakers in England, but the perforation is of hour-glass form and nearly central. Another axe, the profile of which expands on either side of the shaft-hole, was found beside a Cordoned Urn at Oban.[2]

A pestle-shaped mace-head, flattened at both ends and ornamented with mouldings round the shaft-hole, comes from an urnfield at Largs, Ayrshire,[3] and a rougher form with rounded ends was found with a late Cordoned Urn at Cambusbarron,

[1] *PSAS.*, lvii, p. 102.   [2] *PSAS.*, xxxii, p. 59.   [3] *Arch.*, lxii, p. 245.

Stirling. A more specialized type lay between an Enlarged Food Vessel and a pocket of cremated bones near the foot of an upright in the Stone Circle at Crichie. In plan (Fig. 31) the weapon is ovoid, but one end has been ground as if to form a very blunt edge. The distinctive feature of the Crichie type is, however, the waist, seen in the profile view. This has been explained as a technical device to facilitate perforation. If the raw material of the weapon were an oval pebble, the two semicircular indents on the profile could be ground out by simply rubbing backward and forward with, or on, the abrasive. A comparatively narrow section would then be left for perforation.

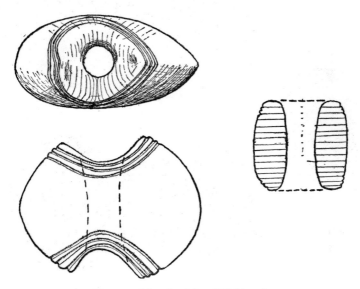

FIG. 31.—Mace-head from Crichie. $\frac{1}{2}$.

Four or five mace-heads of this peculiar form have been found in North-eastern Scotland—one with a Cordoned Urn near Strichen, Aberdeenshire.[1] In two or three examples from Orkney and in one from Coll the perforation is unfinished or not even begun.

Some more elaborate weapons might theoretically be derived from the Crichie type. Stray examples from Fife and Galloway and one, found with a Cordoned Urn at Chapelton, Ardrossan (Fig. 32), come nearer the axe form, the butt being a truncated

[1] *Ant. J.*, vii, pl. lxiii, 4 ; Reid, *Prehistoric Interments*, fig. 21.

cone though the edge remains blunt.[1] A still more ornate form
with mouldings in relief round the central depressions came
from a disturbed cemetery comprising some short cist burials
and Food Vessels at Fossil Grove, Glasgow.[2]

These weapons approximate closely to the so-called Bann River
axes that are found in Northern Ireland. Indeed, the examples
from South-west Scotland might be imports from Ireland. But
they might, as indicated, be treated as the culmination of a local
development, starting with the Crichie type ; in that case the

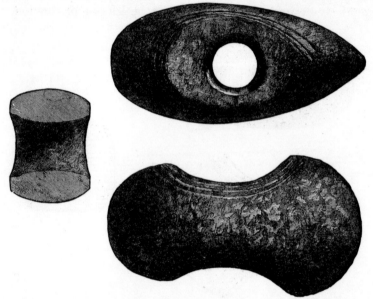

FIG. 32.—Axe-head from Chapelton, near Ardrossan, after Anderson. ½.

Bann River axes would be due to Scottish influence. On the
other hand analogous axes are known from England, and
R. A. Smith[3] has been able with the aid of grave-finds to con-
struct a self-contained typological series leading from genuine
axes with elongated bodies and sharp blades such as accompany
skeletons to the blunt ovoid types associated with cremations.
On Smith's typology the Crichie type would come near the end
of the series, only the Oban axe finding a place near its beginning.

Flint arrow-heads, tanged and barbed, have been found in

[1] Anderson, ii, figs. 288–290.   [2] *PSAS.*, lvii, p. 105.
[3] *Arch.,* lxxv, pp. 90 ff.

Cinerary Urns in Dumbartonshire, Fife, and Banffshire.[1]   No
other distinctive flint implements are associated with urns.
However, flint was demonstrably used in the production of fire.
In two instances the flint flakes were struck against pieces of
iron pyrites—a method of fire-production attested in England
even in Beaker graves.[2]   Once, however, nodular hæmatite
(iron oxide) seems to have been substituted for pyrites
(a sulphide).[3]   The substitution during the period when
Cinerary Urns were in vogue is important for the chronology
of the settlements in Orkney.

Some of the ornaments associated with Cinerary Urns seem
to confirm the idea of continuity in culture.   Beads from jet
necklaces were found with Cinerary Urns in Wigtonshire, Ayrshire, and Kincardineshire.   Buttons with " V "-perforation,

FIG. 33.—Segmented and star-shaped bead, Ardeer (Ayrs) and bone toggle
Seggiecrook, after *PSAS.* ¼.

such as would be expected with Beakers in England, may have
been enclosed in a lost Cinerary Urn from Keith Marischal,
East Lothian.[4]

Southern connections are indicated by segmented beads of
vitreous paste found in a barrel-shaped Biconical Urn at Ardeer,
Stevenston (Ayrshire), and in a Cordoned Urn at Mill of Marcus,
near Brechin.   The beads (Fig. 33) in question are short tubes
divided by notches into from three to four segments and made
of an opaque vitreous material grey or bluish in colour.   They
are indubitably connected with a well-known series of vitreous
paste beads represented in Southern England, South-eastern
Spain, Greece, and Egypt.   Callander [5] and Mann [6] claim that

---

[1] *PSAS.,* lv, p. 40 ; xxxi, p. 221 ; xlii, p. 218 ; cf. p. 69 above.
[2] *PSAS.,* xix, p. 366.
[3] RC. *Berwick.,* p. xxxii ;   there is a parallel from a Derbyshire barrow, Sheffield
Museum, J. 93, 110.   [4] Cf. p. 88 above.
[5] *PSAS.,* lvii, p. 142.   [6] *PSAS.,* xl, p. 401.

the Scottish examples are of local manufacture; even if that be true (and it is most improbable), the idea undoubtedly came from the East Mediterranean. It was even copied in bone in Scotland as in France and Spain; a bone example was probably contained in a Collared Urn from Milngavie, Dumbartonshire.[1]

At Ardeer the segmented beads were accompanied by a star-shaped bead of the same vitreous paste (Fig. 33, 3). And at Low Glengyre [2] a quoit-shaped bead of the same material was found in a Cordoned Urn. Both types recur in the Bronze Age barrows of Southern England and have finer analogies in the East Mediterranean. In Scotland stray segmented, star-shaped, and quoit beads of vitreous paste have been picked up in the sandy tracts of Wigtonshire and Ayrshire and even on Culbin Sands, Elginshire, in Aberdeenshire, and in Perthshire.

An interesting type of toggle or bead [3] was associated with an Overhanging Rim Urn at Overmigvie (near Kirriemuir, Angus), with a Cordoned Urn at Seggiecrook (Kennethmont, Aberdeenshire), and with an Encrusted Urn near Alness (Ross). They are barrel-shaped, bone beads, with mouldings at each end and a small, transverse hole at right-angles to the main axial tube (Fig. 33, 4); the one from Kirriemuir is provided with a loop on the outside opposite to the transverse hole. Exact parallels, also in bone, to these three toggles from North-eastern Scotland may be found in Danish graves of the Late Bronze Age [4]; they may indicate a resumption of intercourse with the Baltic region. One might, however, compare also a gold toggle mounting from the Gold Barrow, Upton Lovell, Wiltshire, or even the bronze toggles found at Glastonbury, and other Iron Age sites.[5]

A crutch-headed pin of bone, rather like that found with Middle Bronze Age weapons in an inhumation grave at Snows Hill, Gloucestershire, accompanied a Cordoned Urn at Balneil, Glenluce. Simpler pins are not rare in Cinerary Urns.

Few metal objects have survived from cremation graves. The most distinctive are the so-called razors [6] found in the urnfields of Magdalene Bridge, Midlothian, Lawpark, St. Andrews, and Shanwell House (Milnathort, Kinross), and in cairns with cremations in Sutherland. They are very thin, double-edged

---

[1] *PSAS.*, xlii, p. 218. [2] *PSAS.*, l, p. 303.
[3] *PSAS.*, lxiv, p. 31. [4] Sophus Müller, *Ordning*, No. 232.
[5] *Devizes Museum Catalogue*, i, No. 52 : Bulleid and Gray, fig. 44.
[6] Anderson, ii, pp. 23, 29, 38.

blades with a short, flat tange ; there is no projecting mid-rib, but the thickened centre is generally very finely engraved with hatched lozenges or other rectilinear patterns (Fig. 34, 1). While not unlike some blades from cremation graves in Southern England, these funerary specimens are conspicuously different from the bifid razors that occur in the Late Bronze Age hoards.

A rough, Biconical Urn at Shuttlefield, near Lockerbie, contained a tapering blade with a distinct mid-rib and a broken tang.[1] It is not unlike the imperfect blade shown in Fig. 42, 5, though much smaller. The curious little blade reproduced in Fig. 34, 2 was found in an Overhanging Rim Urn at Gilchorn near Lunan

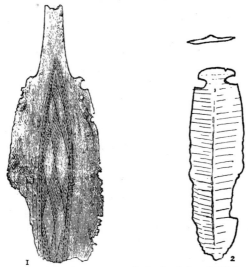

FIG. 34.—Bronze blades from Rogart, Sutherland, ⅝ and Gilchorn Angus, ⅔.

Bay, Angus.[2] It is flat on one face, but has a pronounced mid-rib on the other, while two notches in the butt serve for the attachment of a handle. The blade is thus identical with those from Denmark, Southern Portugal, and South-eastern Spain, mentioned on p. 60, and there attributed to the period of the corbelled tombs and passage-graves ! Such a blade seems out of place in a Cinerary Urn and certainly cannot be used to date the grave to the " Copper Age ". Finally, the Cordoned Urn from Balneil was accompanied by a flat-tanged chisel. Such chisels in England would be assigned to the Middle Bronze Age,[3]

[1] Anderson, p. 29.   [2] *PSAS.*, xxv, p. 459.
[3] Fox, *Cambridge Region*, p. 56.

but, as explained below, the English typology cannot be applied without modification to Scotland.

The foregoing are the only clues available for connecting the development of funerary customs with that of the metal industry after the general adoption of cremation. They are so poor that we shall be forced to describe the tools, weapons, and ornaments of bronze, found in hoards or stray, apart from the sepulchral record. Here it may be stated in advance that in Scotland as a whole no general series of monuments nor of ceramics can be discovered between those described in this Chapter and those attributable to the Iron Age.

It would therefore seem likely that Cinerary Urns remained in use till the Iron Age began. In fact, a jet armlet of specifically Iron Age type was found close to a Cordoned Urn on the edge of the cairn at Drumelzier. And a group of late Cinerary Urns stood in the Iron Age hill-top town on Traprain Law. On the other hand, while in England burials with Overhanging Rim or Collared Urns exceed in numbers those accompanied by Beakers and Food Vessels, I have not been able to trace more than 500 Cinerary Urns in Scotland. Hence, even were the population supposed to have remained stationary, it would be difficult to spread the Cinerary Urns over a longer period than that denoted by short-cist interments. Yet in a cairn, cut through in railway construction at Edderton (Ross), a Cordoned Urn is said to have stood in a trench encircling a central grave, a cist, which contained burnt bones and a blue glass bead with yellow spiral inlays. This bead, deposited before the Cordoned Urn, can hardly be earlier than the La Tène period.[1]

2. Bronze Age Burials in Orkney and Shetland

It will have been noted that neither Food Vessels nor Cinerary Urns have been mentioned from northern and north-western islands off the Scottish coast. Their absence, however, can hardly denote an evacuation of the archipelagos during the period denoted by these vessels on the mainland of Britain. It merely betokens an isolation of the islands, giving opportunity for divergent local developments. This isolation itself may have been due to changes in climate which rendered the prevailing winds less auspicious for voyages to the far north. Or it may

[1] *PSAS.*, v, p. 312.

merely reflect historically changed economic conditions : the Beaker invasions, having established land connections across England and the North Sea with the Continent, may have short-circuited the old coastal traffic round Cape Wrath.

The divergence of the island cultures from those of the rest of Britain, resulting from this isolation, renders it difficult to recognize the funerary monuments of the insular Bronze Age. We have already remarked that the tradition of collective burial probably persisted in the islands for a long time, as happened also in Brittany. The more highly specialized Orkney variants on the burial vault, represented for instance on the Holm of Papa Westray, may well be as late as some interments in Cinerary Urns in Lowland Scotland.

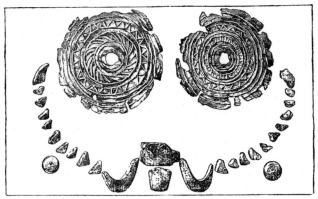

FIG. 35.—Gold discs and amber beads from Huntiscarth, Orkney, after Anderson, ⅓.

On the other hand the practice of individual burial introduced into Scotland with the Beaker-folk reached both Shetland and Orkney. In fact, fragments of two genuine Beakers have been discovered in Shetland,[1] and skulls, comparable in roundness to those of the invaders have been measured both from collective tombs and short cists in Orkney.[2]

Short-cist burials under earthen barrows or without superficial indications are indeed numerous in both Orkney and Shetland, but few have yielded any significant relics. The most important funerary deposit of this sort recorded was found in a short cist with cremated bones at Huntiscarth in Orphir Parish on the

[1] *PSAS.*, lxvii, pp. 34 ff.
[2] *JRAI.*, xiii, p. 82. A sherd, probably belonging to a Beaker, was found in Rousay in 1934 ; p. 45 above.

Mainland of Orkney.[1]   The cist contained two discs of gold leaf about 3 inches in diameter and a necklace of triangular and crescentic amber beads (Fig. 35).   The gold discs resemble, but by no means precisely, the so-called Sun Discs of the Irish Bronze Age and comparable ornaments from South-western Germany. The crescentic amber beads, still more vaguely recall a type found in allegedly " Stone Age " deposits in Norway [2] that may well be equally late.

The idiosyncrasies of island culture illustrated at Huntiscarth are also exemplified by a class of cists peculiar to Orkney and Shetland.   These are two-storeyed.   The upper compartment is generally the smaller and may be walled with coursed masonry instead of slabs on edge.   Its slab floor is itself the lid of the lower compartment, a slab cist of the normal type.   Quite often one compartment is empty while the other may contain more than one body inhumed or cremated.   One such cist on Crantit Farm, near Kirkwall,[3] contained in the lower compartment (3 ft. 1 in. long by 2 ft. 2 in. wide by $1\frac{3}{4}$ feet deep) two heaps of calcined bones and the flexed skeleton of a young person. The upper compartment, only 2 feet long and 1 foot deep, was empty. In the grave was a perforated axe of stag's antler, only 4 inches long, the sole Scottish representative of this type, apart from the Mesolithic specimen illustrated in Fig. 2.   At Little Asta, Tingwall, Shetland,[4] the upper compartment contained a skeleton accompanied by two steatite urns while cremated remains and an infant's skeleton lay in the lower.

The steatite urns introduce another island speciality. They have been found frequently in short cists sometimes with inhumations, more often with cremations, in both Shetland and Orkney.[5] Two main types stand out—one shallow and almost rectangular, save for a rounding of the corners, and the other barrel-shaped, often with a moulding round the rim. Anderson [6] was inclined to treat all the island urns as Viking, but the types used by the Norsemen diverge from those just described, being bowl-shaped. Brøgger [7] recognized that they must rather be Bronze Age, and now Curle has, as we shall see, found such vessels in a settlement in company with moulds for socketed bronze axes.

---

[1] Anderson, i, p. 67.   [2] Brøgger, *Den arktiske Stenålder.*
[3] *PSAS.*, xliv, p. 215.
[4] *PSAS.*, lxvi, p. 72 ; for other examples see lxi, p. 238 ; lxiii, p. 380, etc.
[5] *PSAS.*, lxiii, p. 377 ; lxvii, p. 353.   [6] *Scotland in Pagan Times,* i, p. 77.
[7] *Den norske Bosetningen,* p. 56.

Somewhat similar urns were found in burials of the pre-Roman
Iron Age in the Vestland district of Norway and fragments
even earlier in late " Stone Age " settlements.[1]   But steatite
occurs native in Shetland, and the urns might originate there
as well as anywhere else.   The rectangular form can easily be
paralleled in wood in ethnographical collections, so that the
steatite urns, like so much else in the islands, may be substitutes
in a treeless milieu for wooden vessels.   The extensive use of
the material in Orkney betokens a degree of maritime intercourse
truly surprising in such treeless regions.

A few clay burial urns have also been recorded from Orkney
and Shetland.[2]   One, incomplete, from Flemington, Shetland,

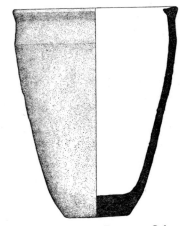

FIG. 36.—Urn from Blows, Deerness, Orkney. ⅛.

bears an incised chevron ornament on the neck and might be
treated as a late and degenerate version of the South-west Scottish
Biconical Urn, and thus connected with the British Overhanging
Rim Urn series (Pl. X, *d*).   Moreover, an Incense Cup is said to
come from South Ronaldshay.   These are the sole funerary
vessels that attest, somewhat ambiguously, a parallelism in usages
with the mainland.

The remaining urns, though built up in sections, like the
mainland Cinerary Urns, seem to denote different traditions.
Three[3] have a sharp shoulder and short neck.   The profile

[1] *Real.,* ix, p. 95 ; xiii, p. 335 ; *Norske Oldfund,* iii, " Ruskenesset."
[2] *PSAS.,* lxvii, pp. 346 ff.
[3] Howan Blo, Deerness, Orkney ; Culla Voe and Papa Stour, Shetland.

(Fig. 36) is reminiscent of the bronze buckets or situlæ [1] that were used as receptacles for cremated remains in the wealthier Hallstatt cemeteries of Central Europe as in Upper Italy. The metal form was translated into clay in Germany and even in Ireland, Southern England, and Norway—perhaps independently. The metal originals, in any case, were so widely diffused by trade that no conclusions can be drawn from the appearance of the type in Shetland and Orkney unless it be that the islands were exposed to other influences than those hitherto detected on the Scottish mainland.

Finally, a curious truncated ovoid urn from a mound at Housegord, Shetland, ornamented with rows of finger-nail imprints, though treated as an Enlarged Food Vessel by Abercromby, falls into no known category. It is said to have been associated with a barrel-shaped bead of blue glass, inlaid with white rings.[2]

Hence there is a sepulchral record in the northern islands, divergent from, but very probably contemporary with, that described earlier in this Chapter. The peculiarities of insular culture it discloses will be made plainer by a consideration of domestic remains in a subsequent Chapter. On the other hand the bronzes from the islands conform to the types current all over the British Isles.

[1] *Infra,* p. 161.   [2] Abercromby, ii, p. 74.

VIII

THE EVOLUTION OF THE BRONZE INDUSTRY

1. The Divisions of the Bronze Age

THE orderly improvement and evolution of tools and weapons makes it possible to divide the bronzes found stray or in hoards between several chronological groups : each group illustrates the fashions prevailing, and the technical standards achieved, at a distinct period of time. The division is thus of the same kind as the division of English history that can be made on the basis of styles of architecture into Norman, Gothic, Renaissance, and so on. In the British Bronze Age Montelius distinguished five periods, but most authorities are content with a triple division—into Early, Middle, and Late Bronze Ages.

The most convenient bases for the division are provided by the evolution of axe-heads, stabbing weapons, spear-heads, chisels, and razors.[1] During the Early Bronze Age the prevailing type of axe-head was the flat celt cast in an open mould ; to the same period are assigned celts with rudimentary flanges, hammered up along the sides. These, like all later bronze axes in Western Europe, were mounted on a crooked shaft (usually called a *knee-shaft*), the celt being fitted into the split downward-pointing end of the crooked stick. The employment of a two-piece (or valve) mould rendered possible various improvements in the axe-head during the Middle Bronze Age. Wide flanges might be cast down the sides on each face of the implement ; they would prevent the axe-head waggling between the prongs of the shaft and reduce the risk of the axe buckling without materially increasing its weight or the quantity of metal required for its production. Sometimes the flanges do not preserve an even width along the whole length of the axe, but expand to peaks and then contract again ; the variant thus produced may be termed a *winged axe* (Fig. 37).

To minimize the chance of the haft splitting, a ridge of metal, termed a *stop-ridge*, may be cast between the flanges on each face to engage the ends of the split shaft's prongs. Such axes are known as *palstavs*. The body of the palstav below the stop-ridge is often filled up solid with metal. But in the early flanged axe

---

[1] A fuller and illustrated account in Childe, *Bronze Age*.

143

the ends of the shaft's prongs had been visible between the flanges on both faces. To reproduce the familiar impression, metallic ridges might be cast on the faces of the palstav below the stop-ridge where the shaft prongs would have appeared. Even flanges may be simulated by low-cast ridges in the same region (Fig. 39, 1). Such ridges imitating more primitive types are likely to be indicative of a relatively early palstav. To facilitate attachment to the shaft by binding thongs, a loop or ear is cast on the side of many palstavs (Fig. 37, 2).

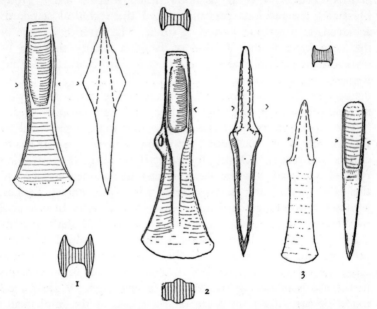

FIG. 37.—Winged axe and palstav from Balcarry hoard, chisel from Perth. ⅓.

Flanged and winged axes and palstavs generally belong to the Middle Bronze Age. In the Late Bronze Age they were replaced by the *socketed axe* in which the end of the shaft fits into the hollow body of the axe-head itself. But in English hoards socketed axes may be associated with palstavs that have smooth faces of triangular plan below the stop-ridge and with others in which, just above the stop-ridge, there are wings hammered over. Both these varieties are therefore assigned to the Late Bronze Age.[1] Similarly, both in England and on the Continent winged axes in which the wings are placed near the butt are normally accompanied by socketed axes and have

[1] Kendrick and Hawkes, p. 123.

accordingly to be transferred from the Middle to the Late Bronze Age. Hawkes suggests that the hammered wings of the late palstavs have been inspired by the last-mentioned winged axes.

The evolution of stabbing weapons can be correlated with that of the axes by means of grave-finds and hoards. With flat axes we should expect to find only flat, triangular daggers cast in an open mould. In the Middle Bronze Age a longer type, ogival in plan, appears and then a regular dirk or short rapier

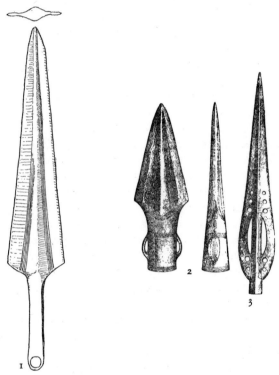

Fig. 38.—Spear-heads from Muirkirk, Ayrs, $\frac{1}{4}$; Dean Water, Angus, $\frac{1}{3}$; and Denhead, Angus, $\frac{1}{3}$, after Anderson.

(still essentially a thrusting weapon). Both daggers and rapiers have broad butts or hilt-plates, on to which a distinct hilt was attached by rivets. Cut-and-thrust swords appear first in the Late Bronze Age together with socketed axes. Flat tangs project from the butt, on to which plates of wood, horn, or other material, were riveted to form the hilt.

Specialized spear-heads appear in England early in the Middle Bronze Age in company with ogival daggers and may be found

L

in inhumation graves. The oldest have a rhomboid blade cast in a two-piece mould with a tang which presumably fitted into the end of the shaft (Fig. 38, 1). A collar or ferrule of bronze might be fitted over the end of the shaft and overlap the butt of the blade. Then the ferrule was cast in one piece with the blade and the tang suppressed. Thus may have arisen the British socketed spear-head of the Arreton Down type. A further improvement was to cast a pair of loops on the socket, presumably to hold thongs attaching the head to the shaft (Fig. 38, 2).

In the Late Bronze Age a new type of spear-head with a leaf-shaped, instead of a rhomboid, blade and attached by two pins or rivets instead of thongs was introduced, but did not supersede the native development of the Arreton Down series ; the new type, however, modified the native evolution.[1] The loops became transferred from the socket to the base of the blade—or incorporated in it (Fig. 39, 2). Eventually they lost all function and became decorative crescentic or lunate openings (Fig. 38, 3). There is some uncertainty as to whether spear-heads with loops on the socket but a small, leaf-shaped blade and those with loops at the base of the blade should be assigned to the Late Bronze Age ; the latter type at least is well attested with socketed celts in England, though it occurs as an import early in the Middle Bronze Age of Germany, and even the former was associated with a leaf-shaped sword at Corsbie Moor, Berwickshire. But the type with lunate openings in the blade is associated exclusively with socketed axes and slashing swords so that it is distinctively Late Bronze Age.

It is a characteristically British type, but was sometimes exported from the islands. Such a specimen was dredged up from the harbour of Huelva, Spain, with a number of other bronzes of various origins. Among them were several Sicilian safety-pins or brooches of a type which had gone out of fashion before the Greeks colonized Syracuse in 734 B.C. Assuming that the bronzes from Huelva really constitute a contemporary group—the cargo of a foundered merchantman—it follows that the Late Bronze Age in Britain was fully established by 750 B.C. This would be the earliest reasonably probable absolute date in British prehistory.

The use of the typological division just described as a basis for chronology depends upon the following conditions :

[1] Cf. *Arch.*, lxxxiii, pp. 194 ff. ; *Mainzer Zeitschrift*, xxix, pp. 56 f.

communications throughout the area for which it is valid must be so regular and continuous that new fashions and ideas may travel evenly and rapidly through it, and the technical equipment must everywhere be comparatively uniform so that the new ideas can be applied in practice. Everyone knows how in the provinces fashions lag behind the metropolis and that Arabs and Esquimaux cannot compete in the armaments race with European and American Powers for lack of technical equipment. The division here described was originally worked out by Montelius [1] in the first instance for Scandinavia and Italy, regions continuously interconnected throughout the Bronze Age by trade in amber. His scheme with minor adjustments is applicable to intervening regions which shared in the amber trade along the Elbe, the Rhine and the Upper Danube. But the further we go east or west of the central amber route the less satisfactorily does Montelius' system work. For England it has needed radical revision. To what extent can the English typology be applied to Scotland?

We have already remarked that types assignable on the usual classification to the Early Bronze Age are widely distributed in Scotland. Middle Bronze Age types also occur. We have not only winged axes and palstavs, but also stone moulds for casting the latter type (two from Galloway and one from Eildon Hills in the Tweed Basin).[2] Moreover some curious adzes or chisels constructed like a palstav, but with the blade parallel to the flanges come from Dumfriesshire, Perthshire, and Argyll [3] (Fig. 37, 3).

Only three true ogival daggers can be cited, coming from Dumfriesshire, Perthshire, and Fife. Corrie [4] has enumerated twenty-five rapier blades, but all come from counties south of the Tay and the majority from south of the Southern Uplands. The early tanged spear-head is represented by only one specimen from Muirkirk in Ayrshire (Fig. 38, 1), but there are some twenty-five spear-heads with loops on the socket. Stone moulds for their manufacture have been found even in Aberdeenshire, but these would produce a weapon with a leaf-shaped blade, and this form of blade is far commoner in Scotland than the earlier rhomboid blade. To the same period may belong flat chisels with a tapering tang of the same thickness as the blade found on Traprain Law and with a Cordoned Urn in Wigtonshire.

[1] For England, *Arch.*, lxi, pp. 97 ff.   [2] *PSAS.*, lvii, p. 142.
[3] *PSAS.*, lxii, p. 151.   [4] *PSAS.*, lxii, p. 142.

Most of the foregoing objects are stray finds, but Callander [1] has described seven hoards of the period, all but one coming from south of the Forth.

Do these sparse and unevenly distributed finds suffice to constitute a distinct period? Fox [2] has pointed out a method of control. It is certain that as the Bronze Age advanced metal became increasingly common. The chances are, therefore, that from each successive period of more or less equal length a larger number of specimens should have survived. Fox finds that this is actually the case in England with regard respectively to flat axes, flanged axes and early palstavs, and socketed axes and later palstavs. In the Cambridge region, for instance, the Early Bronze Age is represented by 26 axes, the Middle by 82, and the Late by 190. No such relation holds for Scotland. We can point to 132 flat axes, but only 120 winged axes and palstavs (some of which would on the English system belong to the Late Bronze Age) and not quite 200 socketed axes. Evidently there is a discrepancy here.

The discrepancy becomes more glaring when the finds which should denote the several periods are classified in accordance with the natural geographical divisions of the country. This can best be done with the aid of a table [3] :—

AXES

	Flat and slightly flanged celts	Winged celts and palstavs	Socketed celts	Tri-angular knife daggers	Rapiers	Swords
Tweed Basin . .	10	14	30	0	4	4
Galloway and Dumfries	21	35 + 2	23	3	15	8
Lothians . . .	10	3	24	2	2	30
Midland Valley to Tay	7	18	13	5	3	19
Fife . . .	4	5	17	4	1	0
Tay to Moray Firth .	60	33	44	8	0	28
Far North . . .	14	7	17	1	0	4
West Coast and Isles from Arran to Hebrides . .	6	5	14	3	0	22
	132	120	182	26	25	115

[1] *PSAS.*, lvii, p. 134. To these should be added one from Dumfries (*PSAS*, lx, p. 28), and one from Arran (*PSAS.*, lix, p. 255). [2] *Cambridge Region,* p. 18.
[3] I have to thank Dr. Margaret Mitchell and Mr. Henderson for the figures for the Early and Late Bronze Ages respectively.

Only in the Tweed Basin, Annandale, Nithsdale, and Galloway do the " Middle Bronze Age " axes bear anything like the proportion to flat axes that should be expected on the analogy of England. No rapiers occur north of the Tay and only six north of the Southern Uplands. Why are they thus restricted ? Why are palstavs so much rarer than flat axes beyond the Tay and the Clyde ? Surely just because the new types of tools and weapons never " caught on " in these northerly districts. The provincial natives were quite content with flat axes and daggers, while their more advanced contemporaries in England and even on the Tweed and in Galloway were using winged axes and palstavs, ogival daggers and rapiers.

In other words, many flat axes and triangular daggers must be assigned to the Middle Bronze Age of Great Britain and be contemporary with English palstavs and rapiers ; the big flat axes with very wide splayed blades and the large triangular daggers described on p. 99 are particularly suited to such treatment. Confirmation of this view may be found in the fact that twelve out of fourteen hoards assigned by Callander to the Early Bronze Age come from sites north of the Southern Uplands, while five of seven hoards of his next period come from south of those ranges. Plainly the northern hoards of Callander's Period II may be the counterparts of the southern hoards of his Period III ! We may conclude that the Middle Bronze Age industry never became established in Caledonia save in the extreme south. Elsewhere its products were only occasionally imported or manufactured.   But the distribution table suggests further considerations.

Neither in Galloway nor in North-eastern Scotland do socketed axes exhibit anything like the excess over earlier types that is to be expected on the analogy of England. And we shall find below that the Late Bronze Age complex arrived in Scotland considerably later than in England. It can only be assumed that " Middle Bronze Age " types and, in the north, even flat axes were still in use in Scotland while socketed axes were already current in England.

An examination of the largest of Callander's Middle Bronze Age hoards, that from Glentrool in Galloway,[1] will confirm this expectation. It comprises a rapier, a palstav (Fig. 39, 1), a spearhead with protected loops at the base of the blade (Fig. 39, 2), two

[1] *PSAS.*, lv, p. 29 ; lvi, p. 20.

bifid razors, a flat-tanged knife (Fig. 39, 3), a torque of twisted bronze wire (very much corroded), a pin with a flat head and a loop on the side of the shaft, and beads of glass and amber. Now the palstav, though the ridge and flanges on the face might rank as early features, looks late; the wings have been hammered over as if in imitation of the Continental winged-and-looped palstav of the Late Bronze Age. The spear-head might be found with socketed axes in England. Bifid razors both in

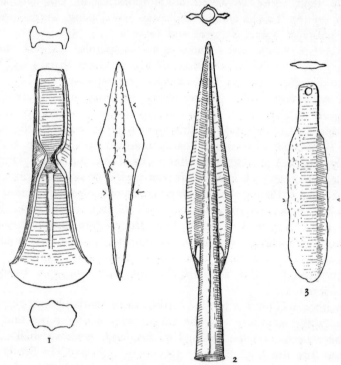

FIG. 39.—Palstav, spear-head and knife from the Glentrool hoard. ⅓.

England and Scotland are normally associated with socketed axes. The Glentrool specimens diverge from the majority (Fig. 42, 3) in the absence of a round hole at the top of the slit. But the same peculiarity is observable on the razors from the very late hoard of Braes of Gight. It is also true that razors did not necessarily reach Britain with the socketed axe from Central Europe but may have arrived earlier from Sicily by the Atlantic route [1] ; in Holland a tanged razor was found in a grave, together with an ogival dagger of Middle Bronze Age type.[2]

On the whole, the Glentrool hoard looks like the product of a backward group, clinging to the rapier-palstav complex when swords and socketed axes were already wielded on the opposite shore of the Solway. In Scotland the Middle Bronze Age types and even some flat axes and knife-daggers must be spread out so as to fill up also part of the time occupied by the Late Bronze Age in England. Hence the limiting date of 750 B.C. for that period need not apply to Scotland.

The table further shows that there is no correlation between the " Middle Bronze Age " types and the Cinerary Urns. The latter are just as common north of the Southern Uplands in Fife and the Lothians as in Galloway and the Tweed Basin. The Urn people may have used palstavs and rapiers, but they cannot have been responsible for their introduction from the south.

2. THE LATE BRONZE AGE

The Late Bronze Age witnesses a radical transformation of equipment and armament throughout Great Britain, and at the same time fundamental changes in the structure of the metal industry. The new types that characterize the period—socketed axes and slashing swords—are not the logical outcome of native developments but were created in Central Europe and brought, fully formed, to Britain. An innovation is the appearance of founders' hoards—collections of scrap metal and old tools designed for re-smelting. Such betoken the advent of a new class of merchant craftsmen and a new organization for the production and distribution of bronzes. The simultaneous emergence of a variety of specialized tools—gouges, hammers, anvils, curved knives—points in the same direction.

The new types in Scotland are spread fairly evenly over the whole habitable area. Their distribution here is, in fact, comparable to that of " Early Bronze Age " types and quite different from that of the " Middle Bronze Age " series. The discrepancy is additional proof that the new industrial types are not the result of a local evolution.

[1] Cf. Childe, *Bronze Age*, figs. 12, 4, and 9.
[2] van Giffen, *Bauart*, p. 88, fig. 78, *c-f*.

The Late Bronze Age of Scotland differs from that of England in several respects. In the first place, founders' hoards, so common in England and on the Continent, are rare. Out of fifty-two Scottish hoards only two certainly belong to this category—one from Duddingston Loch, Edinburgh, and the second from the Island of Islay.[1] Possibly the relative poverty of Caledonia made the sort of trade denoted by founders' hoards unprofitable.

Secondly, certain types, prominent in England, seem unrepresented in Scotland. In England—or at least the Lowland part—three probably consecutive complexes can be recognized.[2] They are characterized respectively by " U "-type swords, " V "-type swords, and Carp's Tongue swords. In Scotland only the " V "-type is effectively represented. Similarly our socketed celts all belong to late forms associated with " V "-type swords. In particular the Continental winged palstav with lateral ear (*Lappenabsatzbeil*), associated in England with the Carp's Tongue sword, is missing as is the socketed axe decorated with cast imitations of wings. In these respects Scotland falls into line with the rest of Highland Britain. The absence of these types may mean that the Late Bronze Age began later in Scotland than in Lowland England, as had been inferred from the numbers of axes. That will not, however, explain the absence from Scotland of Hallstatt types of sword which incidentally reached Ireland and Wales.

Finally, the Scottish hoards include certain Continental forms which are missing in England, though some reappear in Ireland. These types, almost entirely ornaments, denote contacts with the Continent, distinct from those effected through England.

The axe distinctive of the Late Bronze Age is, of course, the socketed celt with a loop. The majority from Scotland, short, plain implements such as are so common in Ireland, would be regarded as late on English standards. No Scottish examples bear cast mouldings imitating wings, but several specimens are decorated with three parallel ridges on each face, a type rather common in Yorkshire.

Together with the socketed axe new specialized tools were introduced : socketed gouges, chisels, and hammers, tanged chisels—the tang may now be thinner as well as narrower than

---

[1] This included two axes, a flanged chisel, a halberd, and a spear-head with loops on the socket, all much worn.

[2] Kendrick and Hawkes, p. 125.

the blade—and a curious socketed knife with a bent blade (Fig. 41). Callander [1] suggests that the gouge and curved knife were carpenter's tools. But they might also have been used by the smith in preparing moulds. A bent knife was actually associated with a small anvil in a hoard at Fresné-la-Mère, Calvados, in Normandy. Incidentally a similar anvil was found stray in Sutherland.[2]

FIG. 40. — Socketed axe from Traprain Law. $\frac{1}{3}$.

The variety of standard tools suggests increased specialization of labour and the development of distinct crafts that had previously been in a rudimentary undifferentiated state. Scottish hoards like that from Adabrock, Lewis (two axes, a socketed hammer, a socketed gouge, a tanged chisel, a riveted spear-head, two bifid razors, two whetstones, and beads of gold, amber, and glass, as well as a fragmentary bronze vessel) [3] from Cullerne, Findhorn (Elgin) (celt, bent knife, razor, two riveted spear-heads) [4] and Monmore, Killin (Perthshire) (two celts, gouge, tanged blade, riveted spear-head, penannular armlet, etc.) [5] look like the kits of travelling artisans. But as each hoard included spear-heads, such evidently went about armed.

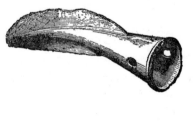

FIG. 41.—Curved knives from Point of Sleat, Skye, and Wester Ord, Ross., after Anderson. $\frac{1}{3}$.

In addition to the curved knife, a two-edged knife with a straight blade, and a short oval socket, likewise pierced by two rivet-holes, was also current (Fig. 42, 2). Estyn Evans [6] has suggested that it was developed from a similarly shaped tanged

[1] *PSAS.*, lvii, p. 150.   [2] Anderson, ii, fig. 222.
[3] *PSAS.*, xlv, p. 27.   [4] *PSAS.*, liv, p. 124.
[5] *PSAS.*, liv, p. 129.   [6] *Arch.*, lxxxiii, p. 190.

knife (like Fig. 42, 1) by the addition of a ferrule, much in the same way as the Arreton Down type of spear-head. Both types of knife are distinctively British though occurring also, like many contemporary British products, in North-western France. Eight socketed knives have been recorded from Scotland, two coming from Orkney. On the other hand, a single-edged socketed knife with recurved blade, found near Crossraguel Abbey, in Ayrshire,[1] is a specifically Continental form particularly common in Switzerland and the Rhône Valley at the beginning of the Hallstatt period.

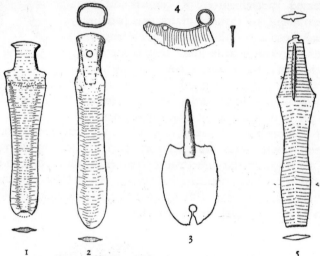

FIG. 42.—Knives from Jarlshof (Shetland) and Quoykea (Orkney); razors from Quoykea and Traprain Law, blade from Killin. ⅓.

The only bronze sickle recorded from Scotland (from Dores, Inverness) belongs to this period. It is of the peculiarly British socketed type. The rarity of this agricultural implement in Scotland may indicate that agriculture was still relatively unimportant as compared with hunting and stock-breeding.

Maple-leaf or bifid razors are a very common element in Late Bronze Age hoards from Galloway to Orkney. As in England and Ireland, these are wide, double-edged blades of very thin bronze, fitted with a stouter tang. There is always a slit at the end of the blade and generally a circular opening just above (Fig. 42, 3). As noted above, the closest parallels to the British razors come from Sicily, though they have relatives in

[1] Munro, *Prehistoric Scotland*, fig. 89 ; cf. Dechelette, *Manuel*, ii, fig. 92, 6–7.

Central Europe and France. A well-known razor, found in a gravel pit at Kinleith, near Edinburgh,[1] is also double-edged, but it has an open-work body, crescentic blades, and a loop at the end of the tang. Finally, a single-bladed razor (incomplete) was found on Traprain Law (Fig. 42, 4). It belongs to a group of lunate razors, derived from Italian models and familiar from Hallstatt graves in Western Europe. Cognate types are known even from England and Wales,[2] but the closest parallel to the Traprain specimen with the same moulding on the back of the blade comes from Denmark.[3] The whole series belongs explicitly to the Hallstatt cycle, and our razor is the only immediate derivative of that culture known in Scotland.

In armament the most distinctive innovation of the Late Bronze Age was the leaf-shaped sword adapted to slashing as well as thrusting. A tang, usually splaying out at the end and provided with low flanges down the sides, projects from the base of the blade. To this plates of horn or other material were riveted to form the grip. There is generally a row of distinct rivet-holes along the centre of the tang and two or more in the shoulders of the blade. But in four or five specimens[4] the holes in the tang have joined up to form a slit, while the flanges have virtually disappeared. These peculiarities may be due to the influence of the foreign Carp's Tongue sword.

With the exception of one from the mouth of the Tay (Fig. 43, 1), the shoulders of all Scottish blades are straight. This feature is distinctive of the so-called " V "-type swords as contrasted with the " U "-type in which the shoulders of the blade are rounded. In nearly all Scottish swords the edges of the blade, immediately below the shoulders, have been blunted and nicked. This feature, termed in Italian the *ricasso*, was designed to allow the swordsman's thumb to rest on the blade, the notch serving as a guard.

In addition to the swords with horn-plated grip, Scotland has yielded five swords with metal pommels and hilts (Fig. 43, 3). In each case the hilt and pommel seem to have been cast on the tang of an ordinary " V "-sword. In at least one instance the pommel is only a thin sheet of bronze cast over a clay core that is still in position. These weapons are doubtless inspired by the solid, bronze-hilted swords of Central Europe, but are

[1] Anderson, ii, fig. 23.   [2] Wheeler, *Wales,* fig. 81.
[3] Montelius, *Vorklassische Chronologie Italiens,* fig. 637.
[4] Corsbie Moor, Berwicks. ; Polder Moss, Stirling ; Forse, Caithness.

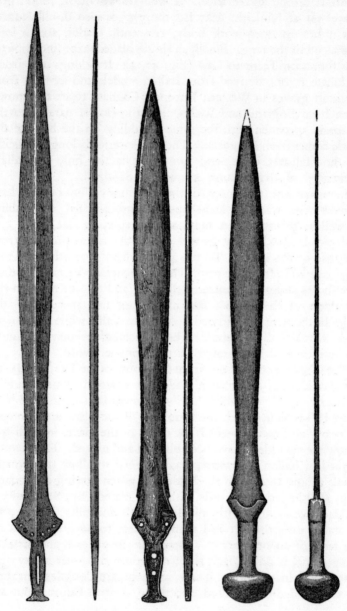

FIG. 43.—Swords from Migdrum Is., in Tay; S. Uist and Leadburn, Peebles, after Anderson. ⅕.

probably of British manufacture. There are a few similar swords from England and one from Sweden.[1] The casting-on process was very popular among the British and Irish bronze-smiths.

The swords were carried in scabbards of wood or leather, terminating in a metal chape. All the surviving chapes from Scotland belong to the tongue form—a small, metal box shaped like a truncated and much flattened pyramid—which is common also in the rest of the British Isles and in North-western France.[2] It goes with the "U" and "V"-type swords. The purse-shaped chape, proper to Carp's Tongue swords, and the winged chape of the Hallstatt type are alike unknown in Scotland, though represented in England.

The imperfect blade from the Monmore (Killin) hoard, here reproduced in Fig. 42, 5, may have been a weapon. The curious ridge on each face of the tang must have been designed to facilitate the attachment of the handle or hilt. The type is well known in Ireland, and a very similar blade was found at Scarborough in Yorkshire. The blade found with a Cordoned Urn at Shuttlefield near Lockerbie, seems to be of a similar type, but very much smaller and lighter—perhaps a model for funerary use.

In addition to swords, the Late Bronze Age warrior carried one or two spears. A type that appears first in this period has a leaf-shaped head and was fixed to the shaft by pegs or thongs through the socket. Side by side therewith go developments of the native looped spear-head—notably the type with crescentic opening in the blade (Fig. 38, 3). This form in Scotland is confined to the east coast from the Ness to the Tweed; its distribution coincides with that of the spear-head with protected loops incorporated in the blade, whereas the type with basal loops is best represented in Galloway and the Tweed Basin. The spear-shafts were shod with tubular bronze ferrules expanding trumpet-wise at the butt. A type with a spiked butt is also known; both forms were riveted or lashed on to the shaft.

Defensive armour appears first in the Late Bronze Age in the form of circular shields or bucklers of hammered bronze.[3] The Scottish specimens consist of a single sheet of beaten bronze. They are strengthened by a hoop of stout wire over which the rim is hammered, as well as by concentric ridges and rings of

---

[1] Montelius, *Minnen*, 120.   [2] Childe, *Bronze Age*, fig. 9, 2.
[3] Cf. Sprockhoff, *Handelsgeschichte der germanischen Bronzezeit*, pp. 4-12.

bosses hammered up from the inside.   At the centre a hemi-spherical boss, about 4 inches in diameter, has similarly been hammered up.   The hollow behind the boss is spanned by a strip of metal, riveted to the shield at each end, which serves as a handle.   Nine or ten such shields have been recorded from Scotland;   all come from three hoards found respectively at Yetholm (Roxburghshire), Lugtonridge (Ayrshire), and Auch-maleddie (Aberdeenshire).   Similar shields are known from England, Wales, and Ireland, as well as two from Denmark.

There is no necessity for assuming that the round shield was introduced from Central Europe with the socketed axe and the slashing sword;   for the Central European shields—all belonging to the Hallstatt period—diverge substantially in their decoration from the British.   A derivation from the East Mediter-ranean by the Atlantic route would be more plausible.   Round shields are depicted in Egyptian and Mycenæan paintings by the end of the thirteenth century B.C. and are carried by Sardinian statuettes a few centuries later.   But in Egypt the round shields are born by raiders from the north.   The British and Continental bucklers may be just translations into metal of older targes of leather or wood.   A round leather shield was actually found in a bog in Ireland, and the outline of a circular targe of some perishable material, probably wood, was discerned under a Middle Bronze Age barrow in Würtemburg.[1]   The latter shield was decorated with small bronze knobs.

In any case shields of the particular type represented in the Scottish hoards are essentially British products.   But their creation owes something to foreign influence—the technique of hammered bronze work which is distinctive of the Late Bronze Age–Hallstatt complex on the Continent.

The same technique was a precondition of the manufacture of metal cauldrons and buckets [2] which likewise appear in this period.   The cauldrons go back to Greek and Italian models which may begin as early as the eighth century B.C.   They are globular vessels, like the Greek cauldrons, and built up out of three or more sheets of thin bronze, riveted together.   The ring handles are Hellenic in form, but attached in a barbarian technique; the staples that hold them have been cast on to the rims instead of being riveted.   Leeds happily suggests that the maker was

[1] *Prähistor. Blätter,* 1906, p. 50 ; Childe, *Danube,* p. 298, n. 7.
[2] Leeds in *Arch.,* lxxx, pp. 1 ff.

trying to imitate Mediterranean models, in which the handles had been brazed on, without knowing the latter technique.

Leeds distinguishes two groups of cauldrons. In the earlier (A) the neck is strengthened by corrugations. The staple is a half-tube with three or (later) more corrugations on the top, and was cast with " T "-shaped tongues of metal projecting downwards on both sides of the neck. Scotland can boast three such cauldrons,[1] England only one, but Ireland eleven. In the later type (B), the rim is bent sharply outwards and its edge turned over into a roll (Fig. 44). The half-tubular staples are

DU 1, 2.

FIG. 44.—Cauldrons from Kincardine Moss, and West Highlands, after Anderson.
$\frac{1}{14}$.

again cast on, but the tongues of the castings are made to wrap round the brim, and the whole is strengthened by struts descending vertically from below the rim to the belly of the cauldron on to which they are riveted. There is one example of this type from the west of Scotland, but fourteen from Ireland, and one from Wales. A pair of staples and rings included in a hoard found at Poolewe, in Wester Ross, belongs to a rather different

[1] Dulduff, Ayrs. ; Hattenknowe, Peebles., and one uncertain.

class (B2) represented by four Irish and two English cauldrons ; in all these the staples have been cast separately and subsequently attached to the rim. The Poolewe hoard comprised also a penannular ornament or fibula with trumpet ends. This confirms the inference from the distribution that cauldrons in Great Britain were mainly of Irish manufacture.

FIG. 45.—Bronze bucket from Cardross, Dumbartonshire, after *PSAS*. $\frac{7}{50}$.

The buckets, with their sharp shoulders and short necks, agree in profile with the Italian and Hallstatt *situlæ*. But the handles are not Italian, but Hellenic, in form and, like those of our cauldrons, have been cast on. The British and Irish buckets, in fact, represent a local hybrid in which Hellenic handles have been attached in barbarian technique to Italic bodies. We have examples from Duddingston Loch, Edinburgh, and from Cardross, Dumbartonshire (Fig. 45). Ireland has produced nine buckets, but England only three. That from Cardross, like one from Heathery Burn Cave in County Durham, has been strengthened by a wheel-shaped plate riveted on to the outside of the base.

Buckets of the same form but different structure were widely diffused from Upper Italy throughout Central Europe. In the rich cemetery of Hallstatt they were used to contain cremated remains. Cinerary urns of clay, imitating such bronze ossuaries, are common in the Early Iron Age and peripheral survivals of the Bronze Age in Central Europe and extend as far as Holland, Norway,[1] and even Ireland.[2]

Over against these vessels of beaten bronze, we have fragments of bowls of cast bronze from the hoards of Adabrock, Lewis, and of Balmashannar near Forfar,[3] and a third from Ardoe on the Dee,[4] in Aberdeenshire. The latter was found in the same sand hill as two Collared Urns and several short cists, one containing a Beaker.

Most of the new fashions in personal ornament which emerge in the Late Bronze Age are immediately inspired by Irish usage. Indeed most of the gold ornaments of the period may rank as imports from Ireland [5] though bronzes of the same form may be local copies. Specifically Irish are penannular ornaments, varying in diameter from ½ to 2 inches and all provided with extravagantly large trumpet-like terminals. Some eight examples in gold and one in bronze are known from Scotland, all coming from the west coasts from Galloway to Ross. The smaller specimens in particular resemble in outline Danish fibulæ or brooches of the Late Bronze Age.[6] But though some sort of connection may be suspected, the Scottish and Irish ornaments lack the loose wire pin of the brooches.

The larger specimens in fact approximate to a well-known

---

[1] *Oldtiden,* iii (1913), pls. iii, 22, iv, 23 (La Tène).

[2] *PRSAI.,* 1932, p. 85, pl. xix, A.

[3] *PSAS.,* xxvi, p. 182.

[4] Abercromby, ii, p. 21 ; cf. the cast vase from Homburg in Hesse, *AuhV.,* v, p. 144.

[5] For Scottish specimens see Callander's list in *PSAS.,* lvii, pp. 163 ff. ; for Irish parallels see Armstrong, *Catalogue.*

[6] Childe, *Bronze Age,* fig. 14, 17.

M

class of massive penannular armlets of bronze or gold; for these, too, expand to circular buffer- or slightly cup-shaped terminals at each end. This type of armlet, though commoner in Western than in Central Europe, was very likely introduced into the British Isles together with the socketed axe and the sword. But it soon became naturalized, particularly in Ireland. Some sixty specimens in gold are known from Western Scotland,[1] as well as a pair in bronze from the Monmore hoard near Killin (Perthshire). From the east we have a pair found with a rough stone cup or mortar at Hillhead, Caithness,[2] two from St. Abb's Head (Berwickshire),[3] and perhaps others from Gallows Hill, St. Vigeans (Angus), and Galla Law, East Lothian. Finally, one of a pair found on the top of a cist in the urnfield at Alloa (Fig. 46, 2) belongs to this type, while the other is connected with the Central European series distinguished below.

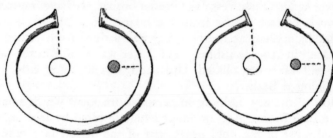

Fig. 46.—Gold bracelets from Alloa. ⅓.

Irish, too, must be the hollow penannular gold ornaments of triangular section, varying in diameter from ¾ to nearly 2 inches.[4] Of the nine Scottish specimens four come from the Balmashanner hoard (Angus), one from Gogar near Edinburgh, and the rest from the west coast between Galloway and Mull. The example from Mull[5] (Pl. XII, 4) is composed of three distinct strips of thin gold—a tubular centre and two flat strips—held together by folding over the edges and re-inforced by a ribbon wrapped into a tube along the outer edge.

With the Mull example was a bronze disc, ornamented with concentric grooves and bands of small circles (Pl. XII, 1–2). It

[1] In the case of specimens that no longer survive, it is impossible to distinguish western from eastern types.

[2] *PSAS.*, xlvii, p. 134.

[3] *PSAS.*, lxv, p. 26.

[4] *Ant. J.*, v, p. 143 ; in *Rev. Arch.*, xxviii (1928), p. 30, Favret describes cognate objects from France one associated with Hallstatt types.

[5] *PSAS.*, lxviii, p. 192.

PLATE XII

GOLD OBJECTS FROM MULL

National Museum

had been coated with gold leaf and represents the sole example of a " sun disc "—an object common in Ireland and supposed to be ritual.

Very small penannular rings, tapering off at both ends are common in Ireland and are generally termed ring-money. Some are of solid gold while others are of copper coated with gold leaf. The latter sort of base money is represented in Scotland [1] by stray rings or small lots from Galloway, Skye, Covesea (Elgin), Fuaraig Glen (Banffshire), and the Balmashanner hoard. Traces of string or possibly hair were observed on the Covesea specimens ; their owner must have carried his " money " tied together or worn it in his hair.

Finally, some forty-five torques, formed out of a single twisted ribbon of gold wire, have been recorded in Scotland. Such ribbon torques are far commoner in Ireland. Though generally assigned to the Late Bronze Age, specialized examples were found at Shaw Hill near the head of the Tweed with a gold sceptre mount that can hardly be older than the beginning of our era.

Over against these western ornaments a few types with a different ancestry are known. Sunflower pins [2]—i.e. pins with a disc-head set parallel to the shaft which is bent at the top— though not rare in Ireland, are Scandinavian and Central European in origin. The specimens from Ythsie, Aberdeenshire, and Grosvenor Crescent, Edinburgh, may therefore be regarded as on the way to Ireland rather than imports thence. The same may apply to a pin with a cup-shaped head from Gogar.

More interesting is a group of Central European ornaments restricted to the east of Scotland. All the relevant types are illustrated in a hoard from Braes of Gight, near Methlick, Aberdeenshire.[3] This comprised three penannular neck-rings of stout, circular bronze wire terminating in cast loops each carrying a small ring. One (Fig. 47) was adorned with eighteen pierced projections or loops jutting out from the outer edge of the wire. Each originally carried a small ring. A fragment of a similar necklet was included in the hoard from Wester Ord, Ross.[4]

These necklets are unique in the British Isles, and I can find no exact parallel abroad. But closed neck-rings with small ringlets attached to loops on the outside are characteristic of the Late

[1] PSAS., lvii, p. 163 ; lxv, p. 181.   [2] Childe, Bronze Age, fig. 14, 8.
[3] PSAS., xxv, p. 135.
[4] With socketed celt and curved knife, PSAS., lix, p. 113.

Hallstatt Selz-Dangstetter culture of Alsace and the Middle Rhine.[1] Our examples must be regarded as derived from this Late Hallstatt type; they are therefore later than 600 B.C. and illustrate the overlap between the Late Bronze Age of Scotland and the Early Iron Age of Central Europe.

The Braes of Gight hoard contained further three rings joined together by links of narrow bronze ribbon. Similar linked rings occur as girdle chains in the Late Bronze Age and Hallstatt lake-dwellings and urnfields of Switzerland and Upper Bavaria.[2]

Finally the same hoard contained six massive penannular armlets with expanding ends. The terminals do not expand all round as in the groups described on p. 162, but outwards

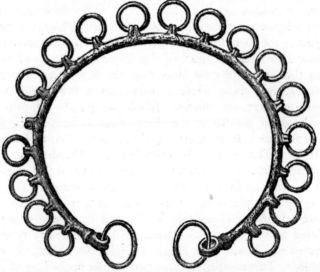

FIG. 47.—Necklet from Braes of Gight, Aberdeenshire, after *PSAS.* ⅜.

only (Fig. 46, 1). The type in Scotland is confined to the east, particularly to counties round the Moray Firth,[3] but appears also in Heathery Burn Cave, Co. Durham, and in the Alloa cemetery side by side with a specimen of the western type. The treatment of the terminals is characteristic of the Bronze Age of Central Europe and persists in Alsace [4] into the Hallstatt period.

[1] *PZ.,* xi, p. 174; Schaeffer, *Les Tertres funéraires . . . de Haguenau,* ii, p. 217.
[2] Childe, *Danube,* p. 344 and fig. 203.
[3] Auchtertyre and Covesea, Elgins; Wester Ord, Ross.; Connage, Banff.; Balmashanner, Angus, *PSAS.,* lxv, p. 185.
[4] Schaeffer, *Tertres,* ii, fig. 98, *c.*

The whole group is of Central European origin and illustrates connections between the Continent and Scotland which did not affect Lowland Britain where other "Hallstatt" types are relatively so common.

3. THE RANGE OF THE BRONZE AGE

The hoards from Braes of Gight and Wester Ord indicate that the Late Bronze Industry in Scotland was still flourishing as late as 500 B.C.—the end of the first Iron Age in Central Europe. A bluish glass bead mottled with white from the Adabrock hoard will add another couple of centuries on to the local Bronze Age ; for such a bead would not be expected before the second Iron Age or La Tène period of the Continent. How much longer did bronze remain the principal industrial metal in Scotland ?

To answer this question fairly we must rid our minds of any misapprehension as to the superiority of iron over bronze. It was a long time before people learned to forge a really good axe or sword of iron. The technique of iron-working is quite different from that of bronze-casting. The earlier iron tools and weapons of Europe were certainly inferior to the bronzes with which they had to compete. The victory in the competition was won for iron not by its intrinsic superiority as a cutting metal but solely by its cheapness. Iron ores are widely distributed ; copper ores are not common, tin is absolutely rare. Under normal circumstances only rich men could afford bronze tools or weapons, anyone could buy iron ones.

But in the British Isles circumstances were not normal. Cornwall is one of the richest tin-producing districts in Europe and Western Asia ; copper is abundant, particularly in Ireland. The combination of Cornish tin and Irish copper had made possible a flourishing industry early in the Bronze Age. By the Late Bronze Age the economic organization was probably good enough to make metal relatively cheap. (It must be noted, however, that many late bronzes in England seem to have been adulterated with lead.[1]) People, controlling such resources and accustomed to use good bronze tools, would not readily abandon them for inferior iron ones. It would need the advent of a people, inured to the use of iron in less favoured regions, to suppress the well-tried bronze arms and implements.

[1] Information from Dr. A. Raistrick.

Now we shall find that no bands of iron-using invaders can be traced in Caledonia before the third century B.C., and even then such occupied only restricted areas.   Outside the latter, bronze would presumably remain the favoured metal.   The bronze-smith who cast swords on Traprain Law need not have shut up shop much before the beginning of our era.   A socketed axe of bronze was found in the Roman camp at Ardoch.[1]   Some of Galgacus' soldiers may have still fought with bronze weapons at Mons Graupius !   The end of the Bronze Age in Caledonia (and also in Ireland) may then be relatively very late—at least as late as the latest Cinerary Urns cited on p. 138.

Implements or ornaments of Late Bronze Age type have never demonstrably been found in burials associated with Cinerary Urns (still less with Food Vessels).   The distribution of isolated specimens and of hoards is again entirely discordant with that of Cinerary Urns, as may be seen by comparing the table on p. 148 with Map III.   But neither isolated weapons and tools that may have been lost in a battle or on a journey, nor yet hoards belonging to travellers and merchants that might have been hidden at danger-points on the road, give any accurate idea of the distribution of settlements.

But at least nine Scottish hoards comprise only a couple of tools, weapons, and ornaments.   Each may well represent the personal possessions of an individual or a household.   The hoards from Quoykea (Orkney),[2] Adabrock (Lewis), Wester Ord (Easter Ross), Point of Sleat (Skye),[3] Monmore near Killin (Perthshire), and Torran on Loch Awe,[4] belong to this class. It is difficult to see why any of these should have been deposited where they were found by chance wayfarers.   It appears more likely that the objects were buried in the vicinity of their owners' dwellings while the latter were engaged on some expedition from which they never returned.   Granting this, such hoards could be used to determine the distribution of settlements with more confidence than other hoards or than isolated finds.   They illustrate a distribution radically different from that disclosed in Map III with its conspicuous blanks from the Clyde to Orkney,

[1] *PSAS.*, xxxii, pp. 461, 470. Anderson insists that there is " no reason to doubt that the association (of bronze and iron implements) is a genuine case of contemporary occurrence ".
[2] Socketed knife and razor.
[3] Two leaf-shaped spear-heads, a sword, a curved knife, and a cup-headed pin.
[4] A leaf-shaped spear-head and a gouge.

and in fact foreshadow a distribution characteristic of the Iron Age, Map IV.

In other words it looks, on the basis of Map III alone, as if the introduction of the socketed axe and the sword marked, not only innovations in fashion, technique, and economic organization, but also a new distribution of settlement. However, as indicated on pp. 138 f., the Cinerary Urns plotted on Map III do not mark all burials assignable to the Late Bronze Age; at least in Orkney and Shetland we have from the same period burials in short cists or in urns of a different series. It is to that extent doubtful how far the discrepancy denotes fresh settlement or a mere re-establishment of commercial relations on lines already foreshadowed in the period covered by Map I. The truth seems to be that, throughout the Bronze Age, there is no exact correlation between the metal industry and the several groups of funerary pottery. It really looks as if the bronze tools and weapons were at no period an integral part of the cultures, represented in the graves—as if the bronze-smiths had never been members of the communities to whom the graves belonged, but had rather formed a craft or guild, working indiscriminately for all communities.

Yet the Late Bronze Age seems to mark such a complete revolution in armament, dress, technical equipment and economic organization, that many authorities invoke an invasion to explain it. The theory of one or more invasions by " sword-bearers " sweeping over Britain, first adumbrated by Crawford [1] in 1922 and elaborated by Peake [2] in the same year, has subsequently gained increasing acceptance among prehistorians in England and Ireland.[3] It has even been suggested that the invaders were the first Kelts to land on these islands and introduced to Great Britain and Ireland the Goedelic branch of Keltic speech, which survived only in Ireland.

But it must be insisted that new types of tools, weapons, and ornaments can be introduced quite simply by trade without any mass immigration whatsoever. Even new techniques could be taught by relatively small numbers of immigrant craftsmen who need not even remain permanently settled in the country. And a reorganization of the metal trade, such as that denoted by the founders' hoards, might be effected by itinerant merchants

[1] *Ant. J.*, ii, pp. 27 ff. [2] *The Bronze Age and the Celtic World.*
[3] Kendrick and Hawkes, pp. 119, 135, 140 ; Mahr, article " Archæology."

visiting these shores in quest of Cornish tin, Irish gold, and any old scrap metal. Even if such settled down, they might be only a trifling fraction of the total population and need not enjoy such social prestige or political status as would enable them to modify seriously language or religion or even domestic industries like pot-making.

Again, the innovations distinctive of the Late Bronze Age do not by any means all come from the same quarter. If the socketed axe and leaf-shaped sword point to Central Europe, razors and cauldrons may rather have reached us coastwise from the Mediterranean. Finally, many of the innovations such as the socketed knives and perhaps the bucklers have no direct foreign prototypes, but must be admitted as developments of a native tradition, albeit modified and stimulated by new technical processes. And such British types, though centred in the British Isles, spread to adjacent regions of France and the Low Countries to such an extent that Breuil [1] could speak of a Britannico-Sequanian province of Bronze Culture.

If there had really been an invasion in Peake's sense, it would be expected that the invaders would have left their mark also on the ceramic and sepulchral records. Now in the English lowlands at least four intrusions during the period when Late Bronze Age types were current can be distinguished with the aid of pottery and burials. But none can have arrived early enough to account for the rise of the Late Bronze Age industry if the limiting date of 750 B.C. for its establishment be accepted. Even the earliest groups who introduced the globular and bucket urns into Southern England cannot have arrived appreciably before that date. And in fact a leaf-shaped spear-head of Late Bronze Age type was found on a ground surface older than that in which the urnfield of Pokesdown (Hants) [2] had been dug. Nor have these invaders left any unambiguous record of their presence in Upland Britain including Scotland and Ireland. In other words no changes in pottery nor burial rites can be connected with the foreign bronze types associated with the " U "-sword series.

Since this early group of " foreign " bronzes is unrepresented in Scotland where the Late Bronze Age begins only with the later, thoroughly British types, no fresh light on the question of Peake's invasion is to be expected here. It only remains to ask whether,

---

[1] *L'Anthr.*, xiv, p. 517.　　　　[2] *Ant. J.*, vii, p. 470.

and how far, the introduction here of the developed British series coincided with the advent of fresh colonists. A consideration of distributions in time and space has shown that the makers of Cinerary Urns could, as they probably did in fact, use socketed axes and swords. But it still left loop-holes to be filled by new settlers. And during the last five years the novel bronze types have been found with domestic pottery, distinguishable from that of the Cinerary Urns. It may be taken as the symbol of a Bronze Age invasion, though the invaders need not be identified with the first bearers of the Late Bronze Age types.

IX

THE LATE BRONZE AGE INVASION

1. FLAT-RIMMED POTS

DURING the period when socketed axes and swords were current in England, several intrusive groups, settling in sufficient numbers to affect the ceramic and sepulchral records, have been recognized. It is indeed likely that an almost continuous stream of invaders was flowing into England from the Continent, but two principal waves, each with two crests, can be distinguished—the Urnfield [1] and the Hallstatt invasions [2] respectively. The first group of urnfield invaders, settling principally in Wessex, introduced what are termed globular urns from the Rhine Valley ; a second group, occupying East Anglia and Southern England, brought the so-called bucket urns, decorated with finger-tip impressions on raised mouldings, again from the Rhine Valley. This wave did not certainly reach Upland Britain at all, though the decoration of our Encrusted Urns is thought by Fox to be inspired by the bucket-urn people.

The Hallstatt invasion is best represented by the All Cannings Cross groups that occupied Wiltshire and introduced pottery allied to the latest Hallstatt (Jogassian) wares of North-eastern France. The most characteristic vases are often covered with a red hæmatite wash, polished and decorated with incised patterns ; these sometimes preserve the angular profiles inspired by metal models, such as the situlæ. But associated with the fine wares goes an abundance of coarse gritty pottery (Radford's Class 1), largely " Bronze Age " in tradition, but distinguished by harder firing, a peculiar flattening of the rim, and finger-printing on the walls of the vases as well as on applied mouldings. The All Cannings Cross folk introduced the use of iron, of ring-head pins, and of shale or lignite for armlets,[3] as well as a series of textile implements hitherto unknown in Britain. But they still used socketed axes and bifid razors of bronze.[4]

---

[1] Kendrick and Hawkes, pp. 143 ff. ; *Ant. J.*, xiii, pp. 436 f. ; cf. *Oudh. Med.*, xv, p. 63.

[2] Kendrick and Hawkes, pp. 150 f., 154–174 ; Radford, in *CPPS.*, pp. 147 f.

[3] Cunnington, *All Cannings Cross*, pl. 26.

[4] Cunnington, *All Cannings Cross*, p. 119 ; *P. Sp. Soc. U. Bristol,* iv, 1931 pl. iv, *a*.

A more or less parallel movement from the Low Countries best represented at Castle Hill, Scarborough,[1] but according to Radford affecting also Southern England, is characterized by pottery allied to Dutch urnfield types influenced by Hallstatt forms of the Rhine and probably also by Teutonic (Harpstedt) forms from farther east. Here again, coarse, flat-rimmed pottery, indistinguishable from Radford's group 1 at All Cannings, predominates. The settlers at Scarborough used iron and spindle-whorls and jet armlets, but still employed socketed axes, tanged chisels, and other pure Bronze Age implements.

The Hallstatt invasions reached England only in the sixth, or probably the fifth, century B.C. when the La Tène culture was already beginning in South-west Germany and Eastern Gaul. In the south the waves reached the Mendips in Somerset. Wheeler[2] has suggested that the settlement in Heathery Burn Cave, County Durham, is connected with the Scarborough invaders. Yet the relics from the cave include, besides antler cheek-pieces for bridle-bits and jet armlets, a very typical set of Late Bronze Age implements including a mould for a socketed axe.

During the last five years flat-rimmed pottery, allied to Radford's Class 1 ware of England, has been found associated with relics of the Late Bronze Age in Scotland. The first discovery of this kind was due to Miss Benton.[3] In 1929 and 1930 she excavated the Sculptor's Cave on the shore near Covesea, Elgins. In addition to relics of the Romano-Caledonian Iron Age, and in places stratified below such, she found objects of Bronze Age type—namely bracelets with expanded terminals of the eastern form and false ring-money—together with bone implements and flat-rimmed pottery. The bone implements included netting-needles, made by splitting the metatarsal of a red deer longi-tudinally and piercing the articulation (Fig. 48, 2) as well as piercers and a needle made from the metapodials of sheep (like Fig. 51, 1). Identical netting-needles were found at Heathery Burn.[4]

The contemporary pottery is coarse, the paste comprising large stone and garnet grits, but is superficially rather smoother than most Cinerary Urns and is distinctly harder fired. The commonest form was a squat barrel-shaped pot (Fig. 48, 1) that

---

[1] Rowntree, *History of Scarborough*, pp. 20 ff. ; Elgee, *North-East Yorks*, p. 179 ; *Arch.*, lxxvii, pp. 179 ff.
[2] In Rowntree, *History of Scarborough*, p. 404.   [3] *PSAS.*, lxv, pp. 177 ff.
[4] In Scandinavia the type goes back to Boreal times, *Oldtiden*, ix, p. 131.

recurs in "Hallstatt" sites in Southern England [1] and survives
in Yorkshire [2] into the full La Tène period. The rims are most
distinctive. Some show an internal bevel, reminiscent of native
Bronze Age practice, and others an incipient eversion fore-
shadowing the Iron Age type; the typical rims are, however,
flattened down as if the potter had pressed her thumb on the
top of the brim while the forefinger rested against the wall just
below; there is, thus, often a slight ledge on the inside or outside,
sometimes on both sides.

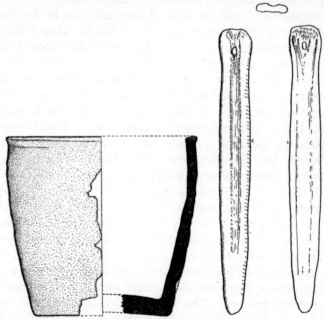

FIG. 48.—Pot and netting needle, Covesea. ⅓.

In the light of Miss Benton's discovery the same fabric can
be recognized among miscellaneous sherds both from the east
and the west of Scotland.[3] Nothing like it, however, is to be
found among the Cinerary Urns from cemeteries in the east of
Scotland. On the other hand at least, one urn from the urnfield

---

[1] e.g. *Ant. J.*, iv, p. 355.   [2] *Arch.*, lx, p. 263, fig. 9.
[3] The curious Cinerary Urn associated with gold armlets and smaller gold rings
at Duff House, Banffs., probably belongs to this class; certain sherds in the National
Museum come from Sordale Hill (Caithness), Tentsmuir (Fife), Traprain Law,
Glenshee (Perths.), Bragar and Port of Ness (Lewis), Rudh' an Dunain
(Skye), Coll.

at Largs, Ayrshire, closely approximates to the barrel type, just described. The same pottery has begun to turn up in Northern Ireland.[1] It seems, then, clear that flat-rimmed pottery here is not a direct evolution of the native Bronze Age fabrics but an intrusive group due to fresh settlers. On the other hand both at Old Keig in Aberdeenshire, and at Jarlshof in Shetland the fabric in question has been found in monuments that look like the outcome of autochthonous traditions. To understand the complication thus introduced we shall have now to survey areas hitherto ignored since Chapter III.

2. RECUMBENT STONE CIRCLES

In North-east Scotland within the roughly triangular area between the coasts and a line drawn from Speymouth to Bervie Bay there are traces of over seventy megalithic circles all sharing common peculiarities.

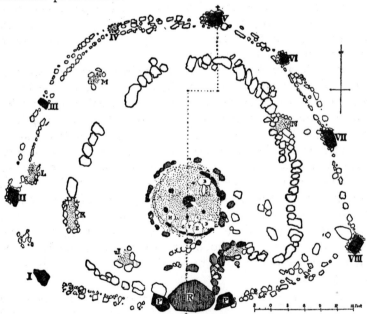

FIG. 49.—Plan of Garrol Wood Circle, after *PSAS*.

All appear to have been multiple circles consisting of three more or less concentric rings (Fig. 49). The outermost ring, generally very irregular, varies in diameter from 60 to 110 feet.

[1] Typical sherds from a cave on the shore at Ballintoy and from Rathlin Island.

As in the case of circles round cairns of the Clava type, the two tallest uprights, that may exceed 9 feet in height, usually lie to the south-south-west; the rest diminish progressively in size till the pair on the extreme north-north-east may be only 4 feet high each. Often the uprights are connected by or stand in a stony bank, but it is uncertain whether the bank is an original feature.[1]

Between the two tallest uprights there always lies a huge block, prostrate or on its edge. It may be 16 to 18 feet long and weigh up to 20 tons and is known as the *Recumbent*; the two uprights are accordingly termed Flankers. The ends of the recumbent generally fit close against the inner edges of the flankers, while its top is usually flat and exactly horizontal. Often the recumbent and flankers would lie well within the circumference of the ring were it a true circle.

In several cases [2] there is a conspicuous platform of stones heaped up against the base of the recumbent on the inside. And at least once [3] this platform was flanked by large slabs on edge at right angles to the recumbent. Cup-marks have been noted on the stones in several circles.[4]

Within the area delimited by the great circle there are frequently traces of a low cairn, hollow at the centre. The outer edge of the central cairn may be marked by a peristalith of uprights (which in denuded examples constitute the " second ring ") or by a simple kerb of tilted stones. The central hollow may be similarly delimited by an innermost ring of uprights. Sometimes the central hollow had been paved.[5] Owing to the ruinous condition of most of these monuments it is impossible to give average dimensions for the central ring cairn and its enclosed hollow. The following figures may, or may not, be representative; they give in feet the diameters of the recumbent ring, the central cairn, and the enclosed hollow respectively: Clune Hill [6] 58, 44, 18 ; Seanhinney,[7] 87 × 81, 64, 8 ; Garrol Wood, 63 × 51, 40 × 38, 12½.

---

[1] The uprights were not deeply embedded in the subsoil ; at Old Keig a pillar 9½ feet high rested in a socket 4½ by 3½ feet across but only 9 inches deep. The stone was really held in position by wedgers cleverly disposed round the edge of the socket.

[2] Castle Fraser, Hatten of Ardoyne, Tomnagorn, Dyce, *PSAS.*, xxxviii, p. 300 ; xxxv, p. 242 ; xxxiv, pp. 174, 190.

[3] Auchquhorthies of Manar, *PSAS.*, xxxv, p. 227.

[4] *PSAS.*, xxxv, p. 230 ; xxxvii, p. 134 ; lii, pp. 121 f.

[5] Castle Fraser, *PSAS.*, xxxviii, p. 300.

[6] *PSAS.*, liii, p. 70.   [7] *PSAS.*, xxxiv, p. 185.

The similarity of these recumbent stone circles to monuments of the Clava group [1] in which the central chamber and entrance have been suppressed is patent. Significant points of agreement are the central ring cairn with its peristalith of stones on edge, the reduction in the size of the orthostats from south to north, and the presence of cup-marks. Moreover, all the circles stand in the vicinity of good agricultural land. Though not juxtaposed in cemeteries, they do cluster round favoured regions ; thus there were six or seven round the Haugh of Alford. Finally, all that have been excavated yielded sepulchral deposits, generally of cremated remains, in the central hollow.

At Garrol Wood [2] the principal deposit was contained in a funnel-shaped depression in the central area, 2 ft. 2 in. across and 10 inches deep, lined with wedge-shaped blocks of granite. Four other deposits were found in pockets in the ground in the central area while in and outside the ring-cairn were little enclosures of stones, all empty. At Old Keig [3] I found in the innermost enclosure an irregular area of burnt earth which possibly marked the site of a funerary pyre. A trench grave, $4\frac{1}{2}$ feet long by $2\frac{3}{4}$ by $\frac{2}{3}$ ft., had been dug through the burnt earth. The site is known to have been disturbed in the seventeenth century, but fragments of burnt human bone were found in and around the central trench grave. Central graves are mentioned in connection with several other circles.[4]

From a purely architectural standpoint, therefore, one would conclude that the recumbent stone circles were a specialized local development of the Clava type. As was indicated on p. 52 the architects of those latter monuments occupied the Nairn, Ness, and Spey alluvia at a relatively early period and there developed their sepulchral traditions in isolation, scarcely affected by the Beaker invasion. At some time the inhabitants of these districts must have spread eastward into the coastal plain.

The relics from Old Keig somewhat complicate this picture. Urns have been reported from a number of circles, but prior to the excavation of Old Keig no fragments, large enough for diagnosis, had been preserved. Indeed prior to 1932, the only significant relics even vaguely connected with circles of the recumbent stone type were a wrist-guard, pierced by three holes,

---

[1] *Supra*, p. 51. [2] *PSAS.*, xxxix, pp. 195 f. [3] *PSAS.*, lxviii, p. 387.
[4] Candle Hill, Rayne ; Ardoyne, Anderson, ii, pp. 108 f.

allegedly found at Old Rayne (Candle Hill) [1] and stone cups with handles found in or near circles in the Alford district.[2] At Old Keig we secured numerous sherds. Most of the pottery was collected near the edge of the central trench-grave, but sherds were also found in front of, and under, the recumbent, under the east flanker and under the bank. All the sherds belonged to the hard ware already familiar from Covesea. Distinctive were squat, barrel-shaped urns with flattened rims and shallow bowls with rounded, inturned rims. Traces of finger-printing on the vase's neck immediately below the rim were observable on two sherds. The only other relics were small, round flint scrapers and a fragment from a thin flake, pressure-flaked on both faces, possibly an arrow-head, and a segment from a lignite armlet. The latter type, though foreign to the pure Bronze Age, was represented at Heathery Burn Cave and became popular on the Continent in the Hallstatt period.

Thus the culture of the builders of Old Keig and of the chief as whose burial-place it was erected was that of the " Late Bronze Age invaders ". Yet the idea of the circle itself and the technique of its construction belonged to a much older tradition, going back in Scotland perhaps a thousand years earlier to the chambered cairn-builders. If the flat-rimmed pottery really mark the advent of foreign intruders, these must have rallied to their support the survivors of the collectivist tradition who had maintained themselves apart from the Beaker-folk. Indeed, the new-comers for all their prestige, have evidently adopted much of the religion and funerary ritual of their native allies. Though cremation may be proper to the new-comers, the megalithic circle is the direct descendant of the " Neolithic " collective tomb. Here, then, we have before our eyes a striking instance of the absorption of an intrusive culture. In Aberdeenshire at least, the Hallstatt invaders fuse with the autochthonous stocks to produce a composite culture. Some recumbent stone circles may of course be earlier than this fusion.[3]

3. Bronze Age Villages in Orkney and Shetland

Similar conclusions may perhaps be drawn already from the results of excavations which A. O. Curle is still conducting at

---

[1] Anderson, ii, p. 109.   [2] *PSAS.*, i, p. 116.
[3] A few sherds of Beaker and perhaps of Food Vessel came to light at Loanhead of Daviot in 1934, but the bulk of the pottery belonged to the Old Keig type.

Jarlshof, Shetland. To understand these we must consider aspects of the island cultures hitherto ignored. The archipelagos provide ideal pasture land for sheep and excellent bases for fishing and for catching sea-fowl. But the severity of the climate obliged the islanders to devise substantial shelters to protect them against the constant gales. The scarcity of timber compelled them to use stone for building material and to translate into stone articles of furniture and structural elements that elsewhere would be made of perishable wood. Finally, sand-dunes have preserved some of these dwellings and their furniture for our inspection. In recent years two regular villages belonging to the Bronze Age have been examined. They give us a picture of aspects of island life, denied to us in the rest of Britain.

Skara Brae[1] in Orkney, though of very uncertain age, gives such a full picture of life under literally neolithic conditions that it may be described first. The village in its final form consisted of eight huts. It had been rebuilt several times so that four structural periods could be recognized, but no substantial differences in architecture or equipment could be distinguished between them. The huts were all built of unshaped stones from the beach, though thin slate or freestone slabs were used for special purposes, such as roofing. Some of the earlier huts may have been built in hollows excavated in the sandy soil and were certainly girt with relatively flimsy walls, backed up against sand or refuse. The later hut-walls might, however, be massive constructions 4 feet thick. Even so, when not backed up against the walls of the next dwelling, they were protected externally by a platform of heaped rubbish, usually kept in position by an outer revetment wall (Pl. II).

The several huts were connected by narrow passages, roofed with horizontal slabs 4 to $5\frac{1}{2}$ feet above the flagged floor. The passages, like the huts, were buried in refuse so that in its final stage at least the village was entirely underground, though the ground beneath which it lay was artificial—peat-ash and kitchen refuse mixed with sand.

Each hut was a self-contained unit varying in floor-space from 21 by 20 to 14 by 13 feet square (Fig. 50). The sides are straight and roughly parallel, but the corners are rounded. The walls corbel inwards, like those of collective tombs, particularly at the corners, but even at 8 feet above the floor

[1] Details in Childe, *Skara Brae.*

the highest surviving course in a corner overhangs only 2¾ feet, so that it is very doubtful whether the whole area (here 17 by 16 feet) was ever covered by a beehive roof of stone. Opening off each hut are from one to four small cells in the thickness of the walls. They are roofed either by corbelling, as in the cells at Quoyness, or by flat lintels. In three huts a drain-channel

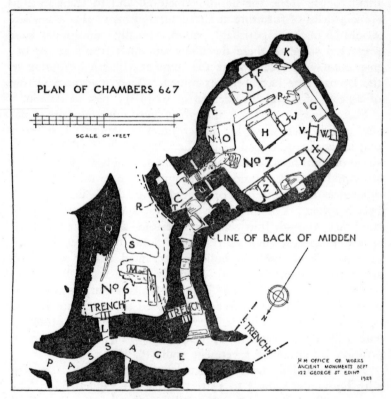

FIG. 50.—Hut 7, Skara Brae.

covered by flagstones runs out from one cell so that the cells in question may be regarded as privies.

Each hut was entered through a doorway, about 3¾ feet high and less than 2 feet wide, provided with checks and a bar-hole to keep the door in position. In the centre of the floor is a square hearth, bordered by kerbstones set on edge. Against the wall on either side of the hearth stands an enclosure formed of slabs on edge; these enclosures agree precisely with the fixed plank beds of Norwegian peasants and, strewn with grass and heather, doubtless did serve as sleeping-places. Stone pillars at the enclosure's corners supported a sort of bed-canopy while recesses or ambries in the wall behind may have been used by the bed's occupants as keeping-places for personal possessions, precisely as in Hebridean shielings last century.

Built out from, or let into, the rear wall are two tiers of shelves, supported by three pillars or piers and resembling a kitchen dresser. Several cists of thin slabs with the joints luted with clay to keep them water-tight are let into the floor near the hut's corners. The floor was of stamped refuse, but the entrance, one or two corners, and the beds were always paved.

The village seems to have belonged to an isolated and self-sufficing community. Its inhabitants lived principally on the flesh of calves and lambs, shell-fish gathered on the shore and presumably milk. No evidence was found for agriculture, for fishing with a line or with a harpoon, nor for hunting. The cattle and sheep were certainly domesticated, but belonged to peculiar specialized breeds, conspicuously different from the Neolithic and Iron Age cattle of Britain; gelding was practised. Peat was probably the sole fuel employed, and fire was kindled by striking flint or chert against nodules of hæmatite,[1] as by the Cinerary Urn folk on the mainland. Metal was neither worked nor used in the village.

Ground stone celts served as axes, split beach pebbles as knives, ox-scapulæ as shovels and the metapodials of sheep or deer, split longitudinally from the distal end or obliquely near the proximal end, as awls. The celts might be mounted in perforated hafts of antler. Chisel-like tools were made from the metapodials of oxen. Generally the proximal end of the bone was split off obliquely and a small oval hole pierced just below the distal articulation (Fig. 51). More rarely the proximal end was utilized; and the transverse perforation omitted. Small tools like thin celts were also made from slices of cattle marrow-bones; they agree precisely with those from Kenny's Cairn in Caithness, and the beaker grave near Cawdor Castle.[2]

Pottery was manufactured. The paste comprises very large rock fragments, and the firing is inadequate. The vessels were built up out of superposed rings, like Peterborough bowls and

---

[1] p. 135 above; cf. Callanders, *PSAS.*, lxv, p. 99.
[2] pp. 72, 99 above.

Cinerary Urns. Most sherds seemed to belong to large cooking pots, but reconstruction was impossible. The rims were internally bevelled like those of Food Vessels and Cinerary Urns. The commonest mode of decoration was the application of strips, rings, or pellets of finer clay, precisely as on Encrusted Urns. Incised sherds were found in the lower layers only. One bore cord impressions. Generally the patterns were drawn with a blunt instrument on a slip of finer clay. The designs include

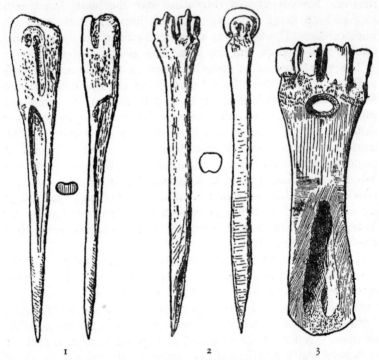

1   2   3

Fig. 51.—Piercing tools (⅔) and bone adze (⅜). Skara Brae.

the sole example of a spiral ever found on a hand-made pot in the British Isles. The pots were covered with circular lids, roughly chipped out of slate. Basins and paint-pots were fashioned out of whales' vertebræ while mortars, paint-pots, and troughs were hammered out of blocks of sandstone.

No implements indicative of a textile industry were discovered in the village and very few needles of bone. The villagers must have dressed in skins. Such would be fastened with bone pins. These generally have a loop on the side of the shaft and pre-

PLATE XIII

CARVED STONE OBJECTS, SKARA BRAE $\frac{5}{7}$

[face p. 180

sumably copy bronze pins, like that from the Glentrool hoard. The person was painted with white, red, blue, and yellow earth-pigments, conserved in little receptacles of stone or whalebone. Strings of beads were worn. The beads were made from cows' teeth, from segments cut off the marrow-bones of sheep, or from walrus ivory. The teeth of killer whales and ivory pendants of the same shape were worn as amulets, as among the Esquimaux.

Finally the site yielded several enigmatical stone objects very accurately and skilfully shaped by hammering and grinding—a double axe of shale replete with a handle in the same material, several spiked objects and stone balls carved with knobs or flat bosses (Pl. XIII). The last-named belong to an extensive group widely distributed over Scotland and even to Westmorland and Northern Ireland, but commonest in Aberdeenshire. No specimens have been found in a datable context, but the distribution would be compatible with a date shortly after A.D. 400 for the mainland specimens. These curious objects, like many rougher implements of flagstone found so abundantly in the islands, may be largely translations into stone of wooden artifacts.

It is still impossible to assess the role of Skara Brae in Scottish prehistory. Its occupants evidently constituted an isolated and exclusive community and had developed a highly specialized adjustment to their peculiar environment. The blending of "Neolithic" and Bronze Age traditions suggests contact with the mainland down to the time when the Encrusted Urn began to develop there. At the same time there are hints of connections with Scandinavia and the Baltic lands going back far beyond the Vikings to the "Arctic" culture or its older ancestor of the Boreal forests—i.e. the perforated antler hafts, the bone chisels, the double-axe, and spiked implements.[1]

The village, now being explored by Curle at Jarlshof,[2] in its situation among the sand-hills on the shore and in its construction of natural boulders from the beach recalls Skara Brae. But the culture is definitely in advance of that just described. This need not imply any very material difference in date ; the Shetland Islands possess natural resources—copper lodes and steatite—that might attract progressive colonists earlier than the more southerly archipelago. Several contiguous dwellings have

---

[1] Parallels to the latter from Finland are illustrated in *Skara Brae,* pl. lx.
[2] Preliminary reports, *PSAS.,* lxvi, pp. 113 ff. ; lxvii, pp. 83 ff. ; lxviii, pp. 224 ff.

been uncovered, but they were not as a whole occupied simultaneously. Four structural phases at least have been recognized. All seem anterior to the erection of an adjacent broch—a type of fortress distinctive of the Early Iron Age in

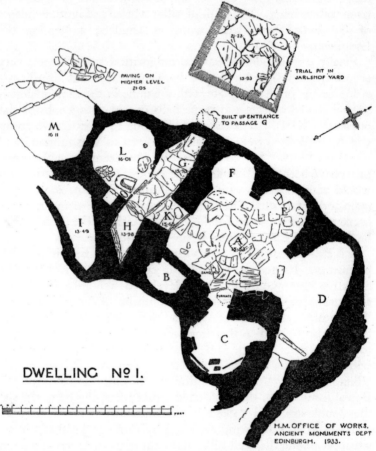

PAVING ON
HIGHER LEVEL
21·05

TRIAL PIT IN
JARLSHOF YARD

BUILT UP ENTRANCE
TO PASSAGE G

M
16·11

L
16·01

G

F

I
13·49

H
13·98

K
13·6

E

A
13·03

B

J

D

C

DWELLING Nº I.

....f....

H.M. OFFICE OF WORKS,
ANCIENT MONUMENTS DEPT
EDINBURGH. 1933.

FIG. 52.—Dwelling at Jarlshof, after *PSAS*. The original entrance had been at
K through passage G : the door in D is secondary.

the north—but iron was already coming into use locally at the time of the latest occupation, and known even earlier.

Like the earliest structures at Skara Brae, the Jarlshof dwellings were sometimes erected in hollows excavated to a depth of 2 or 3 feet, in the sandy soil or in the refuse from earlier occupations.[1]

[1] *PSAS.*, lxvii, p. 94.

The excavations would be lined with a boulder wall, faced on the inside only, but above ground an outer face was added bringing the thickness of the wall up to 3 or 4 feet. Only natural boulders were employed in these walls, and in the earlier houses pinnings—small stones used to fill up corners and crevices between boulders—were lacking; in the latest buildings the boulders might be laid in clay mortar. As far as it is permissible to generalize from the existing data, the prevailing type of house consisted of a large chamber or court, in one case about 10 by 9 feet square, with a couple of curvilinear cells or deep bays opening off either side and a larger compartment at one end. Both the "court" and the accessory chambers might be paved, and a hearth, formed of a horizontal slab with a slab on edge behind it, was found in one cell. The terminal compartment in one case at least served as a byre.

Attached to a house of phase II was a ruined Earth-house or *souterrain*—a curved gallery, 1¼ to 2½ feet wide, excavated in the ground and walled, like the houses, with boulder masonry. A complete Earth-house with the lintels of its roof still in position was found communicating with a later dwelling.[1]

The Shetland villagers possessed cattle and sheep, some similar to those kept in the islands to-day and others larger, and also ponies.[2] Moreover, they certainly cultivated barley (bere) which they may have ground in very deep saddle querns or troughs. Shell fish—particularly cockles and limpets—were collected and eaten, but fish bones are surprisingly rare. As in Orkney, peat was used for fuel, but the bronze-smith employed charcoal, derived from oak and other trees.

Knives and saw-like tools were made of slate, and clubs, axes, adzes, and hammers of grit and pebbles, but in no cases were the edges of the axes finished by grinding, as in the celts from Skara Brae. Scrapers were made of quartz, there being no flint in the islands. Adze and chisel-like tools were made from the metapodials of cattle. Some were hollow throughout, the articulating surface of the proximal end having been broken through, producing a sort of socketed chisel—a type familiar on the Baltic from Boreal times[3]; in others the distal articulation is preserved and the implements agree exactly with Fig. 51, 3, save that the transverse perforation is lacking.

[1] *PSAS.*, lxviii, pp. 238, 247.   [2] *PSAS.*, lxvii, pp. 128 ff.
[3] *MSAN.*, 1919, p. 306; 1926–7, p. 51; *Real.*, xiv, p. 519.

Awls were made from the metapodials of sheep cut off obliquely near the proximal end as in Fig. 51, A 2, but were less common than at Skara Brae. For shovels, which must have been constantly needed for clearing away the sand, the villagers used not only ox scapulæ but also heart-shaped slabs of slate perforated near the centre with an oval hole affording a very convenient hand-grip.

Bronze was, however, used at Jarlshof, and even worked there. Indeed by phase II (no moulds or bronzes have been yet found in a hut of phase I), a bronze-smith had established his work-shop in the house explored in 1931. This is remarkable ; prior to that year one minute blade was the sole bronze known from the Shetland Islands. At Jarlshof Curle has found countless fragments of moulds for socketed axes, " V "-type swords (with " T "-pommel and ricasso), a socketed knife, and a disc-shaped pin-head with a conical boss in the centre as well as a double-edged tanged knife (Fig. 42, 1). All the types are those proper to the Late Bronze Age of the British Isles. Only the pin may have had a Scandinavian ancestry, but the type had become acclimatized in North Britain and Ireland.

The processes of manufacture employed seem also to be the same as are attested for Yorkshire and the Scottish Lowlands. These processes have been thoroughly elucidated by Curle's [1] masterly study of the mould fragments and jets. Most of the fragments belong to valve moulds of baked clay—the stone moulds, employed in the casting of Middle and Early Bronze Age types, have been abandoned. A pile of the clay used for their manufacture together with the stone trough in which it was kneaded was found in the house.   The valves—halves of the mould—had been built up on a pattern, sometimes of wood. After preparation, the two valves were keyed together and wrapped in an envelope of coarser clay while a funnel or gate was fitted to one end. The mould was then baked before the metal was run in.

In the case of a socketed axe the clay core, to represent the hollow socket of the axe, was probably modelled only after the valves had been baked. Grooves were cut in the butt end of the core to serve as ducts through which the metal might be run into the cavity between the core and the valves (Fig. 53). The moulds when completed were stood upright in a hollow in the house floor filled with sand and the metal poured in.

[1] *PSAS.,* lxvii, pp. 118 ff.

The mould would, of course, have to be broken to extract the casting.

It is thus clear that Late Bronze Age tools and weapons were being manufactured in Shetland on a considerable scale. The requisite copper might have been mined in the islands; the tin at least must have been imported and probably the wood or charcoal necessary for the furnaces.

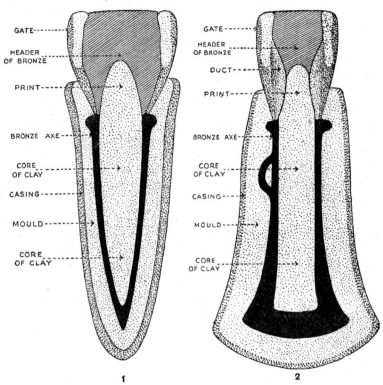

GATE
HEADER OF BRONZE
PRINT
BRONZE AXE
CORE OF CLAY
CASING
MOULD
CORE OF CLAY

GATE
HEADER OF BRONZE
DUCT
PRINT
BRONZE AXE
CORE OF CLAY
CASING
MOULD
CORE OF CLAY

1   2

FIG. 53.—Reconstruction of the mould for a socketed axe by A. O. Curle, after *PSAS.*

But in addition to bronze, the islanders were acquainted with the production of iron. Iron slag [1] was found in a deposit of phase II. But evidently the islanders found bronze cheaper and more efficient; it was not till phase IV that iron began to oust bronze in the island's economy. So Jarlshof offers a brilliant illustration of that overlap between the two metals, anticipated on theoretical grounds.

[1] *PSAS.,* lxviii, p. 303.

The pottery associated with this Late Bronze Age industry and appearing already in phase I—i.e. before the moulds—belongs to the flat-rimmed class already described. But owing to the use of steatite temper the Jarlshof vessels, especially in phase I, often appear much finer than anything hitherto described. They may be highly polished and sometimes very thin. On later sherds we have traces of the angular shoulders characteristic of the English "Hallstatt" wares. One sherd from the oldest house was decorated with a grooved chevron, thoroughly Hallstatt in effect. A rim, flattened to form an internal flange, is also interesting owing to parallels from All Cannings Cross in Wiltshire; it belongs to phase III.[1]

Besides pottery the villagers used vessels of steatite and other stone. Among the latter was a fragmentary vessel of sandstone, four-sided, quite like the steatite urn from Little Asta, mentioned on p. 140. It establishes roughly the date of the burials with steatite urns in the northern isles.

Two whorls from the latest occupation are the sole indications of a textile industry, but steatite beads and armlets were common.

Architecturally, Jarlshof illustrates a house-type which has striking parallels as far afield as Cornwall and Wales.[2] But the southern specimens are not demonstrably older than the Scottish. Indeed, this sort of house is so well adapted to a windy northern clime that it might well have arisen on the islands. In fact, if the collective tombs of Quoyness and Kewing Hill copy the houses of the living, the plan in question would go back to Neolithic times in Orkney. The huts at Skara Brae with their cells grouped round a central room could be assimilated to the same plan, as Hencken has noted.[3] It must not, then, be assumed off hand that the Jarlshof houses were introduced by the invaders; they may rather denote an autochthonous type that the latter took over.

The Earth-house raises more complex problems. We shall find such common in Northern and North-eastern Scotland during the Iron Age. But even on the mainland we shall see that the idea must be older than the local Iron Age. Outside Scotland, Earth-houses are very common in Ireland, where they

---

[1] Cunnington, *All Cannings Cross*, pl. 36, 1.
[2] Hencken, *Cornwall*, pp. 138, 152.
[3] *Arch.*, lxxxiii, p. 281.

are termed *souterrains*, and, under the name of *fogous*, in Cornwall,[1] while there are analogous refuges in Gaul,[2] most numerous in the modern Poitou, the region occupied in Cæsar's day by the Pictones. No Cornish or Gaulish examples have yielded relics certainly earlier than the second century B.C. Indeed the Earth-house is the sort of refuge that is most likely to have been created in a cold and windy environment like that of the far north. MacRitchie[3] has insisted on its resemblances to the winter houses of the Esquimaux. And comparisons with structures of un-certain age among the Lapps[4] are worthy of note.

The steatite vessels from Jarlshof and the socketed bone chisels open vistas of possible contacts with Norway and the Baltic; they might, however, be explained, like those noted at Skara Brae, as due to ancient participation of the northern isles in the Arctic Stone Age of Scandinavia. The Jarlshof bronzes are essentially British or Britannico-Hibernian, and the pottery too can be paralleled, though not necessarily exclusively, in England and Northern Ireland.[5]

4. THE EXTENT OF THE LATE BRONZE AGE INVASION

The Late Bronze Age invasion must be considered in the light of all the facts here marshalled. The flat-rimmed pottery suffices to indicate a considerable influx of new settlers to Cale-donia during the period when socketed axes and swords were current and to establish links with Northern Ireland. In Shetland it is possible, but by no means certain, that the bronze types were introduced by the new settlers. On the Scottish mainland that is still less certain. Such uncertainty is peculiarly regrettable since by itself flat-rimmed pottery is not distinctive enough to establish the origin of its makers.

Miss Benton was evidently inclined to associate her pottery at Covesea with the eastern (Central European) group of orna-ments described on p. 163, and thus to deduce an invasion of Eastern Scotland from the Continent, coming direct across the North Sea without touching England. Such a movement is

[1] Hencken, *Cornwall*, pp. 140 f.
[2] Blanchard, *Les Refuges souterrains de la France*.
[3] *PSAS.*, li, p. 192.
[4] *Finskt Museum*, xxxv (1928), pp. 1-24.
[5] *Ant. J.*, xiv, p. 182.

still possible. It would be parallel to that which impinged upon England at Scarborough, but would presumably start rather further north from North-west Germany. With a little straining even the Norwegian parallels to our steatite vessels might be connected with such a movement. The Irish souterrains, perhaps even the Cornish and Gaulish ones, would have to be connected with the same migration. It would thus resemble, both in scope and direction, the Viking expansion a thousand years later. The invaders would have annexed the north-eastern coasts and islands of Scotland and from these bases have descended upon Ireland and Cornwall, just as the Viking raiders actually did.

The explicitly Britannico-Hibernian character of the bronzes associated with the flat-rimmed pots is a serious, but not fatal,[1] obstacle to this thesis. On the evidence of the metal types the invasion of Scotland should be an extension of the " Hallstatt " invasion of England, already impregnated with distinctively British traditions. And most likely it would reach us coastwise via Ireland ; the numerous slashing swords and hoards from the West Highlands and islands and the flat-rimmed sherds, noted on p. 172, would then mark the route of the invaders. Naturally, the idea of the Earth-house would arrive from Ireland at the same time. On this view the settlements at Covesea and near Old Keig would mark the last ripples of the wave, not its first impact on Scottish shores.

Both alternatives must for the moment be left open. But three points may be taken as established. The " Late Bronze Age invaders " were in fact iron-users, but, having established a footing in Ireland and Cornwall, preferred bronze tools and weapons for reasons already set forth. Secondly, the invasion established a continuity of culture between the coastal plain south of the Moray Firth and the coasts and islands north thereof. This continuity was, we shall find, interrupted by the advent of the " castle complex " to the far north ; in the islands and Caithness the full Iron Age was completely dominated by the broch culture ; in Aberdeenshire contemporary developments were based mainly on the " Late Bronze Age " tradition, and many Iron Age types common to this region and the islands must be regarded as belonging culturally, if not in time, to this " Late Bronze Age ".

---

[1] Our " pre-Vikings ", using Shetland as a base for descents on Ireland, might have brought back thence captive smiths who would produce bronzes of Hibernian type !

Finally, the same cultural unity also embraced Ireland, at least Northern Ireland, again before the rise of the " castle complex ". To this period of unity must be assigned the primary diffusion of the Earth-house idea which is only accidentally connected with the castle complex.   And so the Cornish fogous must belong to this phase at least culturally — and very likely chronologically too, since its culture presupposes a combination of Cornish tin with Irish copper. In a later Chapter we shall see that the Earth-house, set in this context, would provide one possible solution for the Pictish question.

X

KELTIC FORTRESSES AND REFUGES

1. THE DISTRIBUTION OF IRON AGE POPULATION

THE Late Bronze Age invasion was but the first of a series of intrusions which enormously augmented the total population of Scotland. During the long centuries of the Bronze Age we can recognize only tiny scattered groups of peaceable herdsmen and peasants. By the time of Agricola the land was intensively settled by sedentary, if warlike, farmers. According to Tacitus [1] the Caledonian army at Mons Graupius mustered 30,000. The historian has doubtless exaggerated the figure to magnify the glory of his hero and the Roman arms. But the archæological data, as represented on Map IV, would be quite compatible with soberer inferences from written history. The map reveals a dense population filling up most of the areas chosen for rural settlement throughout later historical times in striking contrast to the chequered picture presented by Maps II and III.

It is true that the character of the record has changed. Instead of burial cairns and funerary vases, we have to rely now exclusively on settlement sites. And admittedly these have often a better chance of survival than sepulchral monuments. A cairn or stone circle can be all too easily removed from a field or a roadway ; an earthwork or even a stone fort can only be completely obliterated with extravagant labour, and such obliteration is seldom necessary.

Moreover, we admittedly lack any guarantee that the monuments here plotted are contemporary ; indeed, unless our unit of time exceed three centuries, the reverse must be assumed. Very few of the monuments have been scientifically excavated, and such as have, were exceedingly poor in relics. Still nearly all the monuments here considered conform to types, representative examples of which have yielded evidence of occupation at some time between 200 B.C. and A.D. 200. We are therefore

---

[1] Agricola, c. 29.

justified in drawing certain conclusions from our map of them : the population must have been vastly increased ; its distribution has been radically altered ; the whole economy of the country has been transformed.

The increase in population may in part reflect an increased food supply due to improved methods of cultivation, but is so great as to imply immigrations into Caledonia on a large scale. Actually, as in England, the anthropologists [1] agree that the physical character of the average inhabitants had been entirely changed between the Early Bronze Age and the Iron Age. Such mass migrations may be the outcome of ethnic movements and political events on the Continent during the last centuries before our era. The great expansion of the Kelts and the subsequent westward spread of Germanic tribes are known from Greek and Roman writers. The advance of the legions under Cæsar supplemented the blinder forces of folk-migration. The more reckless would seek to preserve their freedom in barbarism beyond the seas rather than submit to the blessings of civilization under the *pax romana*. In A.D. 43 the same pressure was applied to Britain. Forty years later the legions crossed the Forth.

While such events provided motives for the retreat of Keltic tribes into the fastnesses of Caledonia, the use of iron alone made that possible. Cheap and relatively durable iron tools for tree-felling and ditching were an indispensable presupposition for intensive settlement on our heavily wooded and marshy soils.

Moreover, the Romanization of France and England opened up fresh opportunities, even for barbarians living beyond the frontiers. Under the *pax romana* Gallia and Britannia soon waxed rich ; they formed a market for the slaves, beasts, pelts, and wool, that northern barbarians could supply. The fat provinces and the trade to their ports offered rich booty to raiders and pirates.

Finally, the natives of Scotland themselves were brought into immediate contact with the Roman conquerors.[2] Already in A.D. 81 Agricola had established a series of guard-houses (*præsidia*) and permanent forts from the Forth to the Clyde, closing the isthmus and " banishing the foe as it were to another island ".[3] Two years later the Governor crossed the Forth and, after the victory at Mons Graupius, advanced into Aberdeenshire, while

[1] *Biometrika*, xviii, p. 101.
[2] On the Romans in Scotland, see *JRS.*, ix, pp. 111 ff. ; *BRGK.*, xix, pp. 20 ff. ; Macdonald, *The Roman Wall in Scotland*, 1934.
[3] Tacitus, Agricola, c. 23.

his fleet sailed round the island. By no means all the territory traversed was retained in any sense ; only marching camps are known from Angus and further north. But permanent garrisons were installed in Perthshire at Ardoch, Strageth and as far as Inchtutil near Perth, and Dalginross, near Comrie. A regular road guarded by watch-towers linked these outposts to the fort at Camelon on the isthmus, which was itself connected with the better pacified Province by the road through Lauderdale, past Newstead, and across the Cheviots near Carter Bar to Corbridge on the Tyne.

These outposts in Scotland were held for about thirty years. But the Romans' grip on Scotland was precarious ; the posts had to be rebuilt twice after attacks by natives and were eventually abandoned about A.D. 115, when the legions were withdrawn at least to the Tyne-Solway line. This line was definitely established as the frontier of the Empire by Hadrian about 122. But after a serious revolt in North Britain in 139, the legions returned again into Scotland under Lollius Urbicus, and in 142 the Forth–Clyde frontier was re-established. The isthmus was defended by the great ditch and turf bank, known as the Antonine vallum. Along it nineteen permanent forts were erected on the sites of Agricola's old stations ; a harbour was equipped at Dumbarton ; and a second road to the western end of the vallum via Annandale and Clydesdale was constructed to supplement the old one through Newstead to Corbridge.

But Galloway was left unsubdued on the flank, and the subjugation of the more easterly tribes can hardly have been thorough. In 155 there was a rising when the Roman hold on Scotland was more or less interrupted for some three years. About 180 a still more serious disturbance broke out, and by 185 the Antonine vallum was finally abandoned, the frontier of the Empire being withdrawn for ever to the Tyne–Solway line.

Therewith, any Roman occupation of Scotland ceased. But about 207 Septimius Severus undertook punitive operations on a large scale against the tribes north of the Forth. He may even have reached Aberdeenshire. But no annexation followed, and the troops were withdrawn.

Though purely military in character (like the British occupation of Baluchistan and similar frontiers of India), the Roman occupations profoundly affected the life and culture of the natives. The military posts with their attendant camp-followers and merchants provided the barbarians with an example of civilization, with a mart for their products, and with a source for obtaining urban manufactures. On the other hand, military intervention must have disrupted tribal organization and impoverished its victims terribly. Incidentally, the occupation enormously complicates the archæological record. And its vicissitudes are a warning of the extent of tribal displacements to be expected during the period under review.

With the available material it is hopeless to try and disentangle details of such movements. We shall here survey the monuments known to have been erected or occupied before, or shortly after, the Roman conquest with a view primarily of ascertaining the origin of the pre-Roman settlers. The monuments in question might provisionally be divided between three main groups: defensive constructions—forts and castles; refuges—crannogs and earth-houses; and undefended villages. Over 1,500 constructions of the first group are still visible. It is premature to attempt a rigorous classification, for the percentage excavated or even accurately planned is infinitesimal. But certain well-defined groups do stand out and do afford clues as to the origins of their builders.

2. Forts

(i) Gallic Forts

Three forts, possessing conspicuous architectural peculiarities and a significantly restricted distribution along the east coast, constitute a group which claims pride of place since one of its members has yielded the oldest definitely Iron Age relic found in Scotland or indeed north of the Tees. All three are girt with double-faced walls of good masonry, the faces being tied together by wooden beams at right angles to the line of the walls. This method of construction caught Cæsar's attention in Gaul and is termed the *murus gallicus* technique.

At Burghead (Elginshire)[1] on the Moray Firth, the inner wall enclosed an area of 520 by 300 feet. It was 24 feet wide, faced with quarry-dressed freestone slabs internally and externally. The facing walls themselves were each 3 to 3½ feet wide and were tied together by transverse beams of oak, 6 to 9 inches thick. The transverse beams were joined together by beams

[1] *PSAS.*, xxv, pp. 436 ff.

and planks, laid parallel to the wall faces, which were clamped together with iron bolts and supported layers of rubble.

Two forts, overlooking the Tay estuary on spurs of the Ochils, each termed Castle Law, behind Abernethy and Forgandenny respectively, illustrate the same structural principles applied to smaller citadels. At Abernethy [1] there was an " inner bailey " 180 by 90 feet in area, girt with a wall 18 to 25 feet thick. In the outer face a double row of rectangular holes for beams, 12 by 10 to 10 by 8 inches across, was visible (Fig. 54). The channels for the beams could be followed well into the mass of the wall, but did not run through the inner face. An outer rampart, joined to the inner one by a traverse, exhibited a similar structure. There was a rock-cut cistern in the inner court, while beyond the outer wall an earthen bank seems to have extended the fortified area to include a small loch.

FIG. 54.—Walls of Gallic fort near Abernethy showing holes for beams, after *PSAS*.

The acropolis at Forgandenny [2] (Fig. 55) was a rectangle with rounded corners, 228 by 65 feet in area and girt with two built stone walls 18 and 15 feet thick respectively. Beam-holes, as at Abernethy, were visible in the inner wall but on both faces, and post holes were also recognized right against it inside and outside. The gateway through the outer wall, 10 feet wide, was equipped with jambs and holes for a bar ; no entrance to the innermost enclosure was located. This stone-built citadel stood within a complex system of banks, some with ditches outside them.

The Abernethy fort yielded the oldest Iron Age relic discovered in Scotland, a bronze brooch of La Tène I type, and other objects of specifically pre-Roman character. No Roman relics have been recovered from any fort in this group.

[1] *PSAS.*, xxxiii, pp. 18 ff.   [2] *PSAS.*, xxvii, pp. 16 ff.

The *murus gallicus* construction is represented only by one possible example from England, Corley in Warwickshire.[1] But it is common throughout France and Belgium.[2] Our forts therefore probably mark the landings of small bands of invaders who had crossed the North Sea from Gaul direct to the Moray Firth and the mouth of the Tay (there is a fine harbour at Burghead). They mark probably the earliest landings of La Tène Kelts in Scotland.

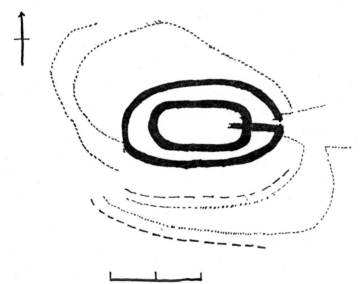

FIG. 55.—Plan of Gallic fort near Forgandenny.

(ii) *Vitrified Forts*

Over sixty stone-built forts in Scotland exhibit vitrifaction[3]; the stones forming the ramparts have been fused and thus cemented together. Such forts are found on the east in Angus and Aberdeenshire, and round the Beauly and Dornoch Firths, then in the Great Glen, and along the west coast from Skye to Kintyre, Islay, Arran, and Galloway. There is one isolated example on the Lammermuirs in East Lothian. Vitrified forts

[1] *Antiquity,* v, p. 84.
[2] *Dechelette,* iv, pp. 491 ff.
[3] List with plans in Christison, pp. 170 f. ; add Trudernish Point, Islay, An Knap (Sannox), Arran (*PSAS.,* lxii, p. 240), and Harelaw (RC. *E. Lothian,* No. 254). Many of Christison's examples, though included in Map IV, are doubtful.

always occupy hilltops but generally follow a regular plan—
a rectangle or elongated oval with parallel sides—regardless of
the contours of the land.[1] At Finavon the wall has been found
running dead straight for over 100 feet quite irrespective of
marked inequalities in the underlying rock (Pl. XIV, 1).   In the
eastern counties the enclosures attain a length of from 400 to
600 feet with a width of 100 to 150 feet.   There is seldom, if
ever, an encircling fosse, but the principal enceinte may be subdivided and provided with a rock-hewn well.   At Dunagoil in
Bute the entrance was provided with checks and holes for
a bar.

At Dunagoil [2] the wall was faced with coursed masonry on
both sides, the mass of vitrified material lying between the faces.
Mann believes that the facing walls were raised to a height of
3 feet or so, with rubble between them.   Then brushwood was
piled on the rubble, sealed down with clay and set alight.   The
core thus heated would have been converted into a sort of
molten cement to bond the faces together.   When it had set,
the process would be repeated till the desired height of wall
had been reached.   At Duntroon, Crinan,[3] the inner wall face
and the core showed vitrifaction, but not the outer face.   Wilson
concluded that the heat had been supplied by wood fires kindled
in the interior of the fort where the bed-rock showed the effect
of heat for a distance of 12 feet out from the wall base.   At
Finavon the wall is 20 feet wide at its base.   The inner face,
with marked outward batter, still stands 8 to 10 feet high,
but of the outer face only massive foundation courses rising
perpendicularly survive.   Neither of the built faces is vitrified
but blocks of stones fused together cover the external slope,
and others have fallen from higher levels into the interior.   A
temperature of 1,100° C. was required to fuse the sandstone slabs
composing these walls, and there is no trace of the use of a flux.[4]

La Tène II or III fibulæ were obtained from Dunagoil and
probably from Dun Fheurain.   Neither Finavon, Dunagoil, nor
Duntroon, yielded any relics of the Roman period, but *terra
sigillata* and other first-century relics were found at Dun Fheurain.
The Mote of Mark (Kirkcudbright) [5] was certainly occupied both

---

[1] e.g. Finavon (Angus), Tap o' North (Aberdeens.), Craig Phadrig (Inverness),
Dunagoil (Bute), Carradale (Kintyre), Cnoc Farrell (Ross).
[2] T. Bute, *NHS.*, 1925, p. 60.   [3] *PSAS.*, xxxix, p. 275.
[4] From tests carried out by the courtesy of Mr. Wallace Thorneycroft.
[5] *PSAS.*, xlviii, p. 165 ; lxvi, p. 284.

PLATE XIV

1 INTERIOR MASONRY OF WALLS AT FINAVON

2 FORT ON DRUIM AN DUIN

in the first or second century A.D. and again in the eighth or
ninth, but it, like other vitrified forts from Galloway, is anomalous
in many respects. On the whole the foundation of the forts in
Eastern Caledonia and even on the west coast north of the
Clyde must go back well beyond the beginning of our era to
a date not far removed from that of the Gallic forts. Since
vitrified forts are not known in England, but common in the
Keltic lands of the Continent as far north as Belgium, it may
be inferred that they were introduced by invaders who came
direct across the North Sea. These would have settled first on
the east coasts north of the Tay and thence spread across to the
west through the Great Glen and possibly also through the
Tay or Tummel gaps and via Loch Awe. Arrived on the west
coast, they must have taken ship for Islay, Kintyre, Arran, Bute,
and eventually Galloway, Ireland, and North Wales.

(iii) *Castles*

Under the term " castle " may provisionally be grouped
together a very miscellaneous assemblage of stone-built forts,
all seemingly later than those hitherto described. All are characterized by the excellent masonry of the massive walls and their
small size. The space comprised within the enceinte is normally
less than 100 feet across and, indeed, rarely exceeds 65 feet.
Such small enclosures could not, even in emergencies, house
many families ; they cannot be villages or tribal refuges, but
can only have served as the domicile of a war-like chief and his
retainers.

While many of these castles crown a natural eminence or are
perched on a precipitous cliff, others stand on quite low ground
beside modern farmhouses without any natural defences. Even
so, ditches and other outworks are abnormal, though certain types
of castle regularly stand within a fortified enclosure. The distribution of such structures is significant. They are common all
along the west coast from Galloway to the Hebrides. From the
west they may be supposed to have spread eastward—coastwise
round Cape Wrath to Orkney, Shetland, and Caithness, and by
land up Loch Awe to the Tay Basin and Angus. Such a distribution is significantly like that of the chambered tombs ; the
significance of the analogy is enhanced by the fact that individual
castles often stand close to convenient landing-places. It may

justify a provisional treatment of a number of diverse structures as an unit.

Some simple castles are strictly circular and preserve this plan irrespective of natural contours : an area 35 to 90 feet in diameter is girt with a double-faced ring-wall of stone 10 to 12 feet thick. Thus far, the ring castles exactly resemble Irish cashels. But their doorways seem always to have been provided with checks, a feature by no means often visible in cashels. Ring castles are not rare in Western Galloway,[1] Arran,[2] and Argyll, and some of the Western Isles.[3] From Argyll they extend across Central Perthshire [4] to Angus, and perhaps to Fife.[5] A well-preserved example near the Mull of Kintyre is provided by Borgadail [6]; its wall, still standing 7 feet high and 11–12 feet thick, encloses a space 36 feet in diameter, and is pierced by a doorway 4½ feet wide internally and 3½ externally. The ring forts in Strath Tummel and adjacent Perthshire glens attain an internal diameter of 50 feet ; the wall widens from 10 to 13 feet on either side of the entrance, which does not exceed 5 feet in width, but is provided with checks. Most Central Perthshire forts stand low down on slopes ; but Watson notes that many command the mouth of a pass. In Angus and perhaps in Fife, similar ring forts stand within larger enclosures. Kemp's Castle on Turin Hill (90 feet in diameter) is a good example.

The only datable relic from a ring castle is a sherd of first-century *terra sigillata* from a fort 30 feet in diameter and girt with a 15 ft. wall, supplemented by an external ditch, at Aitnock near Dalry, Ayrshire.[7] But flat-rimmed pottery of Hallstatt aspect is reported from the ruined ring of Rudh' an Dunain, Skye. Watson attributes his Perthshire group to the Verturiones, a branch of the Picts not mentioned before A.D. 300. The ring forts here and farther east may, in any case, be regarded as intrusions from the west ; indeed, the whole series may possibly denote Irish infiltration.

On the other hand, the majority of stone castles both in Galloway, Bute, and Argyll, and in the Western Highlands and

---

[1] e.g. RC. *Wigtons.*, Nos. 5, 71, 72, 140, 143, 147, 179, 180.
[2] King's Cross Point, Torr an Chaisteal, *Book of Arran*, pp. 183 and 187.
[3] Also in Glenbeg and Kintail in Western Inverness, *PSAS.*, xxix, pp. 180, 188.
[4] *PSAS.*, xlvii, pp. 30 ff., and xlix, pp. 18 ff. ; Pityoulish Hill on the Upper Spey belongs to the same group, *PSAS.*, xliv, p. 193.
[5] RC. *Fife*, Nos. 106, 243.
[6] *PSAS.*, xxxvi, p. 611.
[7] *PSAS.*, liii, p. 130.

islands and many even in Central Perthshire [1] and Strathspey [2] show nothing of the regularity so tenaciously maintained by the Irish cashels. Though built in the same style as, and in similar situations to, ring forts, such are not circular but irregular in plan, the walls being accommodated to the contours of the ground. In some cases indeed, notably in Islay, the masonry wall merely cuts off the neck of a tiny promontory naturally protected by cliffs and sea. Such irregular castles may have two entrances, but these are provided with checks and bar-holes. In a castle, built along the edge of a cliff on the Mither Tap of Bennachie, 1,700 feet above sea-level in Aberdeenshire, a fine

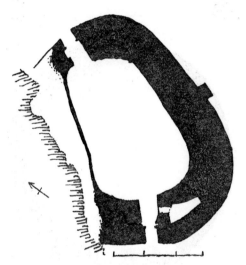

Fig. 56.—Plan of Druim an Duin.

parapet walk is still preserved—a feature to be assumed in most ruinous examples.

In all types of castle, whatever their plan, the space between the wall faces, instead of being entirely filled with loose rubble, may be utilized for chambers. In Dun Bhuirg, an oval enceinte perched on a rock on the shores of Loch Scridain, Mull, there is a cell in the wall that opens off the central space to the right of the entrance ; from the cell a flight of steps begins to mount *clockwise* as if to lead to a gallery over the doorway of the castle. At Druim an Duin (Pl. XIV, 2),[3] south of Loch Crinan and looking

[1] *PSAS.*, xlvii, p. 57.   [2] Near Aviemore, *PSAS.*, xliv, p. 194.
[3] *PSAS.*, xxxix, p. 286.

down Loch Sween, a wall, 14 feet thick and pierced by two
doorways 5 feet high, encloses an irregular area of 48 by 33 feet.
In the thickness of the wall on the right of the south door is
a guard-chamber, 12 feet long but only 4⅔ feet high. A ledge
or scarcement runs along the inner face of one wall, 5 feet from
the ground. It was designed to support a veranda round one
side of the court. The castle yielded a rotary quern that probably
betrays Roman influence.

Ardifuar,[1] standing on low ground in a modern farmyard on
the opposite side of Loch Crinan, is a circular fort with an

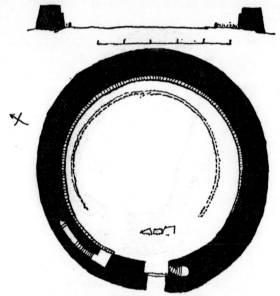

Fig. 57.—Plan of fort at Ardifuar.

internal diameter of 65 feet (Fig. 57). The wall is 10 feet thick
at the base, and again there is a scarcement to support a circular
veranda. In the thickness of the wall is a guard cell on the
right of the doorway (which is 6 feet wide outside), while on
the left a stairway led up, presumably to a parapet walk.
Dunburgidale on Bute [2] agrees with Ardifuar in area and width
of entrance. But in its walls, 10 to 14 feet thick, is a more or
less continuous gallery 2¼ feet wide. The four " semibrochs "
on Tiree [3] and Dun Burg on Mull agree precisely with

[1] *PSAS.*, xxxix, p. 260.   [2] *PSAS.*, xxvii, p. 287.
[3] Beveridge, *Coll and Tiree*, pp. 73 ff.

Dunburgidale save that the central court is here only 35 to
40 feet across.

The same idea is applied in the Borgue of Castlehaven,[1]
a subrectangular fort right on the rocky shore of Wigtown Bay
in Galloway (Fig. 58). The inner bailey, 60 feet long by 35 feet
wide, is girt with a wall 11 to 15 feet thick, in which are three

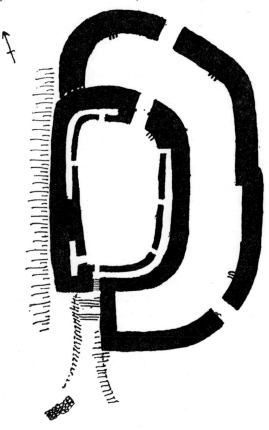

FIG. 58.—Plan of Castlehaven fort.

discontinuous galleries roofed with horizontal slabs. Projecting
stones, like the steps of a stile, lead up to a rampart walk on
the top of the galleries. Similar steps presumably once led to
a rampart walk on the outer wall which is only 8 to 10 feet thick.

In the *galleried duns*[2] of the Hebrides and of Glenelg on the

[1] RC. *Kirk.*, No. 64.   [2] RC. *Hebrides*, p. xxxvi; *PSAS.*, xxix, p. 182.

mainland (opposite Skye) the rampart walk has become a covered gallery. In fact in them we have the idea of enclosing an irregular space with a high, hollow rampart composed of two parallel walls tied together at intervals by horizontal slabs. This extremely ingenious structural device may conceivably have been inspired by the *murus gallicus* technique, the wooden beams being replaced by stone slabs owing to lack of timber.

The most perfect and most typically Scottish application of the principals above described is the *broch*.[1] Its basal portion is in plan a ring fort—a massive circular wall 12 to 16 feet thick, pierced by a single door never more than 4 feet wide and enclosing a circular space from 30 to 40 feet in diameter. In the thickness of this wall there is practically always a guard-chamber at the doorway and an elongated cell opening on to the courtyard on the left; there may be two other cells in addition. But this solid wall is only the foundation for a tower that might attain a height of 40 feet. The latter consists of two walls with a hollow between, but tied together every 5 or 6 feet of their height by horizontal slabs bonded into each. These form floors to the so-called galleries which are, however, sometimes so narrow that they must be regarded as merely structural. A spiral staircase, starting in the left-hand cell on the ground floor, winds up between the walls (Fig. 59). There are no apertures in the outer wall, but in the inner wall a series of slits is left over the door and the cell entries. They may have been designed primarily to relieve the pressure on the lintels. The tower walls do not converge so that the tower must have been open at the top in contradistinction to the Sardinian *nuraghe*. On the other hand, there was a veranda all round the central court. The outer ends of its rafters rested on a scarcement running round the inner wall of the tower 5 or 6 feet above the ground; the inner ends were supported by a ring of posts.[2] In the open space near the centre of the court there might be a hearth. Generally, there is a well or cistern in the court; it may be very deep and reached by a flight of steps.

Save in the western isles, the broch seldom stood alone. The vast majority of brochs both in Shetland, Orkney, Caithness, and Sutherland, and also in the Lowlands, stand in a fortified

[1] Curle, in *Antiquity,* i, pp. 290 ff., summarizes the evidence.
[2] In treeless Orkney the posts were replaced by stone pillars and the veranda roofed with slabs, *CPPS.,* p. 285.

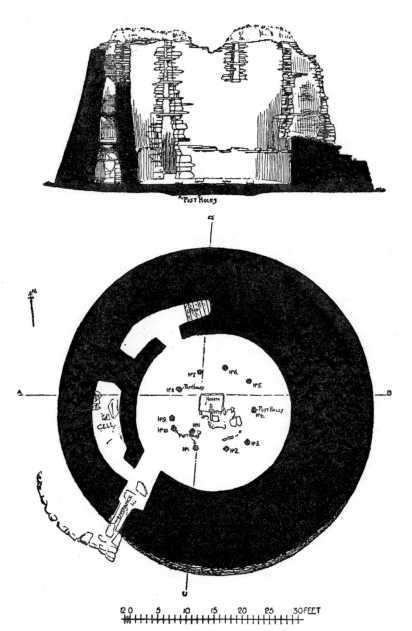

FIG. 59.—Plan and section of broch of Dun Troddan, after *Antiquity*.

enclosure. The outworks consist of ditches and banks of earth, rubble, or built masonry. At Nybster [1] the outer rampart's masonry is identical in style with that of the tower, and stone steps, built on to the inner face, lead up to a parapet-walk along it. If the broch was the castle of a chief, his retainers lived in this fortified enclosure outside the tower. The remains of rough stone huts are often to be seen between its walls and the outworks.

Judging by the relics found in them, most brochs must have been erected by the first century A.D. But in the north the sites continued to be occupied till the fifth or sixth centuries. In these centuries the original tower was often substantially reconstructed, sometimes with very inferior masonry and so as to distort or frustrate the original design.[2] The cistern might be blocked up, new entrances hacked through the walls and internal stair-cases added to supplement or replace those between the tower walls. Such unintelligent reconstructions in masonry that often recalls Skara Brae or Jarlshof rather than the true castles, look like the work of barbarian descendants of " Bronze Age " stocks. They suggest that the broch builders were a conquering minority, soon absorbed by an older subject population.

The broch was, however, an essentially northern creation. There are traces of no less than 145 brochs in Caithness, eighty in Sutherland, seventy-eight in Orkney, seventy-five in Shetland, and forty-four in Skye and the Hebrides.[3] In the north-eastern counties brochs are often closely juxtaposed but always on good agricultural land, and, when near the shore, in the vicinity of convenient landing places. In many instances brochs stand barely ¼ mile apart. At Keiss in Caithness there are four within a square mile ; two of these yielded sherds of *terra sigillata*, and the available evidence points to contemporary occupation of them all. Such a concentration and juxtaposition of immensely strong fortresses must reflect peculiar social conditions. Anderson and Curle regard the brochs as a system of defence against sea-raiders. W. Mackenzie and I prefer to explain them as the castles of a conquering aristocracy designed, like the Norman keeps, to overawe a subject population. The effect of blood-feuds such as arise in a clan society, as in Albania to-day, must also

---

[1] *PSAS.*, xxxv, p. 140.

[2] e.g., Anderson, i, pp. 219, 228 ; *Arch. Scot.*, v, pp. 99, 341 ; *PSAS.*, xxxv, pp. 113 ff. ; *CPPS.*, p. 286.

[3] See the Royal Commission's reports on these counties.

be borne in mind. In any case the broch is eloquent of dangerously unstable conditions under which the farmer and fisherman might at any moment have to retreat into an impregnable refuge.

The broch castle, created in the far north, was carried south presumably by bands of raiders who settled in those richer lands. There are three doubtful brochs near the mouth of the Tay behind Dundee,[1] two certain examples near Stirling,[2] two overlooking the Gala Water near Galashiels, and one on the Whitadder in Berwickshire. On the west there are certain brochs on Mull, Lismore, and Islay. Three alleged brochs on the western coasts of Wigtonshire may be only castles of the type of Dunburgidale or Druim an Duin, though one[3] boasted a guard-cell in its walls and the quantity of debris suggests a broch.

To the eastern Lowlands the castle-builders had brought the idea of the broch with them fully developed from the north. The date of their arrival accordingly provides a *terminus ante quem* for the development of the broch type in its northern homeland. Now a re-examination of the pottery from the broch of Tor-woodlee near Galashiels has convinced Dr. Curle[4] that the structure was already standing in the first century A.D. Hence, though nothing unambiguously pre-Roman has ever been found in a broch, the type must be regarded as going back to, or beyond, the beginning of our era.

The broch marks the culminating point in the development of the castle type. But it need not be later in time than the simpler castles, none of which has yielded any earlier relics. The broch has no parallel outside Scotland. But the architecture of the castles in general embodies the same traditions as are seen in the terrific stone forts of the northern and western coasts of Ireland[5] and of Cornwall,[6] with perhaps remote echoes in the *oppida* of the maritime Veneti[7] of Brittany, the *castros* of Galicia and the *nuraghe* of Sardinia. All were strongholds of maritime folk, at once traders and pirates, farmers, and free-booters which is precisely the impression produced by the Scottish castles. But, whereas the great Irish and Cornish forts look like the

---

[1] Hurley Hawkin, at Liff, St. Bride's Ring and the Laws, Monifieth (*PSAS.*, vi, p. 210 ; iii, p. 440) ; none show stairs to-day ; Laws stands in a large enclosure with powerfully built ramparts, perhaps partly vitrified.
[2] *PSAS.*, ix, p. 29 ; vi, p. 259 ; both show stairs.
[3] *PSAS.*, xlvi, p. 182.   [4] *PSAS.*, lxvi, p. 341.
[5] Macalister, *Ireland*, pp. 265 f.
[6] Like Chun Castle, *Arch.*, lxxvi, pp. 206 f. ; Hencken, *Cornwall*, pp. 125.
[7] Brøgger, *Den norske Bosetningen*, p. 73.

citadels of well-knit communities, our tiny castles might be the refuges of scattered families. And perhaps their builders were in fact splinters from larger units, shattered by the Roman conquests in Gaul and Britain and the disturbances thereby created.

In any case the architectural parallels hint at a south-western origin for the castle-builders. That would accord admirably with the parallelism between the distribution of their monuments and that of the collective tombs. We shall find some confirmation of this theory in the relics distinctive of the brochs and the castle-area as a whole.

(iv) *Hilltop Towns*

Only a small proportion of the defensive constructions in Scotland conform to the type of hilltop fort that is the commonest in Southern England and Gaul. Such are the fortified townships forming the capitals of tribal groups, the nearest approach to a city achieved by the Kelt. They normally occupy the summits of isolated hills, comprise an area of 10 or more acres, sufficient for a permanent population of several hundred families, and possess a more or less regular water-supply. Dunpender or Traprain Law is the best Scottish example. The area comprised within the walls is 32 acres, and excavation has demonstrated prolonged and intensive occupation. Several other forts in the Lowlands conform in situation and size to the above requirements—notably Kaimes Hill, Midlothian,[1] White Melville, and Cademuir Hill, near Peebles, Walls Hill, near Kilbarcolm, Renfrewshire,[2] Burnswark [3] (Fig. 60) in Annandale, Eildon Hill, near Melrose, Bonchester Hill, Roxburghshire,[4] and Cockburns Law, Berwickshire. In the hill country of Galloway hilltop towns are totally lacking ; the westernmost in this direction crowns Moyle Hill [5] overlooking the Solway plain and the lower Nith. On the whole west coast, the Doon, a promontory fort on the west of Arran,[6] is an isolated instance though large enough to serve as a metropolis for the whole island. North of the Forth, only the fort on Turin Hill, near Forfar,[7] really comes up to the standards of size here adopted. The White Catertun in the same county and Burghead, near Elgin, could

[1] RC. *Midlothian*, No. 216.
[2] Christison, p. 265 (28 acres).
[3] RC. *Dumfries*, No. 272 (17 acres).
[4] *PSAS.*, xliv, p. 226 (13 acres).
[5] RC. *Kirkcudbright*, No. 121 (13 acres).
[6] *Book of Arran*, p. 189 (15 acres).
[7] *PSAS.*, xxxiv, p. 97 (14 acres).

be brought within the requirements only by including the outworks surrounding a citadel of essentially different character.

The towns' defences are always quite simple—generally a single
stone rampart rarely supplemented by a shallow outer ditch.
At Traprain the rampart is built of large undressed blocks the
foundation being formed of a double row of great slabs on edge.
At Kaimes Hill, Bonchester Hill, and perhaps in a few other
instances there is a citadel defended by an inner rampart and

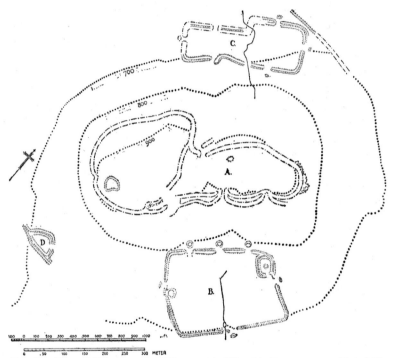

Fig. 60.—Plan of hilltop town of Burnswark (A), with Roman camps (B and C)
below : contours every 100 feet.

a wide, outer bailey below it. Hut-circles are visible in several
towns like Bonchester Hill, Kaimes Hill, and Eildon Hill, but
on Traprain the dwellings were constructed of wattle and daub.

Bonchester Hill yielded no Roman relics but an iron pin of
early La Tène type. Burnswark [1] was besieged and captured
by the Romans in the first century, perhaps under Agricola
himself. Traprain, though inhabited down to the fourth century

[1] *TDGAS.*, 1925-6, pp. 47 ff.

A.D., was occupied already in the Late Bronze Age. It is accordingly clear that the foundation of hilltop towns in Lowland Scotland antedates the Roman invasion; the habit of living in such towns cannot have been introduced here by the conquerors, as may have been the case in Wales.

(v) *Small Forts*

The remaining defensive constructions can only be classified as " small forts "; the vast majority of the forts, over 850 in all, between the two " Roman Walls " in Southern Scotland and Northumberland belong to this class. These are easily distinguishable from the hilltop towns by their small size, their situation on spurs or slopes rather than on isolated summits, and the absence of any obvious provision for water-supply. Often two of these small forts stand within half a mile of each other at different elevations.[1] Occasionally there is a small fort within the same distance from a hilltop town.[2]

Such forts are most abundant on the slopes overlooking the valleys of the Tweed and its tributaries, of the Annan and of the Clyde and the Lothian plain. They seem, moreover, to cluster in a significant way round the head-waters of rivers as if guarding the passes from one valley to the next. Thus, there are twenty within a radius of 2 miles round Moffat at the head of Annandale, and sixteen in an area of 8 square miles along the Tweed near Peebles. Such aggregations have suggested to Ogilvie[3] a common system of frontier defences. The groups of small forts might mark tribal boundaries; Watson made the same suggestion about the simpler ring castles of Central Perthshire which exhibit similar grouping and are likewise contrasted with hilltop castles or forts. The small forts of the Lowlands lie adjacent to the Roman roads that followed the valleys. I[4] therefore suggested the Romans as the enemy against whom the small forts were erected.

The assumption of a co-ordinated plan in the location of these

---

[1] e.g., in East Lothian, Blackcastle and Greencastle, RC., Nos. 46, 50, and Nos. 48, 49; near Heriot, RC. *Midlothian*, Nos. 108, 234; in Peebles., Drochil (Lyne Water), Harehope Hill, Chargelaw, Holmswater, Kilbucho Burn; in Lanarks., north spur of Tinto, on Coulter Water, and opposite Abington, in Clydesdale.

[2] e.g. on West Cademuir Hill, Peebles.

[3] *Great Britain*, pp. 435, 484.

[4] *Ant. J.*, xiii, p. 10.

works is not, however, inevitable. They may perfectly well be
the Lowland equivalents of the western and northern castles—
in other words, the fortified manors of chiefs who with their
dependents tilled the slopes below the fort; many of these stand
close to modern farms and on the edge of land still cultivated.
One or two stone forts on the Upper Tweed and Manor Water,
for instance, might pass for castles built by intruders from
the west.

Hardly any small forts have been excavated. Externally they
exhibit great variety. The majority are girt with two or more
ramparts and ditches. Nearly all have more than one entrance.
In two cases [1] these were defended by *chevaux-de-frise*—pointed
stones set on end to impede the progress of cavalry. The same
device is seen in some Irish and Welsh forts.[2] While some small
forts have ramparts of earth, others of stone, too much significance
must not be attached to the distinction, which depends largely
on local conditions. In Ireland the circular stone cashels on rocky
country are just the counterparts of the earthen raths of other
districts. It must be remembered that so-called earth ramparts
were not structureless banks, but were sustained and consolidated
by timber revetments and palisades. Such defences may have
been quite as elaborate and imposing as stone walls.

Castlelaw on the Pentlands near Glencorse [3] illustrates this
point. The typical small fort was defended by two " V "-shaped
ditches, cut in the rock, and by two, or in places three, banks.
The " middle bank " was composed of the earth and broken
rock from the ditch immediately behind it; the material had
been piled against the timbers of an external revetment. Of course
only the groove in which they stood and the heavy boulders
that had reinforced their bases survived. The inner rampart,
composed of earth, was terribly effaced, but the post-holes showed
that the gate, $7\frac{1}{2}$ feet wide, had been of the barbican type.
Such is compatible with a parapet walk continuing over the
gateway, as in the stone castles.

On more rocky country the ramparts must be composed mainly
of rubble for which a dry-built stone wall is a more appropriate
revetment than timber. The East Fort at Earnsheugh,[4] near
St. Abb's Head, provides a good illustration. It was girt by

---

[1] Dreva and West Cademuir, on Upper Tweed; the same feature outside the
town on Kaimes Hill.
[2] Macalister, *Ireland*, p. 269.
[3] *PSAS.*, lxvii, pp. 362 ff.   [4] *PSAS.*, lxvi, pp. 152 ff.

two banks and two " V "-bottomed ditches. The inner rampart, of earth and rubble over a core of rammed soil, was supported by a revetment wall of large, quarry-dressed blocks. The outer rampart, composed of earth and stones in alternate layers, was bounded by a kerb of tilted stones on the inside, but a built revetment like that of the inner rampart, faced only one section. Connected with this fort was a larger one on the east. Its inner rampart, perhaps 15 feet wide, consisted of rubble over a core of packed soil, faced on the inside by a built wall still standing 3¼ feet high, while the outer face had collapsed into the ditch. The core of the outer rampart in the same fort was a built wall of small slabs, only one course deep and faced on the inside only. It was backed up against a clay and rubble packing which was repeated on the inside.

The age of such small forts is still indeterminate. Relics of the second century were obtained both from Earnsheugh and Castlelaw. But at the latter site they came from a secondary Earth-house erected in the inner ditch which was thereby robbed of all defensive value. The fort must accordingly be older. So at Channelkirk in Lauderdale,[1] a Roman camp had disturbed an older, native fort which had, however, been reconditioned after the abandonment of the camp. A small fort—an oval enclosure of 100 by 70 feet, girt with two ramparts, separated by a ditch and entered by a single gate flanked by a bank—had been incorporated in the camp (B in Fig. 60) erected by the Romans for the siege of Burnswark.[2] This type, represented by other examples in the Lowlands, and reminiscent of the Gallic fort at Forgandenny, must accordingly be regarded as pre-Roman. Finally, A. O. Curle[3] has suggested a Bronze Age date for certain simple circular forts, girt with an earthen bank and a ditch cut only in the earth, that closely approximate in form to the normal Irish rath. A hoard of bronze rapiers is said to have been found in 1837 in the ditch of such a fort at Drum-coltram, Wigtonshire,[4] while flint arrow-heads have been ploughed up near a similar fort at Overhowden, Lauderdale. On the other hand, certain " forts ", the interior of which has been excavated to below the level of the surrounding land, are generally held to belong to the second century or later.[5] One was erected at

[1] PSAS., lxiv, p. 325.   [2] RC. Dumfries, No. 272 (iii).
[3] Rhind Lectures ; cf. RC. Dumfries, p. liii.
[4] PSAS., lxii, p. 141.   [5] RC. Dumfries, p. lv.

the foot of Burnswark after the siege (Fig. 60, D). These hollow forts are now termed *enclosures*. Again, a small fort on Ruberslaw, Roxburghshire, had been partly constructed of dressed stones taken from an abandoned Roman post.[1]

3. CRANNOGS AND EARTH-HOUSES

Xiphilinus' abridgement of Dio Cassius [2] speaks of the Caledonians " living in bogs for many days ". His curious story was perhaps suggested by lake-dwellings or *crannogs* such as are found also in Ireland, England, and on the Continent. In Scotland there are examples of uncertain age in many Highland lochs, but a number in Galloway and Ayrshire were demonstrably inhabited as early as the first century A.D.[3]

These are generally situated on small, very deep lochs, the bottoms of which are filled to an unknown depth with yielding peat. The dwellings are not therefore erected on a platform supported by piles but on a sort of sunken raft. This consisted of undressed trunks of birch and similar trees. The raft was floated on the surface of the loch and perhaps anchored by means of oak posts driven through it. Brush wood and rubble were then piled on it till it grounded. The process was repeated till the top of the mass emerged above water.

The top of the artificial island thus formed might be occupied by a rectangular or oval pavement or platform, 40 to 60 feet square, formed of oak logs, trimmed like railway sleepers. The pavement was surrounded by two or three rings of stout oak piles. The piles were joined together by oak beams, mortised into one another and into the piles. The rings of piles, thus elaborately clamped together, may have helped to give stability to the island and to diminish erosion by waves, but they served primarily as the basis for a stockade surrounding the central platform.

The stockade itself might consist of wood and stone combined. At Buston Munro [4] found between the uprights of the inner ring two courses of stones with a horizontal oak beam above them ; the latter carried three more courses of stones above which came another beam and then more masonry.

---

[1] *PSAS.*, xxxix, p. 219.   [2] Dio Cassius, lxxvi, 12.
[3] Data set out by Munro, *Ancient Scottish Lake Dwellings*, 1882 ; cf. also *ACAG.*, vii, pp. 59 f. ; *PSAS.*, xxxiii, pp. 377 ff. ; xliv, pp. 12 ff., and xlvii, pp. 257 for additional sites.   [4] Munro, *ASLD.*, p. 200.

The sleeper platform was apparently covered over with turfs or clay to form the actual floor of the habitation. The Scottish evidence does not suffice to determine whether each platform carried more than one dwelling. But probably the stockade enclosed an open space in which only one hut stood. A gangway bordered with piles led to the platform from the shore.

Most crannogs actually explored seem to have been isolated structures standing on tiny lochs, now dry. But at the west end of Dowalton Loch, Wigtonshire, there was a regular lacustrine hamlet[1]—a group of four crannogs—and a fifth on the south shore of the loch. Curiously enough, a small fort stands on the land less than half a mile from the hamlet.

The relics found in the crannogs attest their occupation during the Roman period. Since as many as four superposed hearths were noticed at Buston, the " islands " must have been inhabited for a considerable period. A cauldron ring from Dowalton Loch is, however, the only object suggestive of a pre-Roman occupation.

Pile-dwellings on meres or rivers, going back in the Alps and on the Rhine to the " Stone Age ", were adopted by the urnfield folk from East Central Europe in early Hallstatt times ; the Hallstatt moor village at Buchau on the Federsee (Würtemberg)[2] already approximates to a crannog in structure. Traces of pile-dwellings near Brentford in the Thames, at Ulrome in Holderness and at Costa Beck, near Pickering,[3] suggest that the idea was introduced into Britain by Urnfield or Hallstatt invaders. In any case, Glastonbury in Somerset provides a classic example of a pre-Roman La Tène crannog settlement in England. But since none of the typical Glastonbury relics has been found in Scottish crannogs, these must be connected rather with the Yorkshire group. Our crannogs look like the retreats of small bands of refugees who had sought shelter in the heart of the damp oak-woods of Galloway and Ayrshire.

The Earth-house or *weem* again is a sort of refuge—from the cold as well as from enemies. We have already met such constructions in a Late Bronze Age context in Shetland, but during the Iron Age they spread even to the Lowlands. The Earth-houses of this period are often built in a wide trench, cut in the living

---

[1] Plan in *ACAG.*, v, pl. xviii.
[2] Reinerth, *Der Wohnbau der Pfahlbaukultur* ; *Real.* iii, p. 246.
[3] Elgee, *Yorkshire*, p. 103.

rock and obviously presupposing the use of iron tools. But the
masonry with which the trench walls are faced is still " Bronze
Age " in style—natural boulders, piled on a foundation of great
undressed slabs on edge, in contrast to the quarried blocks that
face the ramparts of forts and castles. The survival of " Bronze
Age " traditions is further emphasized by the inclusion in the
walls or roofs of stones adorned with cup-and-ring markings.[1]
Though these need not have been carved by the Iron Age builders,
the latter must at least have collected them deliberately and did
employ them in significant positions, for instance at doorways.

The Iron Age Earth-house remains in essence a long gallery,
always curved, entered by a flight of steps and a doorway about
2 feet wide and sometimes less than 2 feet high. Towards its
end the gallery generally widens out to an elongated chamber
that may be 10 feet wide and from 5 to 6 feet high. The walls
usually corbel inwards, and the narrower passages are roofed
with stone lintels. The chamber is often so wide that the possibility of spanning it with stone slabs has been doubted and a
timber roof postulated.[2] In Orkney, where no timber was
available, the stone slabs covering some chambers were supported
by pillars.[3] In Orkney, too, there are slab-roofed and pillared
galleries cut in the rock without masonry facing to the walls.[4]

In a normal Earth-house the gallery is from 40 to 90 feet long,
but the one at Pitcur near Coupar Angus (Fig. 61) attains a
length of 190 feet and boasts in addition an annex 60 feet long.
Several Earth-houses are more complicated. In those at West
Grange of Conan (Angus),[5] and Castlelaw (Midlothian)[6] the gallery
is connected with a subterranean beehive chamber, 10 to 12 feet
in diameter, and in the first instance corbelled over $7\frac{1}{2}$ feet from
the floor. A precisely similar beehive was attached to the
Cornish fogou of Chapel Euny.[7]

Earth-houses are most numerous in Orkney, Caithness,
Sutherland, and the Hebrides. Otherwise their distribution
is quite different from that of brochs or other " castles ". There
are large groups in Aberdeenshire and in Angus between
Arbroath and Coupar Angus, with outliers near Kingussie in
Strathspey, and at Fortingal in Strathtay. Five are known in

---

[1] e.g. Pitcur and Tealing, *PSAS.*, xxxiv, p. 208 ; x, p. 287.
[2] *PSAS.*, xxxiv, p. 204 ; Thorgill's *Saga* presupposes a wooden roof over an
Irish souterrain.
[3] *PSAS.*, li, p. 187 ; lxi, p. 296.   [4] *PSAS.*, lxii, p. 156 ; lxiv, p. 222.
[5] Anderson, i, fig. 259.   [6] *PSAS.*, lxvii, p. 378.   [7] Hencken, *Cornwall*, p. 141.

Fife,[1] and about six south of the Forth.[2] The southernmost example seems to be that at Newstead near Melrose (Roxburgh-

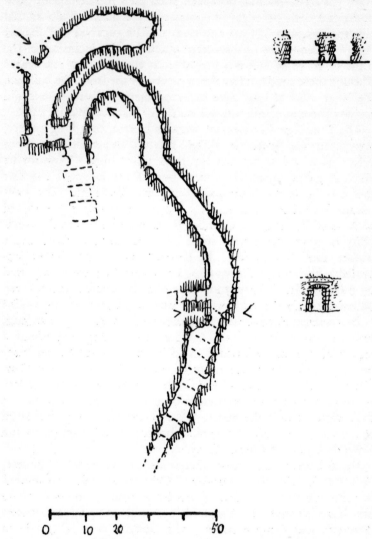

FIG. 61.—Plan of Earth-house, at Pitcur, Angus, after *PSAS*.

shire), the westernmost near Carnwath (Lanarkshire),[3] but

[1] RC. *Fife,* p. xxxiv ; one has since been discovered.
[2] Anderson, i, pp. 300 ff. ; RC. *Berwicks.,* p. xxxvi ; *Midlothian,* p. xxxv.
[3] *PSAS.,* lviii, p. 339.

Corrie[1] mentions a very dubious example in Buittle Parish (Kirkcudbrightshire).

Stones, plundered from abandoned Roman camps, had been used in building the Earth-houses at Crichton[2] and Newstead; these structures can therefore hardly have been erected before A.D. 180. Even that at Castlelaw, though yielding second-century pottery, was later than a small fort. On the other hand, the Roman vases from West Grange of Conan are rather earlier, belonging to the first half of the century.[3]

Clearly the Earth-houses south of the Forth belong to intruders, and these arrived only in the second century and therefore later than the broch-builders. They presumably came immediately from Angus. But the true home of the Earth-house in Scotland was the far north. The builders of the ones in Aberdeenshire and Angus must have come thence; the monuments indeed reflect those relations already mentioned on p. 188.

Such subterranean refuges or habitations can never have existed alone, but must always have been connected with some dwelling above the ground. Only one Scottish weem lies in a fort—at Dunsinane, east of Perth[4]—whereas many Irish raths contain souterrains. Most of ours must therefore have been attached to undefended huts or hamlets. The pavements of such alone were traceable at two sites in Angus,[5] but in Aberdeenshire and Sutherland Earth-houses have been found opening out of normal hut-circles.[6] Some of the latter must therefore be assigned to the Iron Age.

4. OPEN VILLAGES

Hut circles may go back to the Early Bronze Age as shown on p. 118. But they were still being made in the Iron Age; they are found for instance in many forts. They still occur also on open moors far away from any defensive construction. Sometimes they are grouped together in regular hamlets, often surrounded with flimsy banks that would be useful in keeping out beasts but could serve no strategic purpose. While there is a fine group of this kind high up the Whitadder in East Lothian,[7] such hut-villages are exceptional in the Lowlands but

---

[1] *TDGAS.*, 1927, p. 291.   [2] Anderson, i, p. 300; *PSAS.*, lix, p. 95.
[3] *PSAS.*, lxvi, p. 287.   [4] Anderson, i, p. 281.
[5] West Grange of Conan and Tealing; *PSAS.*, iv, p. 49; x, p. 287.
[6] *PSAS.*, xxxviii, p. 110; xlv, p. 20.   [7] RC. *E. Lothian*, No. 184.

are far commoner in Galloway,[1] in the Highlands of Perthshire, in Aberdeenshire, and in Sutherland. Particularly in Perthshire and Aberdeenshire they are found far beyond and above the range of any other type of prehistoric settlement. W. Thorney-croft[2] has recently located sixty-one hut circles in the valleys of the Ericht and the Isla—all just above the 1,000 ft. contour. They are divided between 8 clusters, the largest, near Dalrulzion, comprising nineteen huts, the smallest, in Glen Beany, only two. Two groups, between Loch Davan and Loch Kinnord (Aberdeen-shire) that were planned by General Ogston,[3] comprised six circles each and were surrounded by low banks.

On the Whitadder, as further north, small enclosures adjoin the circles ; they presumably mark cultivation plots—querns proved the practice of agriculture both in Perthshire and Aber-deenshire. In Galloway and the northern counties small cairns are numerous in the vicinity of the villages. Such might be merely dumps of stones cleared from the fields ; it is more likely that they once covered the skeletons of the villagers, as Elgee[4] has argued in the case of Yorkshire. But the acid soils have destroyed the bones completely, and there are no satis-factory records of anything but minute fragments of charcoal under such small cairns.

The circles themselves exhibit much variety. The simple penannular ring, oval or circular, of earth and stones is universal. Double circles, composed of two concentric rings, occur both in Perthshire and Aberdeenshire ; three out of nineteen at Dalrul-zion, and three out of six at Old Kinnord could be assigned to this type In an example, excavated by Thorneycroft, the space between the two rings was like a penannular gallery, $3\frac{1}{4}$ to $6\frac{1}{2}$ feet wide ; it was closed at each end to leave a passage-way from without into the central circle and entered from the latter by a gap more or less opposite the entrance. The central ring enclosed a space 35 feet across with a hearth near the middle.

Another type, found from Perthshire to Sutherland, appears as two circles, the outer of which is tangential to a smaller inner circle.[5] Sometimes two circles are backed up against one another

---

[1] Some such may be quite modern shielings ; cf. RC. *Wigtowns.*, p. xxv ; *PSAS.*, liii, p. 83.
[2] *PSAS.*, lxvii, p. 189.
[3] *Antiquities of Cromar*, 3rd Spalding Club's publication, 1931, pp. 12 ff., figs. 11 and 25.
[4] *North-East Yorkshire*, p. 99.
[5] RC. *Sutherland*, Nos. 36, 63, 498.

while others are divided by internal walls.[1] Some circles from
Sutherland look like variants on the courtyard house of Jarlshof.[2]
Finally, both at Kinnord in Aberdeenshire [3] and in the Strath of
Kildonan (Sutherland) [4] normal souterrains open into hut circles.

Sherds from circles in Glenshee and a jet armlet from one in
Sutherland cannot [5] be earlier than the " Late Bronze Age "
invasion. Pieces of iron from Glenshee and Kinnord and a
weaving comb from Strathardle establish an Iron Age date and
at least the assimilation of the intrusive culture of that period.
But on the whole these villages could be attributed to descendants of the Late Bronze Age population, undisturbed by the
troubles of the migrations and the Roman conquest or driven
thereby to the high ground above the oak-woods.

On the sandy coasts of the isles and the far north the environment demanded a better shelter than was provided by the turf
hut or skin tent that must have completed the hut circle. And if
the dwellings were to be grouped in hamlets there, it would be
well to roof in the streets, as at Skara Brae, in view of the frequency
of sandstorms. The Iron Age villages of the Hebrides, Orkney,
and Shetland, respond to these requirements. In their construction stone replaced wood, since the islands were treeless, but the
fine masonry, characterizing the brochs and castles, is lacking.
The architectural unit is the old courtyard house of Jarlshof,
now enlarged and improved to form the wheel-dwelling.

Unfortunately Scottish archæologists have confused wheel-
dwellings with Earth-houses. In reality, as Captain Thomas [6]
emphasized in the first scientific description of such dwellings,
they are not subterranean, though a true souterrain may be
attached. However their outer walls are in fact very often
backed up against sand-dunes or banks of soil which must have
been partly cleared away or excavated before the dwelling's
erection. In such cases the enclosing wall may be quite flimsy
and only 1½ to 2 feet thick. But at Garry Iochdrach (North Uist) [7]
the house was girt on the seaward side with a massive wall,
8 to 11½ feet thick, that was certainly meant to withstand exposure.

A wheel-house is in essence a walled area roughly circular or
oval and 25 to 38 feet across. This space is divided up into a
number of voussoir-shaped rooms or compartments by radial

---

[1] RC. *Sutherland*, Nos. 129, 279, 351, 499, 503.
[2] RC. *Sutherland*, Nos. 113, 344.   [3] *PSAS.*, xxxviii, p. 112.
[4] *PSAS.*, xlv, p. 20.   [5] *PSAS.*, xlv, p. 22.
[6] *PSAS.*, vii, p. 165.   [7] *PSAS.*, lxvi, p. 34.

walls arranged like the spokes of a wheel. The radials stop
short some 6 to 12 feet from the middle of the "wheel" so as
to leave an undivided central space, 15 to 25 feet in diameter.
This central space may have been a court, open to the sky ;
the compartments set round about it were certainly roofed over,
forming, in fact, the sleeping and living rooms of the inhabitants.

Two types of house are distinguishable according to the
arrangement of the rooms in relation to the central court. In
type I each compartment was entered directly and exclusively
from the court ; in type II several compartments were inter-
communicating, each suite being entered through one compartment which alone opened on to the court. In the first type best

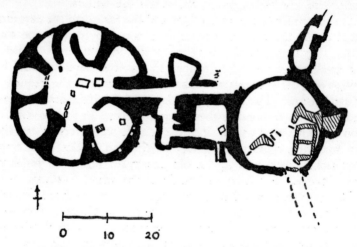

0   10   20

Fig. 62.—Plan of dwellings at Bac Mhic Connain, after *PSAS*.

represented at Bac Mhic Connain [1] (Fig. 62) and in house 1
at Foshigarry [2] in North Uist and by some post-broch houses
at Jarlshof (Shetland),[3] the radials project as piers from the
boundary wall. The piers might be solid structures of masonry,
thick enough to give room for ambries. At Jarlshof the compartments were certainly corbelled over 11 feet above the floor,
the upper courses of both the piers and the boundary wall
oversailing inwards. Beveridge observed a similar oversailing
4 feet above the floor in the boundary walls at Bac Mhic Connain
and Foshigarry, but yet believed that the piers supported horizontal lintels. Flimsy walls, not bonded into the piers, closed

[1] *PSAS.*, lxvi, p. 43.   [2] *PSAS.*, lxv, p. 300.   [3] *PSAS.*, xli, p. 15.

the end of one compartment at Foshigarry and of two at Bac Mhic Connain.

In type II [1] the radials do not as a rule reach the boundary wall; instead there is a gap or doorway, $1\frac{3}{4}$ to $3\frac{1}{4}$ feet wide, between it and most radials allowing of access from one compartment to the next. In compensation most compartments were cut off from the court by flimsy cross-walls joining the ends of the radials. However, in two out of the fourteen compartments at Machair Leathann one radial joined up to the boundary wall while in four others the doorways had been blocked. Similarly only seven of the compartments were walled off from the court.

Captain Thomas actually found the doors between the rooms at Uishnish [2] corbelled over and the compartments roofed apparently by the convergence of the radials (Fig. 63). He adds that the central " court " itself was covered by a beehive roof of corbelled masonry springing from the architraves of the compartments' roofs. As more than half the dwelling had been washed away before his visit, the last statement is puzzling. Beveridge held that the compartments were simply lintelled over, but found no absolutely conclusive evidence. At Howmae in North Ronaldshay,[3] the radials consisted only of thin slabs on edge ; such might carry light lintels but hardly a corbelled vault.

Apart from the arrangement of the compartments, the two types agree very closely. A hearth occupies the middle of the central court. The compartments are often partially paved and provided with ambries in the walls. In the court and sometimes in the rooms there may be sinks. These are floorless boxes formed of four slabs, generally sloped so as to be wider at the mouth ($3 \times 2\frac{1}{4}$ feet) than at the bottom ($2\frac{3}{4} \times 1\frac{1}{3}$ feet). At Foshigarry, and Garry Iochdrach, some of the sinks opened into drains that ran under the chamber floors out to the shore. The best preserved entrance, that at Machair Leathann, was $3\frac{1}{2}$ feet wide and $5\frac{1}{2}$ feet high and equipped with jambs and a bar-hole. It gave on to a wide, walled street or forecourt.

Probably none of the dwellings stood isolated. A long, tunnel-like Earth-house in the hill-side opened into that at

---

[1] Machair Leathann and Garry Iochdrach, Beveridge, *North Uist*, p. 121 ; *PSAS.*, lxvi, p. 34.

[2] *PSAS.*, vii, p. 166.   [3] *PSAS.*, xix, p. 25 ; xxiv, p. 451.

Uishnish, South Uist (Fig. 63). A paved annex was connected by a doorway, with check and bar-holes, to the main dwelling at Garry Iochdrach. At Foshigarry two houses of type II were backed up against one another in such a way that the boundary of each was little more than a semicircle, the common wall being straight. Irregular annexes had been built on to both houses, while under one ran a stone-roofed Earth-house, 42 feet long, but never more than 3 feet high. Within 45 feet of the

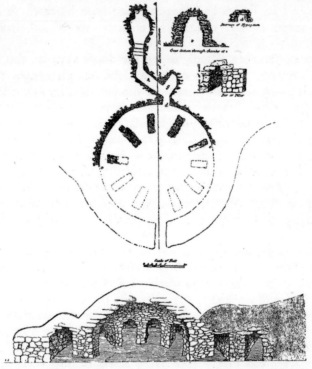

FIG. 63.—Plan and elevation of Wheel-house (with Earth-house) at Uishnish, according to Capt. Thomas.

double house was one of type I with ruins of others in the intervening space. Five larger dwellings with several annexes and cells were preserved at Howmae. Well-built boat-harbours adjoined the settlements of Foshigarry and Garry Iochdrach.

All sites had been occupied for a long time. Two superposed pavements were noted in some compartments at Garry Iochdrach, and there was a deposit of refuse 4¾ feet below the hearth at

Bac Mhic Connain. The last-named dwelling yielded a sherd of *terra sigillata*, proving occupation as early as the second century A.D., but also an Ogham inscription on bone that must be several centuries later. At Jarlshof the houses of type II had been built on to the ruins of a broch and are therefore posterior to its primary occupation.

All the wheel-dwellings have yielded a representative series of typical broch relics. But the architectural tradition embodied in them is definitely older—at least Late Bronze Age. They may be regarded as erected by a native population that was, or had been, subject to the broch-lords and had absorbed their culture.

The *waags* of Caithness embody the same architectural traditions as the full wheel-houses. The classical example, excavated by Curle[1] at Langwell, consisted of a normal hut-circle, $27\frac{1}{2}$ feet in diameter, with an oval chamber 48 feet long attached. The floor of the latter had been excavated a couple of feet into the subsoil. Down its centre at its inner end ran two rows of pillars each 6 feet from the nearest wall from which thin slabs extended to the uprights. Such structures, concentrated in the wildest uplands of the county where no brochs have penetrated, might have been erected by Bronze Age survivors in retreat from the domination of the broch-builders. Rotary and saddle querns indicate occupation into the Roman period.

[1] *PSAS.*, xlvi, pp. 80 ff.

XI

THE KELTIC IRON AGE

1. LIFE IN THE IRON AGE

THE Iron Age culture was introduced into Britain through a series of invasions. In England these can be clearly distinguished by relics as well as by monuments. The Hallstatt invasions, already mentioned, were there succeeded by waves of La Tène invaders—bands of Kelts from Gaul. In Southern England Radford [1] would postulate a late third-century invasion to explain the La Tène elements superimposed upon the culture of Hawkes' Iron Age A group (All Cannings Cross). In any case, towards 200 B.C. large bodies of new settlers occupied South-western Britain right up to Cornwall and South Wales.[2] These created the Iron Age B culture, the culminating expression of which is seen at Glastonbury. The Glastonbury folk presumably came immediately from Western Gaul. About the same time bands of kindred people occupied Lincolnshire and the coasts of Yorkshire, forming what we shall term the Arras group. Their burial rites—the chiefs were interred with their chariots—and their art [3] connect them unambiguously with the authors of the famous Marne culture of North-eastern Gaul. Yet their pottery is essentially Hallstatt in tradition [4] (whether that of the true Hallstatt invasion or Radford's later wave need not be discussed here). Thus the Arras invaders may have been only a conquering aristocracy, a " sprinkling of Keltic heroes dominating the long-established barbarians of the nearer north ".[5]

That the Iron Age culture of Scotland resulted from similar invasions has already been deduced from architectural evidence. Two groups, which must, however, be treated together as the " Abernethy complex ", seemed to have come direct from Gaul. We should turn to the relics to confirm this expectation and to determine how the remaining invaders were related to those who settled in England.

[1] *CPPS.*, p. 148.
[2] Kendrick and Hawkes, pp. 175 ff. The later Belgic invasion (group C) does not affect Scotland.
[3] Leeds, p. 12.   [4] Leeds, p. 3.   [5] Hawkes, *ArchJ.*, xc, p. 151.

222

Unfortunately the relics recovered from Iron Age sites are better suited to the production of a general picture of Iron Age civilization than to establishing distinctions between groups or to determining origins. That is due, on the one hand, to the absolute paucity of relics and to accidental circumstances affecting their apparent distribution, on the other, to the comparative uniformity of La Tène civilization throughout western Europe and to the overpowering influence of Rome upon native cultures even beyond the Empire's frontiers.

The number of relics from native sites in Scotland—and particularly from pre-Roman forts and from castles—is absolutely small. Their distribution in time is just for that reason uncertain. Though four levels could be distinguished in the hilltop town of Traprain, the number of significant types, statistically assignable to a given period, was limited. The four levels should correspond to the first four centuries of our era, yet undoubtedly pre-Roman types could not be distinguished stratigraphically from those of Flavian times.[1] Then local conditions may prevent the survival of certain materials : the salt sea air of the northern isles is peculiarly destructive to iron objects, the acid soils of our hill-tops will consume any unburnt bone. Conclusions from the absence of such substances must be treated with the utmost reserve.

Subdivisions of the La Tène culture are based principally on pottery and decorative styles. Scottish Iron Age pottery is rare, coarse, and seldom decorated ; ornamental bronzes are exceptional.

During the sixty odd years of Roman rule the natives living south of the Antonine wall had ample opportunities of acquiring from the garrisons and from the merchants who supplied their needs, articles of Roman manufacture. As mercenaries, servants, or slaves, they could learn the arts and crafts of the conquerors. At the same time they were brought into close contact with Romanized kinsmen in the Province. The use of these opportunities is abundantly attested by excavations on native sites. Every site, occupied during the first and second centuries, yields Roman coins, Roman pottery or glass, Roman saucepans or tools, and Romano-British fibulæ and ornaments.

The taste for Roman manufactures, thus set up, persisted

[1] The reserve needed in using the stratigraphy of Traprain is emphasized by the excavators in *PSAS.*, lvi, p. 189.

after the withdrawal of the legions and was satisfied by continued
imports from the Province. Even outside the occupied area in
Galloway and beyond the Forth right up to North Uist and Orkney,
Roman coins [1] and manufactures [2] penetrated. They represent
the products of trade, the spoils of abandoned camps and routed
cohorts, or, quite simply, loot. And right up to Orkney Roman
types were clumsily imitated by the barbarians and Roman habits
adopted. A striking instance is the general spread of the flat
Roman type of rotary quern. The idea may have been diffused
by escaped slaves who would have had unpleasant practical
experience of the mill in their days of servitude.

It is thus convenient to indicate briefly common features
of Iron Age economy and industry in the four centuries round
about the beginning of our era, before seeking clues as to the
origins of the groups practising them.

In the first instance agriculture has now come to play a leading
role in native economy. It is true that lyncheted Keltic fields,
such as are so common in Southern England and even Yorkshire,
have so far been recognized at one site only—below the broch
of Torwoodlee near Galashiels.[3] The importance of grain-
growing is demonstrated by the numbers of querns that turn
up at every site of the period whether hill-top town, castle,
small fort, crannog, earth-house, or hut-circle. No less than
fifty were recovered from the broch of Cinn Trolla and thirty-six
from the vitrified fort of Duntroon. All the latter were of the
old saddle type which predominated also in the vitrified fort of
Dunagoil. Such are quite common also in brochs, and at Traprain
occurred still in the third level. Flat, rotary querns are, however,
commoner in later sites of the Roman period even in far northern
brochs, galleried dwellings [4] and wheel-houses and in hut-circles
on remote moors. A few rotary querns from crannogs [5] belong
to the older Keltic pattern in which the upper millstone is shaped
like a beehive. In northern sites [6] and once at Traprain [7] stone
troughs like modern " knocking stones " have been found.
Iron sickles have been found only at Traprain and in the
crannogs.

[1] *PSAS.*, lii, p. 203 ; lviii, p. 325.
[2] *PSAS.*, lxvi, pp. 277–396 with map.
[3] *PSAS.*, lxvii, p. 75 ; cf. Kendrick and Hawkes, pp. 173 f.
[4] Galson, Lewis, and the waag at Langwell Caithness ; *PSAS.*, xlvi, p. 84.
[5] Lochlee, *Munro*, p. 107.
[6] Ousedale Burn broch and Galson Lewis.
[7] *PSAS.*, lviii, p. 247—from bottom level.

The farmyards now included even in Shetland and Orkney cattle and sheep of the same short-horned breed as occurs in South English camps and at Glastonbury. But difficulties were still experienced in carrying young animals over the winter; an excessive proportion of calves and lambs was slaughtered and eaten.[1] In addition to food-animals the Iron Age people

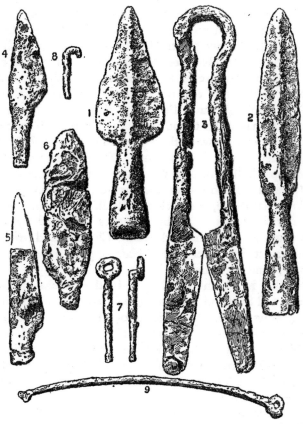

Fig. 64.—Iron tools, weapons and ornaments from Traprain Law, after *PSAS*. ⅖

kept also horses, presumably for riding and driving. Horse bones have been reported from all sorts of castles, hill-top towns, crannogs, and Earth-houses from Galloway to Orkney.[2]

[1] *TBNHS.*, 1914–15, p. 58.
[2] Traprain (*PSAS.*, l, p. 143), Borness Cave, Dunadd (*PSAS.*, lxiv, p. 126), Castlehill near Dalry, the brochs of Kettleburn, Yarrows, and Burwick, Earth-house at Clova, Aberdeens. (Anderson, i, p. 289).

The industrial revolution of the period was the general employment of iron. The metal was worked and even smelted locally
in many (probably in all) settlements. It looks indeed as if each
little community had its own smith who smelted the ore on a
small and uneconomical scale. Even in the second century trade
was not sufficiently organized for the rural hamlets even between
the Roman Walls to be supplied with raw iron from centralized
urban foundries. Within sight of the great hill-top town on
Traprain Law, iron was being smelted at Castlelaw, Glencorse.
In the beehive chamber of the Earth-house there, a small hollow,
only a foot across, had been quarried out of the rock floor. It
was filled with charcoal and iron slag—evidently a smelting
furnace. A bloom of very pure iron lay near the chamber's door.

In Constantine's Cave, Fife, Jehu and Wace [1] found a rather
superior furnace. Its foundations were two concentric rings of
stones with clay between them encircling a stone dish 15 inches
in diameter, and 3 inches deep. The superstructure of clay
had collapsed. The furnace yielded spongy iron and slag. Scott [2]
discovered a still more advanced furnace, based on the principle
of the Catalan forge, in a cave near Rudh' an Dunain, Skye. The
hearth was an area of 15 by 8 inches delimited by stones, a
tall upright forming the back wall. Charcoal and ore could be
piled against the latter and a blast applied by some channel
leading round or under it.

Iron slag has been found even in the brochs of Caithness,
Orkney, and Shetland, and the wheel-dwellings of the Hebrides.
At Bac Mhic Connain Beveridge found a furnace, not certainly
used for iron smelting. It was built of stones and resembled
a rectangular shaft 1 ft. 10 in. square outside, and standing $3\frac{2}{3}$ feet
high with an internal depth of 3 feet. Obviously the fuel needed
for the furnaces would have to be imported into the Hebrides
and the northern isles.

With the new metal new types of tool were introduced, notably
shaft-hole axes. Such are found already at Dunagoil, in the
deepest levels at Traprain and on Burnswark. But iron was not
cheap enough to oust stone at once, even for axes. Ground stone
axes of thoroughly " Neolithic " aspect were found at the Gallic
forts of Abernethy and Forgandenny, in the vitrified forts of
Dunagoil and Duntroon, in the crannogs of Hyndford and
Lochlee, on Traprain Law, and at Foshigarry in North Uist.

[1] *PSAS.*, xlix, p. 241.   [2] *PSAS.*, lxviii, p. 207.

These cannot be dismissed as relics of previous Neolithic occupants or curios picked up by Iron Age invaders, but surely indicate a genuine survival of a " Neolithic " technique and the continued employment of Stone Age tools right into the Iron Age.

Moreover in certain regions, as we shall see, iron had for some time to compete with bronze as an industrial metal. For horse-trappings and ornaments, bronze, of course, continued in use throughout the period. It was worked like iron by local smiths. Crucibles are quite often found in forts, castles, crannogs, and wheel-dwellings. They fall into two groups, both of which are represented in England at Glastonbury. Small, hemispherical crucibles of quite thick clay come from the vitrified forts of Finavon and Dunagoil, from three brochs [1] and from two wheel-dwellings in North Uist.[2] Triangular crucibles of thin fire-resistant clay are common in the second-century level [3] at Traprain and occur in five brochs,[4] and the Buston crannog. Tongs, suitable for handling the crucibles were found in Traprain.[5]

The metal was often cast into flat bars, 3 to 6 inches long and less than half an inch thick, that formed the raw material for working up into ornaments. These were cast in open sandstone moulds such as were used already in the Early Bronze Age. They have been found on Traprain, in the Lochlee, and Buston crannogs, at Mote of Mark, Finavon and Dunadd, and in three brochs, while a bar thus cast lay on the floor of the beehive at Castlelaw, Glencorse. Spear-butts, pins, dress-fasteners, and similar objects were cast at Traprain, Dunagoil, Dunadd, and in the brochs in clay moulds constructed and used in precisely the same manner as those employed by the Late Bronze Age smith at Jarlshof. *Cire perdue* moulds were found at Traprain and Dunadd.

A developed textile industry was introduced by the Iron Age invaders. Spindle whorls are universal in Iron Age sites while a series of specialized weaving tools seems peculiar to the castle complex.

Glass-working and enamelling were generally practised among

[1] Nybster (Caith.), Clumlie (Shetland), Dun Beag (Skye).
[2] Foshigarry and Garry Iochdrar (N. Uist).
[3] *PSAS.*, l, p. 122.
[4] Keiss and Nybster (Caith.), Burrian, Lingrow, and Okstrow (Orkney).
[5] *PSAS.*, xlix, fig. 35, 4.

the La Tène celts of the Continent and England, but these refined arts were only introduced into Southern Scotland during the first century A.D. from the Province.   Small, hemispherical

crucibles with walls about ¼ in. thick were found with alkali-lime silicate glass adhering to them in the second-century level at Traprain.[1] And an opaque, greenish yellow glass for making beads was cast in the small fort of Castlehill near Dalry, Ayrshire, where Roman influence is also pronounced.

Apart from fortification the changes in military equipment effected by the Iron Age invasions are less easily illustrated from the Scottish relics. We know from Tacitus that at Mons Graupius Galgacus's troops used long, iron broad-swords with no point (*sine mucrone*). But no La Tène swords have survived from Scotland though we possess three chapes—from Glencotho on the Upper Tweed, Mortonhall on the Pentlands (Fig. 65), and Bargany House, Ayrshire,[2] and trefoil pommels from Middlebie (Dumfriesshire), Castlehill fort near Dalry, and the Roman station at Newstead.

Xiphilinus mentions the bulbous butts of the Caledonians' spears. Moulds for casting such have in fact been found at Dunagoil and Traprain, and actual specimens in the lowest level at Traprain and in the broch of Harray, Orkney (Fig. 68, 6).

The Keltic chiefs of Gaul had been accustomed to fight from chariots and the practice was introduced into Yorkshire by the authors of the Arras culture. In Gaul the war-chariot went out of use about 120 B.C., but it still survived in England when Cæsar landed there. In Scotland war-chariots are mentioned in connection with the battle of Mons Graupius and as late as the expedition of Septimius Severus in A.D. 207, providing a fine example of cultural lag. No actual

FIG. 65.—Scabbard from Mortonhall, Midlothian, after Anderson. ⅓.

[1] *PSAS.,* lvii, p. 207.   [2] *ACAG.,* vii, p. 48 ; *PSAS.,* xxxiv, p. 254.

chariots survive, but we possess bits and trappings for the steeds that drew them.

A simple type of bit, going back on the Continent far into the Bronze Age, was composed of two cheek-pieces—tines sawn off at the base—united by a snaffle-bar—a piece of wood or a twisted thong of hardened leather, fitting into holes in the tines.[1] In Britain cheek-pieces for bits made from antler-tines appear first at Heathery Burn Cave together with the naves of chariot-wheels. They may mean that the chariot and the bit alike were

FIG. 66.—Bits from Lochlee, ⅓, and Burnswark, ¼.

introduced by the Hallstatt invaders. Perforated tines are common at Glastonbury,[2] but they do not agree accurately with the Continental cheek-pieces and may have been knife-handles rather than parts of bridle bits. However, similar perforated tines have been found in Scotland at Dunagoil, in Archerfield Cave (Midlothian), Borness Cave, and in six brochs.[3] In the specimens from Archerfield, the transverse hole through the tine is square. Apart from these doubtful examples, an iron bit with cheek-pieces, ultimately a metal version of the foregoing type, comes from a third-century level at Traprain.[4]

[1] Childe, *Bronze Age,* fig. 13, 6.   [2] Bulleid and Gray, pp. 441 ff.
[3] Aikerness, Cairston (Bridge of Waith, Orkney), Cinn Trolla, Wester Broch at Keiss.   [4] *PSAS.,* lv, p. 193, fig. 21, 8.

In the La Tène bits the cheek-pieces are replaced by large metal rings as in ordinary bits to-day. In the earliest English examples such as were used by the charioteers at Arras, the mouthpiece was tripartite; two "branches", through which the terminal rings pass, are connected together by a central link of figure 8 shape.[1] In North Britain the type was simplified by casting the branches in one piece with the rings and lengthening the connecting-link. A bit from Lochlee crannog illustrates this development (Fig. 66). The rings and central link are here of iron, but the lateral branches are of bronze and have been cast-on to the rings. The ends of the branches project into the centres of the rings and could be made vehicles for decoration. Since the horses to be controlled were yoked to chariots in pairs, one end of each bit would be more conspicuous than the other and was accordingly more richly decorated. Such decorated bits were elaborated in North-eastern England and are represented only in the Lowlands of Scotland. One, found near Burnswark and perhaps belonging to the chief of that oppidum, is enamelled in champlevé technique. A specimen from Middlebie, in Dumfries-shire (Pl. XV), however, is decorated in the boss style that was developed in North Britain and flourished especially in the second century A.D. It will be noted that the Scottish bits are confined to the area south of the Forth–Clyde isthmus and all go back directly to the Arras type without the intervention of variants that were popular in the Glastonbury complex.

The same remarks apply to the terrets or rein-rings[2] which went in sets of five with each chariot. At Arras the terrets were sub-oval rings, thickened for three-quarters of their circumference and decorated externally with lip-like protuberances. In phases of development, better illustrated in Southern England at Glastonbury and elsewhere, the segment of the ring which was actually attached to the harness became a simple narrow bar separated from the rest of the ring by collars. The Scottish examples all belong to this class, and most are decorated in the North British boss-style, as in the examples found with the bit at Middlebie (Pl. XV). Save for one from the Roman station of Ardoch all come from south of the isthmus—the Tweed basin, the Lothians, the plain of Galloway, and Ayrshire.[3] At Traprain

---

[1] Leeds, pp. 113–17.   [2] Leeds, pp. 118–126.
[3] Add to Leeds' list a stray from Dunure (S. Ayrs.), in Dick Museum.

PLATE XV

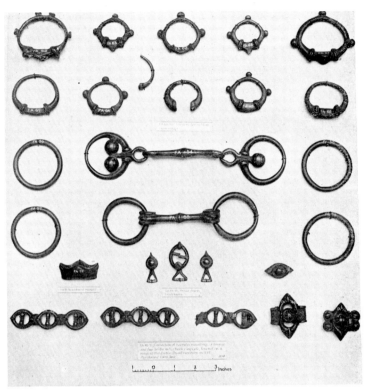

HORSE-TRAPPINGS FROM MIDDLEBIE, DUMFRIESSHIRE

National Museum

one was found in the lowest level,[1] but the others come from the second-century layer to which period the majority should belong.

A rather later type of terret, represented in Northern England and Berwickshire, penetrated even to Aberdeenshire. It is undecorated, while the thickest part of the ring partly conceals an iron bar to which the harness was attached.

The Iron Age did not witness such radical and general changes in dress and ornament in Scotland as in the rest of Western Europe. All the La Tène Kelts of the Continent and England were accustomed to fasten their cloaks with brooches constructed on the principle of the modern safety-pin with a spring pin. The evolution of the *fibulæ*, as such brooches are technically termed, indeed provides one of the most reliable bases for a relative chronology of the Iron Age. The fashion was introduced into

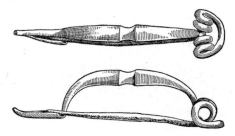

FIG. 67.—La Tène I fibula from Castlelaw, Abernethy, after Ant. J. ¼.

Scotland by the invaders who landed on our east coasts to create the Abernethy complex. A specimen in bronze of late La Tène I form was found in the Gallic fort at Abernethy (Fig. 67). And even on the west coast the vitrified forts of Dunagoil and Dun Fheurain produced iron fibulæ, hopelessly corroded, but probably La Tène II in type.

Curiously enough the fashion never took root in Scotland (nor for that matter in Ireland). The half-Romanized natives living south of the Forth did indeed wear brooches decorated in Romano-British style (Fig. 68, 1, 2), and that even as far from the Wall as Earnsheugh, St. Abb's Head, and Castlehill, near Dalry (Ayrshire). But north of the Wall safety-pins were not adopted.

Brooches of penannular type—a loose pin on a ring—were also worn by the Kelts of the Continent and England. And such enjoyed a rather wider vogue in Caledonia. In pre-Roman

[1] *PSAS.*, xlix, p. 182, fig. 32, 1.

examples from Southern England [1] the ends of the ring are bent back in spirals, but this early form is probably unrepresented here where the terminals are generally cast knobs (Fig. 68, 5). Penannular brooches are found in all levels at Traprain Law, in a grave at Gilmerton, Midlothian, on the Laws, Monifieth, at the vitrified fort of Dun Fheurain, in the crannogs of Hyndford and Dowalton Loch, in the galleried dun of Castlehaven, at

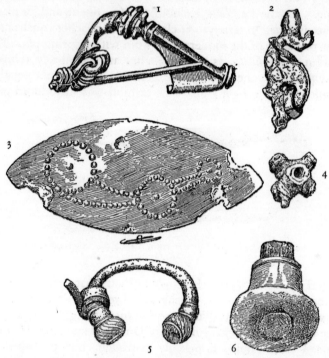

FIG. 68.—Brooches, ornamented bronze plate and bronze spear-butt, Traprain Law, after *PSAS*. ⅔.

Castlehill, Dalry, in the broch of Okstrow, and at the Covesea Cave, Elgin. The type certainly had a long life and survived in the highly decorated forms of the Dark Ages and the later Highland brooch. But it hardly became naturalized in Northern Scotland during the Early Iron Age ; the specimens from Argyll, Orkney, and Elgin, all come from sites where Roman influence was conspicuous.

[1] Cunnington, pl. 18, 1 ; Bulleid and Gray, p. 208.

Simple pins were, however, in general use. Those with ring-heads have considerable value for chronology.[1] The simplest type, derived from the Hallstatt swan's neck pin is made of bronze or iron wire, bent over to a loop at the head and given a kink in the stem just below the loop. The type appears in England at All Cannings Cross and in the Arras group further north, and about the same time in Denmark and Norway.[2] In Scotland it appears, apparently associated with the Abernethy complex in the Gallic fort at Abernethy (Fig. 69, 1), on the Laws, Monifieth, at Dunagoil (Fig. 69, 2) and stray on Loch Moidart in Western Inverness-shire, where vitrified forts are common; but an example from the hill-top town on Bonchester Hill, is best connected with Arras.

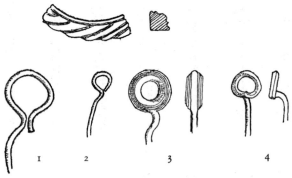

FIG. 69.—Fragment of jet bracelet from Abernethy; pins from (1) Abernethy, (2–3) Dunagoil, (4) Freswick broch. $\frac{1}{2}$.

A variant with a heavy cast ring for the head (Fig. 69, 3) is found in the charioteers' graves at Arras and in Scotland at Traprain[3] and Dunagoil.   In Scotland, apparently in the Abernethy complex, a parallel variant was created in which the head has been bent forward out of the plane of the shaft, as in a modern tie-pin. Examples with looped wire heads come from the Laws at Monfieth, from Dun Fheurain, from Orkney, and perhaps from the cist grave at Gilmerton. Miss Benton[4] has rightly insisted that the shift forward of the head effected in these shouldered pins must have been inspired by the " Late Bronze Age " sunflower pin. The type can therefore have been

[1] Smith in *Opuscula arch. O. Montelio dicata*, pp. 282 f. BM., *Iron*, p. 97.
[2] *Real.*, ix, pl. 154, *a* and *b*.
[3] *PSAS.*, lvi, p. 215 ; the head is solid, not a ring.
[4] *PSAS.*, lxv, p. 194.

created only in Scotland or Ireland and illustrates the overlap
between the Bronze and Iron Ages.

Shouldered pins with the heads similarly arranged but now
cast, not bent, appear in the second-century levels at Traprain,[1]
at Dunadd, in the Ness broch (Fig. 69, 4), Caithness, and stray
on Tentsmuir, Fife, and Culbin Sands and near Coupar Angus.
Still later, in the third-century level at Traprain,[2] the head
becomes a vehicle for decoration. In the Lowlands and at Covesea
(Elgin), it is adorned with pellets in accordance with the North
British boss style, but at Bowermadden broch, Caithness, the
ornament has been reduced to mere cross-ribbing. The series,
thus begun, leads on to the ornate hand-pins of the Dark Ages,
illustrated at Norries Law and in Ireland.

Fig. 70.—Bone pins from the Broch of Burrian, Sanday. ¼.

Bone pins with carved heads, such as were worn also by the
Continental Kelts and at Glastonbury, are very common in
the castle complex (Fig. 70), but occur also in crannogs and
at Covesea. In the south dress-fasteners, such as were used in
pre-Roman times at Glastonbury, came into use in the crannogs
and forts. Though found even in the lowest level at Traprain,
and manufactured there in the second century,[3] these clasps
seem to be the result of influence from the Province after A.D. 80.

Finger-rings were worn by the Kelts of Gaul and England
and introduced by them into Scotland in the Iron Age. Spiral
finger-rings of bronze wire or ribbon occur already in the Gallic
fort of Abernethy, on the Laws at Monifieth, in the crannogs
of Buston, Hyndford, and Lochlee, at Castlehaven, and elsewhere.

[1] *PSAS.*, xlix, p. 171 ; lviii, p. 268.
[2] *PSAS.*, lviii, p. 268, but cf. lvi, p. 221, for an earlier specimen.
[3] *PSAS.*, lviii, p. 264.

Solid bronze finger-rings expanding to a disc in imitation of the bezel of a signet ring were found in the Hyndford crannog and on the edge of a cairn at Muirkirk, Ayrshire.[1] The type goes back to pre-Roman times at Glastonbury.[2] Finger-rings of lignite were also popular in the Scottish Iron Age.

Jet or lignite armlets, appearing in Scotland with the Late Bronze Age invasion, became extremely popular in the Iron Age. All are convex externally and more or less flattened on the inside. One early type, very thick, is decorated on the outside with oblique grooves, producing the effect of Scandinavian torques[3] with alternating torsion (Fig. 69). It might be attributed to the Abernethy complex since specimens come from Abernethy and Dunagoil, but a third was found on the edge of a Bronze Age cairn at Drumelzier on the Upper Tweed.[4] Plain armlets are common in hill-top towns (Burnswark), small forts (Castlelaw Glencorse), crannogs, castles (Castlehill at Dalry and Dunadd), and even in the far northern brochs[5] and hut-circles. They were manufactured at Traprain, the Dowalton Loch crannog and Dunadd and on Shewalton Moor, Ayrshire. Later, glass tended to supersede lignite for bangles in the Lowlands, and glass bracelets were imported even into Skye.

Ornamental metal combs were used by Keltic ladies of the La Tène period on the Continent. During the Roman period bone combs became popular among the natives of Gaul and Britain. They are generally formed of three to five narrow strips of bone riveted on to a pair of transverse bars of the same material. The majority are toothed along both edges, but some have only a single row of teeth, the back being rounded. Double-edged combs are common in the northern brochs and wheel-houses[6] and in the crannogs and occur also at Dunadd, the Laws of Monifieth and St. Ford's Links in Fife.[7] Round-backed combs have been found in the brochs of Burwick and Burrian, Orkney, and in a dwelling at Galson, Lewis.

The picture of Iron Age life deducible from these sparse relics

[1] *PSAS.*, lvii, p. 13.

[2] Bulleid and Gray, pl. 41, E. 111 ; cf. Dechelette, iii, figs. 544, 546.

[3] Childe, *Bronze Age*, p. 123, and fig. 17, 6.

[4] *PSAS.*, lxv, p. 369.

[5] Cinn Trolla and Carn Liath (Sutherland) ; Keiss (Caith.) ; one comes from a hut-circle in Strath of Kildonan.

[6] Jarlshof (Shetland), Burray, Burrian, and Lamaness (Orkney), Elsay, Freswick, Hillhead, and Kettleburn (Caith.), dwellings of Galson (Lewis) and Foshigarry (N. Uist.).

[7] *PSAS.*, xxxv, p. 286.

agrees well enough with what might have been expected from a consideration of the fortresses and refuges from which they have been gathered. In the general insecurity the monuments so grimly attest, the finer arts and industries of higher civilization could find no place. Actually, barbarian squalor reigns everywhere, superficially relieved by a few imports from the peaceful Province. Only in the south in immediate contact with the Romanized provincials are a genuine art and a more sophisticated industry traceable. But even there objects of æsthetic value are rare, and the potter's wheel was not adopted before the end of the fourth century A.D. It remains to fill in the picture by a consideration of the relics assignable to specific cultural groups or peoples and at the same time to try and deduce the affinities of their users.

2. THE SEVERAL IRON AGE CULTURES

(i) *The Abernethy Complex*

The relics derived from Gallic and vitrified forts are too few to allow of the recognition of any distinction between their builders. Indeed they do not suffice to provide any fresh clue as to the origin of these invaders who had come to Caledonia direct across the North Sea, nor even for an accurate estimate of their contribution to Scottish Iron Age culture as a whole.

In addition to their peculiar methods of defensive architecture the invaders certainly introduced a fully developed iron industry, the use of safety-pins (Fig. 67) and ring-headed pins (Fig. 69), of bulbous spear-heads and finger-rings.[1] They exploited the local deposits of lignite and may have created the fluted type of armlet and a curious sort of thick ring. The ring from Finavon is over half an inch thick though the overall diameter is only 1·7 inches, while a specimen from Abernethy is still thicker. The pottery used in such forts was so coarse and soft that earlier excavators missed it altogether or rescued only insignificant fragments. At Finavon I found abundant sherds of cooking-pots, made from very coarse clay comprising large rock splinters and very imperfectly fired. The vessels were flat-bottomed, the rims simply rounded off, and the walls decorated only with casual grooves. For finer vessels wood was doubtless employed.

[1] Above, pp. 233, 235.

Pieces of wooden vessels were actually found at Abernethy. The same site yielded a boulder with an oval hollow, 3 inches long by 2½ inches wide by 1½ inches deep, hammered out in it and a groove for a wick in the rim; a shallow, stone dish came from Finavon. Simple awls, needles, and spatulæ of bone were common at Dunagoil, but Finavon produced only one bone awl and an unfinished handle of antler.

No Roman relics have been found in forts of this type on the east coast, so that they must have been abandoned before Agricola conquered the country. On the west coast the vitrified forts are juxtaposed to the castles, but in Bute and on Loch Crinan it looks as if they had been abandoned before the castle-builders arrived. Nevertheless Dun Macuisneachan[1] and Dun Fheurain were both occupied at least into the first century A.D., and a weaving comb—a type proper to the castles—was found in the latter fort. Here, then, vitrified forts must have co-existed with castles and may even have been occupied by new masters. In Western Inverness-shire and in Ross the roughly exclusive distributions of brochs and vitrified forts suggests that the latter maintained their independence over against castle-builders.

(ii) *The Castle Complex*

In the last Chapter we insisted on the architectural and functional similarities between the northern brochs and the duns or small stone " forts " along the western coasts further south. The brochs have yielded a relatively large number of significant relics. And precisely the same types recur in the wheel-dwellings of the northern isles that have been ascribed to an older subject population. The latter certainly assimilated the culture of the broch-lords. Such stone castles in Argyll, Bute, and Galloway as have been excavated produced scarcely any relics, though one type—the strike-a-light—is common to them and to the brochs. However, in the area of the castles in Bute, Ayrshire, and Galloway are certain inhabited caves, from which a fully representative series of distinctive broch types has been recovered. They perhaps justify the provisional treatment of the whole group of buildings as manifestations of a single culture. They do not exclude the possibility of subdividing that culture in the future and attributing it to several distinct, but allied, waves of colonization.

[1] Angus Smith, *Loch Etive and the Sons of Uisnach*, p. 148.

From a consideration of the distribution of castles and of their architectural similarities to Cornish forts, we inclined to attribute the castle complex to a coastwise movement from the south-west. Distinctive relics from the northern brochs and the southern caves in the castle area provide satisfactory confirmation of this hypothesis. They include a whole series of

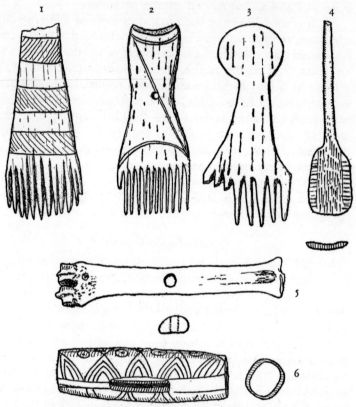

FIG. 71.—Long-handled combs, spatula, bobbin and " toggle " 1, 4, 6. Borness Cave. 2, 3, 5, brochs. ½.

types that are best represented at Glastonbury, but that in some cases appear rather earlier in Wiltshire sites like All Cannings Cross and Swallowcliffe Down, and that all reappear in Roman times in the caves of Western Yorkshire.[1]

The agreements between the Scottish and the South-west

[1] The relics from Dowkerbottom in British, from Victoria and Attermire caves in Settle Museum.

English types are of a nature to prove that our castle complex is in fact the result of coastwise migrations up our western seaboard, essentially similar to those that diffused the Windmill Hill culture in the Stone Age from Galloway to Caithness. But now the pattern is complicated by the reaction on the invaders of earlier settlers—survivors of Collectivist and Beaker stocks, and of the " Hallstatt " invaders as well as of the groups who built the vitrified forts—and by the repercussions of the Roman conquest.

The most conclusive links with the Glastonbury complex are provided by weaving implements. And weaving being essentially a woman's industry, such implements in this instance demonstrate a mass migration just as surely as pottery would. And all the tools in question are specifically British; whatever remote Continental prototypes they may have had, they had already been transformed in South-western England and stamped with its imprint before they reach Scotland.

We have in the first place long-handled weaving combs [1] of antler or, in the northern isles, of whalebone (Fig. 71, 1–3). Some are decorated as at Glastonbury and All Cannings Cross with engraved rectilinear patterns or dots-and-circles. Such combs are found at Borness Cave on the coast of Kirkcudbright, at Dun Fheurain, near Oban, in the brochs of Shetland, Orkney, Caithness, and Sutherland, and in the wheel-dwellings of North Uist, Lewis, and North Ronaldshay. Outside the castle area weaving combs have only been found in the Roman stations of Camelon and Newstead and in one hut-circle in Strathardle, Perthshire.[2] They are conspicuously absent from the crannogs and the caves of East Lothian and Fife, where bone work is well preserved. The examples from the Roman stations presumably belong to British servants or slaves brought from the Province or even from our castle area.

Associated with the combs at Borness cave, in the brochs of Jarlshof, Aikerness, Ayre, Lamaness, Keiss, and Elsay, in the dwellings of Bragar, Bac Mhic Connain, Foshigarry, and Howmae go so-called bobbins. There is a stray specimen from Coll,[3] but none outside the castle area. These are marrow-bones of sheep transversely (but not longitudinally) perforated (Fig. 71, 5) —a common Glastonbury type. Similar bones served as bobbins

---

[1] Bulleid and Gray, pp. 270 ff., Cunnington, pl. 11 ; *WAM.*, 43, pls. viii ; cf. *Revue des Musées,* 1928, p. 139.
[2] *PSAS.*, vi, p. 402.   [3] Hunterian Museum, Glasgow.

on which the weft was wound in the shuttle in the Hebrides last century.[1] In the same connection may be mentioned bone needles which are common in the castle complex, but not confined thereto. The whole textile industry [2] of Glastonbury had been transferred bodily to the castle area of Scotland.

Equally convincing are bone dice (Fig. 72). Dice were used by the Kelts all over the Continent,[3] but differ in form from those found in the Scottish castles. These agree precisely with those from Glastonbury in being parallelopipeds. Our examples come from a cave in Bute,[4] the brochs of Ayre, Burrian, and Hillhead, the wheel-houses of Foshigarry and Bac Mhic Connain, and several unexcavated sites in Orkney.

Tubular sections of bone with a transverse slit through them were found at Borness cave (Fig. 71, 6) and Cleve's Cove near

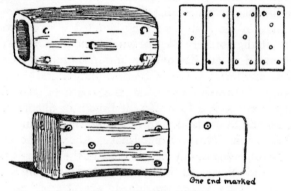

FIG. 72.—Bone dice from the Broch of Ayre, Orkney. ¼.

Dalry, Ayrshire, and a similarly slotted length of whalebone comes from the Road Broch at Keiss, Caithness. The southern examples at least agree precisely with the so-called toggle-like fasteners (they are more probably connected with weaving) from Glastonbury [5] and the West Yorkshire caves. Spatulate pieces of bone from Borness (Fig. 71, 4) again have parallels, much better fashioned, in the spoons from West Yorkshire and, more remote,

---

[1] Bulleid and Gray, pp. 423–6.

[2] Callander (*PSAS.*, lxv, p. 353) suggests that a bone plaque, perforated at the four corners from Skirza Head broch, and round ones with four perforations from Jarlshof and Burrian may have been weaving tablets.

[3] Dechelette, iii, fig. 623 ; cf. Cunnington, pl. 6, 32. Dice like ours were, however, used in Gotland, Almgren, and Nermann, *Die ältere Eisenzeit Gotlands*, pl. 30, 442.

[4] Hunterian Museum, Glasgow.   [5] Bulleid and Gray, p. 460.

in the " spatulate pins " from All Cannings Cross.[1] The tines, sawn off and transversely pierced, and the bone pins with carved heads that have been already discussed,[2] and some buttons or whorls [3] made from the perforated head of an animal's femur, all constitute additional links between the castles and Glastonbury.

In the same direction point, albeit less unambiguously—for they recur also at Arras—dart-heads made from the marrow-bones of sheep.[4] The point is formed by cutting off the bone obliquely near one end; the articulating surface at the opposite end is pierced to the marrow cavity so that a continuous socket runs the whole length of the implement. Exceptionally,[5] as in All

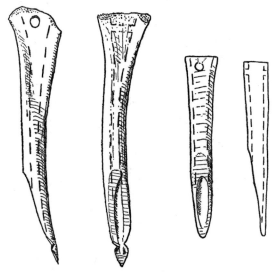

FIG. 73.—Bone dart-heads, Foshigarry. ⅓.

Cannings type B, the butt-end is cut off square below the articulation. Occasionally there are peg-holes transverse to the main axis. In two examples from North Uist [6] a barbed head has been produced by sharp cuts just below the point (Fig. 73). In Scotland such dart-heads are confined to the castle area, but occur within it at Borness Cave, in three brochs and four dwellings.[7]

[1] Cunnington, pl. 6, 24–30.   [2] Above, pp. 229, 234.
[3] Aikerness, Burray, Burrian, Everley, Hillhead, Harbor, and Wester (Keiss) brochs ; Foshigarry and Bragar.
[4] Cunnington, p. 82 ; Bulleid and Gray, p. 421.
[5] Borness cave, Foshigarry, Bac Mhic Connain.
[6] Foshigarry and Bac Mhic Connain.
[7] Aikerness, Keiss, and White Gate brochs ; Bragar, Foshigarry, Bac Mhic Connain, Howmae, and Sanday.

R

Thus a whole complex of significant types, elaborated in pre-Roman times in South-western England, was transferred bodily to Galloway and the far north. Perhaps as ultimate by-products of this essentially coastwise transmission, the same forms reached the dales of Western Yorkshire. Unfortunately, neither ceramic nor artistic evidence can be adduced to reinforce the testimony of the bone-work.

The commonest broch pottery is hard fired and rather thin. The rims are rounded and often everted (Fig. 74). Squat, globular cooking-pots with a very short neck are the most characteristic shapes. This is much the same sort of pottery as is found in the two upper levels at Traprain and on other Lowland sites

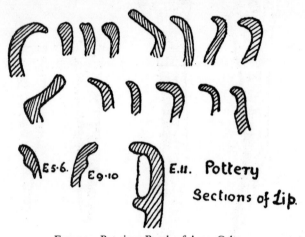

FIG. 74.—Pot rims, Broch of Ayre, Orkney.

occupied in the second century A.D. Even a little vase, shaped like a modern egg-cup, from the broch of Ousedale Burn, Caithness, finds exact parallels at Traprain (bottom level !),[1] at Earnsheugh, and in a cave near Gullane. Even such low-grade wares have not been found in typical castles of Argyll or Galloway.

On the other hand, a considerable quantity of decorated sherds have been collected in the brochs, duns, and wheel-houses of Skye, the Hebrides, and Orkney. Simple incised patterns—alternating triangles, vertical zig-zag bands, divergent lines fringed with short strokes—are common to the duns of Coll and Tiree,[2] the brochs of Dun an Iardhard (Skye), Lingrow, and Ayre

[1] *PSAS.*, lvii, p. 196, fig. 11.
[2] Beveridge, *Coll and Tiree,* plates (unnumbered).

PLATE XVI

a

b

a VESSEL FROM BROCH OF LINGROW
b SHERDS FROM DUNS IN COLL

National Museum

(Orkney), and the wheel-houses like Foshigarry in North Uist. They are frequently combined with applied ribs, crinkled along the edge (Pl. XVI). In Skye and the Hebrides finger-printing on applied ribs or on the pot walls is not uncommon. Circular stamps and applied knobs were also used. A sherd from Foshigarry bears an incised triscele, another from the same site and one from Coll exhibit a naturalistic representation. The best of these is the sketch of a deer incised on a sherd from a dun in Coll (Pl. XVI, *b*). This representation stands alone in the British ceramic art. But painted or incised animals, generally horses, are depicted on La Tène vases [1] from Gaul and, more conventionalized, on the bronze buckets of the Belgae in England. At the same time the Coll stag might be a forerunner of the superbly carved bulls of Burghead and the Pictish stones of the Dark Ages.

None of this northern ceramic decoration bears any significant resemblance to the elaborate Glastonbury style of South-west England. On the other hand, certain simple motives—divergent, fringed lines, double zig-zags with dots or dimples between them [2] —and techniques, like finger-printing, recur in the " Hallstatt " wares of All Cannings Cross. Moreover, as already remarked, pots from native sites of the castle area in the Hebrides are sometimes flat-rimmed as in the English Iron Age A group. From the Hebrides we have examples of the sharp shoulder that would be expected in the same group, and three minute sherds of thin burnished red ware from Everley Broch, Caithness, have a thoroughly Hallstatt look. Again, the everted rims of large vessels decorated in the style already described from the brochs of Mousa and Lingrow, have shallow flutings on the inside. These give the metallic impression of early South-west German and later Central Gaulish Hallstatt vases.[3]

It will be remembered that the pottery of Radford's " early La Tène invasion ", associated in Wiltshire with many Glastonbury types of bone tool, was still largely flat-rimmed and Hallstatt in tradition. Yet the Hallstatt elements in the castles of the extreme north are best explained by a persistence of the Jarlshof tradition among numerous survivors of the pre-broch population. It would confirm our view of the broch-builders as a conquering

[1] Dechelette, iii, fig. 661.
[2] Beveridge, *Coll and Tiree*, plates " Tiree 8 ", " Coll 6."
[3] Childe, *Danube*, fig. 204 ; *Mat.*, 1879 ; figs. 139, 141.

minority. In the northern isles the intrusive castle-folk would
have subjugated, but then tolerated, the older inhabitants with
their more predominantly Bronze Age culture. In Argyll and
round the Clyde the more advanced iron-using occupants of
the vitrified forts must have been exterminated or expelled.

The castle complex thus assumed a new aspect. The conquerors
squatted on every piece of cultivable land near a passable haven
on the western and northern coasts and extended their domains
along natural cross-country routes—along Loch Awe from
Crinan, for instance—and up the straths of Sutherland and
Caithness to the indispensable forests. But, at least in the north,
the old population lived on in their wheel-houses among the
sand-dunes, or joined the new lord's retainers in the fort outside
his broch. The conquerors arrived in sufficient numbers to

Fig. 75.—Quartz strike-a-light, broch of
Lingrow, after Anderson. $\frac{3}{5}$.

establish even there new arts and crafts—the textile industry,
regular iron-working, the new techniques of bronze casting
(indicated by the triangular and globular crucibles [1])—and
perhaps new breeds of cattle and sheep. They were indeed
strong enough to found fresh colonies round the Tay and the
Forth from their northern bases.

But they failed to preserve the higher aspects and finer amenities
of the Glastonbury culture; it cannot be purely accidental that
no product of the flourishing Glastonbury school of art has been
found in the castle area.[2] And if the conquerors imposed so
much of their culture upon their subjects, the latter may have
made contributions of their own to the original broch culture
even before they swamped it. They had at least longer experience

[1] Above, p. 227.
[2] There is, however, a carved wooden tool box from Orkney in Mann's collection.

of the exigencies of the insular environment and had found out how to meet them.

The tradition of replacing wood by stone or whalebone, that had become indigenous in the islands, found abundant expression in the broch period; an extraordinary series of whalebone objects, including flat clubs, often notched along the edges,[1] perforated mallets,[2] and basins,[3] from North Uist and Orkney illustrate the point again. Possibly certain types of object, common in the brochs and sometimes recurring in other castles but certainly not derivable from Southern Britain, should be considered in this connection.

As flint was scarce, quartz pebbles were substituted for use with iron in the production of fire. Such pebbles are grooved on one face and often show traces of rust in the grooves (Fig. 75). They are very common in the northern brochs and in the wheel-houses of the Hebrides. I know examples from the " castles " of Luing,[4] Dunadd,[5] Druim an Duin (Crinan), Dun Breac [6] in Skipness (Kintyre), from Borness Cave, and from sandhills in Northern Ireland, but none from the crannogs or Lowland forts and caves. The type is therefore distinctive of the castle complex as a whole. But it is not English nor Gaulish. The only foreign parallels come from Norway and belong to the early centuries of our era. Whether it reached Norway from North Scotland or *vice versa* is uncertain. In any case the strike-a-lights establish a link across the North Sea in pre-Viking times.

Flat stone discs, $2\frac{1}{2}$ to 5 inches in diameter and carefully smoothed or polished on the faces and edges, have been found in nine northern brochs.[7] In the south they recur in the alleged brochs of the Laws at Monifieth and Hurley Hawkin near Dundee, at Dunadd, Castlehill near Dalry, and the galleried dun of Castlehaven, but also on Traprain Law, in the Lochspouts crannog, and in West Yorkshire caves. At Traprain,[8] seven came from the third-century level and one from the topmost layer.

---

[1] Foshigarry, Howmae, Burrian.
[2] Foshigarry, Bac Mhic Connain, brochs of Cairston and Keiss.
[3] Brochs of Jarlshof, Aikerness, Ayre, Burrian, and Elsay (at Aikerness only in secondary occupations); Foshigarry, Howmae.
[4] *PSAS.*, xxvii, p. 379 (South Fort).
[5] *PSAS.*, lxiv, p. 120.
[6] Petersen, *Gamle Gårdsanlegg i Rogaland*, p. 34.
[7] Jarlshof, Burray, Okstrow, Keiss Road, Nybster, Old Stirkoke, Skirza Head, Cinn Trolla, Dun Beag (Skye); cf. *PSAS.*, x, p. 717.
[8] *PSAS.*, lvii, p. 213.

Cups or ladles of stone, preferably of steatite, are commonly found in brochs, but by no means confined to the castle area. The cup, nearly hemispherical, may be internally $3\frac{1}{2}$ to $4\frac{1}{2}$ inches wide, and $1\frac{1}{3}$ to $2\frac{1}{2}$ inches deep. From it projects a flat or rod-like handle, 2 to 5 inches long, often vertically pierced. Such vessels might well be stone copies of wooden ladles such as have been found in the Lochlee crannog.[1] The translation from wood to stone would be most likely to arise in the treeless islands and especially in Shetland where steatite was available. Examples have been found in seven brochs from Orkney to

FIG. 76.—Stone cup with handle, Dun Beag, Skye. $\frac{1}{2}$.

Skye,[2] in the dwelling at Galson (Lewis), and in the castle of Druim an Duin near Loch Crinan.

But stone cups with handles are by no means confined to the castles ; on the contrary, they are far commoner in Aberdeenshire and in the adjacent counties of Banff and Elgin than in the castle area. And in Aberdeenshire they are said to have been found ' in cairns ", " within a stone circle ", and " adjacent to a stone circle " (of recumbent type).[3] Moreover, there is a specimen

[1] Munro, figs. 102 and 104.
[2] Ayre, Burray, Keiss Road, Kettleburn, Dunrobbin, Cinn Trolla, Dun Telve, Dun Beag.
[3] *PSAS.*, l, p. 148 ; the National and Aberdeen Museums possess thirty specimens from these counties and six from Perthshire.

from Dunagoil which should be pre-castle as well as one from the Hyndford crannog. Outside Scotland there are several examples from Ireland, particularly from the north, one from the Isle of Man, and at least one from Cornwall.[1] In the Middle Ages very similar cups were used in Norway.

In Scotland the type may be regarded as pre-castle in origin and belonging to that " Late Bronze Age " culture which embraced both sides of the Moray Firth before the castle-builders arrived in the north. Are the southern examples due to reactions of the castle-culture along the route which its authors had followed or to that earlier intercourse between North Scotland and Ireland and Cornwall, presupposed in the bronze industry of Jarlshof and illustrated by the souterrains and fogous? Either explanation is possible.

In any case the castle-folk, though inhabiting storm-swept coasts and ultimately reduced for lack of timber to coracles (skin-boats), must maintain contact with the outside world. They must import their tin and copper (and perhaps even iron) and the wood for smelting them. And they did secure Roman coins and vases even in Orkney and the Hebrides ; glass beads and armlets that may have been manufactured at Traprain occur in Orkney and Skye. Shouldered pins of a type evolved in the Lowlands by the third-century have been found in brochs in Caithness and were cast locally in Orkney.

The woollen industry of the islands that has become famous in modern times was flourishing already in the Roman period. But the southern commodities and types must have been obtained more often by piratical raids than by legitimate trade in wool, furs, and slaves. Of such raids we have literary evidence both in Irish and classical sources from the fourth century, but we may infer the like much earlier.[2] By their very situation, perched on a cliff beside a hidden cove, many castles from Galloway to Caithness are marked out as pirate strongholds. For all their intensive agriculture and domestic crafts, the castle-builders were essentially sea-rovers as Brøgger[3] has brilliantly shown. The Lowland brochs may have been built by such raiders who preferred to settle down as overlords among a prosperous peasantry.

[1] Truro Museum.
[2] The references are collected by Watson, *Place Names*, p. 59.
[3] *Den norske Bosetning*, pp. 70 f.

Yet, despite the proceeds of piracy, the castle-folk, especially in the north, must have led a precarious and poverty-stricken existence. They were forced to rely largely on their very limited local resources and make the best possible use of every available material. The skeletons of stranded whales provided a possible substitute for wood and even metal, and such use of whalebone lent a peculiar aspect to the island cultures. Metal ornaments, commonplace in the south, were laboriously copied in this and other materials. A bronze ring dress-fastener, like one from the Lochlee crannog, has been copied in every detail in whalebone at Bac Mhic Connain in North Uist. From Bac Mhic Connain comes a pin of bone with a loose bone ring moving in a perforated head which exactly imitates a late bronze pin that is represented at Covesea, in the brochs, and elsewhere. A whalebone comb from the broch of Bowermadden [1] is plainly a reproduction of

FIG. 77.—Stone lamps, Broch of Okstrow, after Anderson.

a common type of bronze comb. A set of rings carved out of whalebone from the Road Broch at Keiss reproduces a set of three bronze rings cast together at Traprain and regarded as horse trappings. Similarly a stone lamp from the broch of Okstrow (Fig. 77, 1) simulates Roman lamps, as Anderson long ago pointed out.

Perhaps such poverty was confined to the subject population and increased with the lapse of time. As already insisted, the decline in architecture and the unintelligent reconstructions of the brochs denote an absorption of the castle-builders by the older inhabitants of the north, probably already by A.D. 200; perhaps indeed the broch-lords simply sailed away, leaving their towers to their subjects. No stratigraphy renders possible a distinction between earlier and later products in the castle culture. But in general remains of the latest occupation have the best chance

[1] Anderson, i, fig. 205.

of survival. Still most of the relics here considered are likely to go back to a time before decadence set in. The novel forms, as sharply contrasted to those found at Jarlshof as is the architecture of the castles, must have been introduced by the castle-builders ; they confirm the latters' south-western origin.

(iii) *The Inhabitants of Hill-top Towns and Crannogs*

In the Gallic and vitrified forts and in the castles iron and a La Tène culture were introduced abruptly. In the hill-top towns of the Lowlands the replacement of bronze by iron was gradual, and a Late Bronze Age culture was slowly permeated by La Tène elements. In other words, as in North-eastern Yorkshire, the old Cinerary Urn folk may have survived in considerable numbers down to the coming of the Romans. This would seem the most reasonable deduction from relics unearthed in the lowest levels on Traprain Law and the few other objects of pre-Roman type collected in the Lowlands.

Traprain was certainly occupied already during the Late Bronze Age. A small cemetery of late Cinerary Urns was discovered on the hill.[1] Bronze swords of the usual " V " type and other Late Bronze Age objects were cast there by precisely the same processes as were employed by the bronze-smith at Jarlshof. Moulds for their manufacture[2] were found in a " third level " (from the top), though in this section even a " sixth level " (also from the top) could be recognized. In it two socketed axes (Fig. 40) were found together in the doorway of a minute building. Other Late Bronze Age objects, including the Hallstatt razor shown as Fig. 42, were found within the walls of the town.

There is no justification for interpolating an indefinite interval of desertion between this well-documented " Bronze Age " occupation and that during the first century of Roman rule.

FIG. 78.—Iron axe of Bronze Age shape from Traprain Law. ½.

Indeed there are objects from the site that bridge the apparent gap in time and illustrate the gradual transition from a bronze to an iron industry—the ring-head pin like Fig. 69, 3, and above all a socketed axe of iron with loop that faithfully copies the

[1] *PSAS.*, lv, p. 163.   [2] *PSAS.*, lvi, p. 211.

cast Bronze Age form (Fig. 78). It represents, as Rainbow [1] says, " a laborious effort to translate a type appropriate to bronze into a foreign and unsuitable material ". Such an effort is only conceivable where the new metal is still competing with the old in a conservative community, that is, where a bronze industry was still flourishing. The axe from Traprain thus illustrates the gradualness of the transition to the Bronze Age here. The same type is known from Bishop Loch near Glasgow and from Culbin Sands, Elgin. [2]

The earlier pottery from Traprain Law illustrates a similar blending of traditions. The ware is reddish, where not blackened by soot, and as a rule harder fired than normal Cinerary Urns. The rims (Fig. 79) are often internally bevelled in old Bronze Age fashion and flattened inwards or outwards, though less sharply than in the " Hallstatt " ware of Old Keig or Jarlshof. A few sherds show traces of the Hallstatt shoulder and concave neck, though much debased. A couple of fragments from the lowest level reached in 1923 are ornamented with finger-tip impressions below the rim either on the body-clay or on an applied rib. As a whole the ceramic material might be regarded as a Scarborough Hallstatt ware produced by a potter attached to older Bronze Age traditions or a native Bronze Age fabric with Hallstatt elements superadded.

Since pottery of this character is found as high up as the " third (second-century) level ", it undoubtedly represents the normal product manufactured in the town during the Iron Age. If our interpretation be correct, it means that the mass of the townsmen was formed of makers of Cinerary Urns, blended with Hallstatt folk. The latter would be most naturally derived from Yorkshire. And since Cinerary Urns are extraordinarily numerous in the eastern part of that county, a large contingent of mixed people may have migrated thence to Scotland to reinforce the local Cinerary Urn folk. Presumably this account holds good, not only for East Lothian but for the whole of Southern Scotland. Unfortunately the pot-sherds found with the ring-head pin on Bonchester Hill are too small and coarse to demonstrate the truth of this theory in the case of that hill-top town.

Survival of Bronze Age traditions and peoples may be again indicated by the objects of La Tène character found on the edges of Bronze Age cairns—the lignite armlet from Drumelzier

---

[1] *Arch. J.*, lxxxv, p. 173.   [2] *PSAS.*, lvi, p. 217.

and the finger-ring from Muirkirk, Ayrshire.[1] Though not
demonstrably associated with interments in either case, these
offerings at least indicate a continued reverence for a hallowed
spot that might be expected in the descendants of those there
interred.

FIG. 79.—Pot rims from Traprain Law bottom (top row) and second levels. ½.

Other burials may, however, be taken to indicate an infiltration
of La Tène Kelts though perhaps only in the Roman period.
Several inhumation burials are in fact known in Lowland Scotland
at this period. In short cists at Gilmerton[2] and near Dolphinton,[3]

[1] Above, p. 235.   [2] *PSAS.*, xxxviii, p. 427.   [3] *PSAS.*, lv, p. 47.

and under very small, oval cairns at Gullane,[1] the bodies were contracted. The skeleton at Gilmerton was accompanied by a fibula of La Tène IV type, a penannular brooch, and a shouldered pin, all of iron ; it is thereby dated to the first century A.D. At Blackness on the Forth (West Lothian),[2] and at Burnmouth (Berwickshire),[3] the bodies were extended in long cists. At Blackness the skeleton wore a penannular bracelet of bronze ; its ends expand outward as in the Covesea type (Fig. 46, 1), but decorative ribs have been added on the outside. The cist at Burnmouth contained a pair of ritual spoons of bronze decorated in Keltic style ; similar spoons have been found at many sites in England and dated to the first century A.D. The bones of a young pig had also been placed in the grave. Pig bones are a recurrent feature in the La Tène graves of Arras in Yorkshire so that Burnmouth may give a clue as to the affinities of the La Tène elements in Lowland Scotland.

A better clue is provided by the decorated articles of parade which in Scotland are virtually confined to the Lowlands. The Continental Kelts had created out of zoomorphic designs taken over from Hellenic art a purely native style of geometric ornament.[4] The authors of the Arras and Glastonbury cultures had brought this art with them to England and proceeded to elaborate it in a rather insular manner. Few illustrations of the British school of La Tène art can be cited from Scotland.

The earliest and finest is the chamfrein—the helmet for a war-horse—from Torrs in Kirkcudbrightshire (Pl. I). Its rich decoration, engraved and embossed, preserves reminiscences of the Greek palmette from which it is ultimately derived. But this has grown into a series of *répoussé* scrolls branching into leaves and terminating in engraved tendrils with spiral ends or figures like a bird's beak in relief. The nearest analogy to the style of the chamfrein is seen in the decoration of the famous shield from the River Witham, Lincolnshire. It shows connection with the Arras school rather than with that growing up in South-western England (Glastonbury style).

A chape from Glencotho, between the Upper Tweed and Clyde,[5] again illustrates the development of La Tène art along lines proper to the Arras school of the north-east. However,

---

[1] *PSAS.*, xlii, p. 332.   [2] *PSAS.*, lix, p. 117.
[3] *PSAS.*, lviii, p. 143.   [4] For details see Leeds, *Celtic Ornament.*
[5] *PSAS.*, xxxiv, p. 254.

on a collar dug up with a mirror from a bog in Balmaclellan parish (Kirkcudbrightshire),[1] the influence of the Glastonbury school is evident in the engraved " basket-work " filling of the scrolls. The object must indeed be an import from Southern England.

During the first century A.D. the effect of a new development, the outcome of an artist's experiments with compasses, is superbly illustrated by the relief ornament on a beaded torque from Lochar Moss, Dumfries. Such beaded torques are an old La Tène fashion, but the relief decoration is dominated by a purely British motive, the broken-backed scroll. Where the motive originated is uncertain. But on another product of the same school, a scabbard from Mortonhall at the foot of the Pentlands, the scrolls are combined with bosses (Fig. 65). The same combination is seen on a cleverly jointed hinged collar from Stichell in

FIG. 80.—Jointed armlet, Plumpton Castle, Kirkcudbright, after Anderson. ⅔.

Roxburghshire, and on a jointed armlet from Plumpton Castle, Kirkcudbrightshire (Fig. 80).[2] Such a combination of scrolls with bosses is a distinctively North British device, a speciality of the Arras school. It culminates in what Leeds terms the boss style which in his view flourished principally in the second century[3]; it is certainly superbly represented by native manufactures found in the second-century level at Traprain Law and in the Antonine fort at Newstead. According to Hawkes[4] the rise of the style may be traced even before the Conquest in A.D. 50, and in any case its presuppositions are found in the Arras culture, and its development is confined to the north of England and Scotland.

The boss style is handsomely illustrated by the bronze bit and

---

[1] Anderson, i, fig. 105.
[2] Anderson, i, figs. 112–13.
[3] *Celtic Ornament,* p. 117.
[4] Kendrick and Hawkes, p. 191.

five terrets from Middlebie, Dumfriesshire (Pl. XV). But the bit
of the same typological age from a moss near Burnswark is
decorated with red and yellow enamel [1] in a style and technique
that could be paralleled almost anywhere in Roman Britain.
The finest embodiment of the La Tène tradition of decoration
found in Scotland, however, exhibits a style divergent from
anything created in England, but recalling rather Irish and
North-east Scottish art. It is a gold sceptre-head found with
ribbon torques at Shaw Hill on the Upper Tweed (Fig. 81).
Its exact age is uncertain.

The ornate objects here enumerated can only have been the
property of notables, the insignia of chiefs. They must indeed
denote a sprinkling of " Keltic heroes " among the Iron Age
Lowlanders. And these " heroes " were evidently related to the
Arras charioteers. It is possibly they who organized the scattered

FIG. 81.—Gold sceptre-head, Shaw Hill, Peeblesshire, after Anderson. ½.

" Bronze Age " families and induced them to live in hill-top
towns and round forts. The relatively large proportion of ornate
insignia found just where small forts cluster most thickly—for
instance between the Upper Tweed and Clyde—is surely significant. The ornaments may, indeed, have belonged to the chiefs
among whose fortresses they were found. How far such chieftains
contributed to the diffusion of La Tène industries and objects,
like the ring-headed pin from Bonchester Hill, is quite
indeterminable.

The pre-Roman population of the Lowlands would then be
composed of Bronze Age urn-folk mingled with Hallstatt people
from Scarborough and perhaps leavened with rather hypothetical
La Tène chieftains from the Arras group. Such a composition
would approximate very closely to that of the hill-peoples of

[1] Leeds, p. 116.

Northern England whom the Romans lumped together under
the collective name of Brigantes.

The refugees living in the crannogs possessed a very similar
culture. But they appear with a full La Tène culture and complete mastery of iron ; it is impossible to imagine the building
of a crannog without iron axes. It would be natural to connect
the crannog-builders with Glastonbury, since that site is a typical
crannog settlement. But all the distinctive Glastonbury types—
textile implements, dice, dart-heads—so common in the castles,
are conspicuously lacking in the crannogs, as are all products
of the Glastonbury school of art. Yet the crannogs were occupied
at the same time as the castles. And their inhabitants were not
so miserable as to lack all art. Part of a beaded collar,[1] wood
carved in the La Tène tradition,[2] numerous imported ornaments,
like safety-pins and dress-fasteners, have been discovered. The
bit, shown in Fig. 66, is a link with the Arras complex, while
the rest of the Iron Age relics are such as might be expected
in a hill-top town. It will be recalled that there were " Hallstatt "
pile-dwellings in Yorkshire, some occupied into the Roman
period. The inhabitants of the crannogs of Ayrshire and Galloway
can then be regarded as offshoots from the Yorkshire folk,
already thoroughly saturated with the La Tène culture of Arras
before their arrival.

(iv) *The North-eastern Plains*

With the possible exception of the stone cups already mentioned, no explicitly pre-Roman relics of Iron Age type are
known from the fertile plains of Aberdeenshire and the adjoining
counties. Apart from Earth-houses, even Iron Age monuments
are rare here. The number of forts is surprisingly small. Some
of them[3] by their situation should be classed as hill-top
towns but in size and in the complexity of their defences resemble
rather the small forts of the Lowlands ; they may in fact be
late and built by refugees from beyond the Forth after the
Conquest. The scattered vitrified forts are doubtless outposts
of the Abernethy complex, but hardly suffice to dominate the
whole territory. Finally, forts like the Barmekin on the Hill of
Airlie, close to the stone circle of Old Keig near Alford, are

---

[1] Hyndford.   [2] Lochlee.
[3] E.g., Dunideer, the Barmekin of Echt, the Catertuns in Angus.

girt with a very roughly built wall, unsupported by any ditch; such walls might well have been erected by a Late Bronze Age population and are not much superior to the banks round the open villages.

In fact, it looks as if the open village with Earth-houses attached was the prevailing type of settlement throughout the Iron Age in this area. Those that survive on uncultivated moors of course only represent a tiny fraction of the total; Earth-houses, sometimes occurring in large groups as at Kildrummy, are all that remain of others. Does this type of unfortified settlement reflect a better unified political organization—an approximation to a State—or merely the greater security enjoyed by the inhabitants of regions remote from the theatre of the Romans' operations and the depredations of the castle-folk?

In the absence of distinctive relics nothing can be said as to affinities of the Aberdeenshire villagers. The pottery from a comparable village in Glenshee [1] resembles on the whole that from Covesea and Old Keig, though some sherds with an internally bevelled rim or a shoulder come closer to those from the lower levels on Traprain Law. Such features are not sufficient to determine whether the villagers should be regarded as descendants of the Late Bronze Age population of the north-east (Jarlshof–Old Keig group) or outposts from the kindred peoples of the Lowlands.

A survival of Bronze Age traditions of burial in Aberdeenshire may be inferred from objects of the Roman period found in a cist on the edge of a cairn at Cairnhill, Monquhitter.[2] In Strathmore (Angus), however, long cist-graves with extended skeletons, as in the Lowlands, occur in that period.[3] A whole cemetery of such adjoined the Earth-house at West Grange of Conan.[4]

It looks, then, as if south of the Moray Firth the Late Bronze Age population that had once extended continuously from Jarlshof to Old Keig lived on only superficially affected by the Iron Age invasions of the coast and the subsequent expeditions of the Romans. To that population could be ascribed both the Earth-houses and the stone cups, the distribution of which bears no significant relation to that of forts.

The individuality of the area is in any case attested by the

[1] *PSAS.*, lxvii, p. 197.   [2] *PSAS.*, xxxvi, p. 675.
[3] *PSAS.*, xx, pp. 136–9.   [4] *PSAS.*, iv, p. 495.

second century A.D. in its art. When its inhabitants mastered
the technique of enamelling and acquired the skill to cast objects
of parade, they produced forms and a style unparalleled further
south.   These are in particular extremely heavy and clumsy
penannular or spiral armlets of bronze decorated with enamel
plates or studs and patterns cast in relief and engraved.[1] Though
one example comes from Northern Ireland and another from
Roxburghshire the remaining penannular armlets all come from
nine sites between the Forth and Strathbrora. Spiral armlets have
been found at four sites between the Tay and the Moray Firth,
including the Earth-house at West Grange of Conan (Fig. 82),
but there is also one from Stanhope on the Upper Tweed.
Leeds [2] has suggested a date in the first or second century for

FIG. 82.—Armlet, West Grange of Conan, after Anderson. ⅘.

these armlets and has compared their decoration to that of the
Shaw Hill sceptre-head and some gold ornaments from Ireland.

NOTE.—Descriptions of the relics from, and excavations at, the most important
sites here mentioned are published as follows :—

Gallic and Vitrified Forts.
    Abernethy (Castlelaw), Perths., *PSAS.*, xxxiii, p. 29.
    Dunagoil, Bute, *TBNHS.*, 1914–15, p. 74 ; 1925, plates.
    Duntroon, Crinan, *PSAS.*, xxxix, p. 275.
    Dun Fheurain, Gallanach, Oban, *PSAS.*, xxix, p. 281.
Castle province.
    Galloway and Argyll.
    Castlehaven, Borgue, Kirkcud., *PSAS.*, xli, p. 78.
    Borness Cave, Borgue, Kirkcud., *PSAS.*, x, pp. 480 ff.
    Castlehill, Dalry, Ayrs.—perhaps a " small fort "—*PSAS.*, liii, p. 124.
    Ardifuar, Crinan, *PSAS.*, xxxix, p. 260.
    Druim an Duin, Crinan, *PSAS.*, xxxix, p. 286.

[1] Anderson, i, figs. 115–140.   [2] *Celtic Ornament*, pp. 126 ff.

Brochs : Skye.
  Dun Beag, *PSAS.*, lv, p. 110.
  Dun an Iardhard, *PSAS.*, xlix, p. 57.
West Inverness., Dun Telve, Glenelg, *PSAS*, l, p. 252.
Shetland : Jarlshof, *PSAS.*, xli, p. 30.
Orkney : Aikerness, Mainland, N.M.
  Ayre, Mainland, *PSAS.*, xlviii, p. 36.
  Burray, Mainland, Anderson, i, p. 236.
  Burrian, N. Ronaldshay, *Arch. Scot.*, v, p. 340.
  Burwick, Mainland, Anderson, i, p. 238.
  Harray, Mainland, Anderson, i, p. 236.
  Lamaness, Sanday, N.M.
  Lingrow, Mainland, Anderson, i, p. 243.
  Okstrow, Mainland, Anderson, i, p. 240.
Caithness : Bowermadden, Anderson, i, p. 232.
  Everley, *PSAS.*, xxxv, p. 142.
  Kettleburn, Anderson, i, p. 209.
  Keiss—Harbour, *PSAS.*, xxxv, p. 122.
    Road, *PSAS.*, xxxv, p. 135.
    Wester, *PSAS.*, xxxv, p. 120.
    White Gate, *PSAS.*, xxxv, p. 127.
  Nybster, *PSAS.*, xxxv, p. 140.
  Old Stirkoke, Anderson, i, p. 232.
  Ousedale Burn, *PSAS.*, xxvi, p. 355.
  Skirza Head, *PSAS.*, xxxv, p. 145.
  Yarrows, Anderson, i, p. 223.
Sutherland : Carn Liath, Dunrobbin, *Arch. Scot.*, v, p. 105.
  Cinn Trolla, Kintradwell, *Arch. Scot.*, v, p. 95.
On Tay : Hurley Hawkin, Liff., *PSAS.*, vi, p. 210.
  Laws of Monifieth—a doubtful broch standing in a complicated stone fort,
    possibly vitrified, that may be earlier and belong to the Abernethy
    complex—*PSAS.*, iii, p. 440.
On Gala Water : Torwoodlee, *PSAS.*, xxvi, p. 75.

Dwellings : Lewis : Galson, *PSAS.*, lviii, p. 194.
  N. Uist : Bac Mhic Connain, *PSAS.*, lxvi, p. 50.
    Garry Iochdrach, *PSAS.*, lxvi, p. 41.
    Foshigarry, *PSAS.*, lxv, p. 320.
  Orkney : Howmae, N. Ronaldshay, *PSAS.*, xix, p. 30 ; xxiv, p. 455.

Hill-top towns.
  Traprain Law, E. Lothian, *PSAS.*, xlix, l, liv–lviii.
  Bonchester Hill, Roxburghs., *PSAS.*, xliv, p. 233.
  Burnswark, Dumfries., *PSAS.*, xxxiii, p. 247.

Small Forts.
  Castlelaw, Glencorse, Midlothian, *PSAS.*, lxvii, p. 283.
  Earnsheugh, Coldingham, Berwicks., *PSAS.*, lxvi, p. 180.
  The Camps, Edgerston, Roxburghs. (relics at Edgerston House).

Crannogs, Buston, Ayrs., Munro, p. 195.
  Dowalton Loch, *ACAG.*, v, p. 85.
  Lochlee, Ayrs., Munro, pp. 77 ff.
  Lochspouts, Ayrs., Munro, pp. 158 f., 305 f.
  Hyndford, near Lanark, *PSAS.*, xxxiii, p. 382.

XII

SCOTLAND BEFORE THE SCOTS

HERE prehistory should emerge into history : the groups, distinguished by archæology, should be identified with the tribes and peoples who figure in the written record ; their languages should be recoverable from place-names ; their monuments and relics should be explained by reference to folk-traditions. In Scotland too much must not be expected in this direction. The last clearly defined prehistoric period is separated from that described in the earliest coherent native sources and remembered vaguely in popular legend by a Dark Age four or five centuries long.[1] When the veil lifts between the eighth and tenth centuries, Scotland has already received new colonists— Scots, Norsemen, Angles—has changed her religion and, in parts, her language and has been divided up into radically new States.

A few of the prehistoric sites were certainly occupied during the Dark Age—the Mote of Mark, Dunadd, and perhaps some crannogs in the south, many brochs and wheel-dwellings in the far north. But the relics attributable to this period are few and undecisive, and in the north it is doubtful whether the occupation continued down to the time of the Norse colonization described in the sagas.[2] For the rest, the Dark Age is represented by a handful of stray ornaments and a few Early Christian chapels and gravestones that illustrate the spread of a new religion rather than the survival of old traditions. Between the prehistoric record, ending in the fourth century, and the historic an unbridged chasm yawns.

Casual references in Roman writers give us glimpses of Scotland at intervals between A.D. 80 and 400. But each scene thrown upon the screen, as from a discontinuous film, presents new names and fresh groupings of peoples. Such imply tribal movements of a sort which archæology could only hope to grasp after a far more systematic investigation of the Iron Age monuments than

[1] " Gaelic Scotland lacks the historical background that can only be given by a continuous literary tradition," *SGS.*, ii, p. 104.
[2] Brøgger, *Ancient Emigrants*, p. 63.

anything that has hitherto been attempted. At the moment all that can be expected from the literary record is help in the designation in linguistic terms of some of the groups identified archæologically.

The implications of such names must not be misunderstood; they are philological, or at best political, and have no racial significance. They tell us nothing about the physical type of the people and may apply only to small ruling castes who can impose their language and their culture on a subject population. Kelts [1] are people who spoke a Keltic language—a branch of the Indo-European (or Aryan) family of languages; they may be blonde or dark, tall or short, round-headed or long-headed. So Brythons are just those Kelts who changed the Indo-European q-sound into a p, while Goidels preserved the q as a guttural. But such groups may possess a material culture as individual as their language. Throughout Europe the La Tène culture coincides with Keltic speech though not all Kelts need have possessed a La Tène culture.

Scotland takes her name from the Scotti, Goidels from Ireland. But these were late arrivals. In fourth-century writers Scotti seems still to mean exclusively Irish; the first Scottic settlement in Argyll, perhaps at Dunadd, is traditionally dated to A.D. 500. And even in the time of Bede their dominions are supposed to have been restricted to Argyll, though an extension across the Central Valley to Angus is possible. The Western Lowlands were Anglian or Brythonic; East Scotland and the far north were in possession of the Picts.

The linguistic and cultural affinities of the Picts are the subjects of bitter and prolonged controversy. Succession to the kingship was apparently not transmitted to the king's son, and the queen normally sought a husband in a different community—tribe or clan.[2] The system of transmission through the female is familiar to ethnographers under the name of *matriarchy* and is often combined with *exogamy*—obligatory marriage outside the community— and totemism—the cult by the clansmen of some animal or plant from which the clan is supposed to be mystically descended and from which it actually takes its name. Traces of totemism can, in fact, be discerned in the tribal or clan names of the Picts. And the latter used the skin-boat or coracle. Matriarchy, exogamy, and totemism, are not normal in Indo-European societies, and

---

[1] Huberts, *The Celts*, p. 33.   [2] Fraser, *SGS.*, ii, p. 179, questions even this.

the skin-boat seems appropriate to the Esquimaux and perhaps to the prehistoric "Arctic" folk of North Europe.

Partly for these reasons many historians have regarded the Picts as pre-Keltic—descendants of Mediterraneans or "Iberians" or allied to the Esquimaux and the Arctic peoples of Scandinavia. Leading authorities like Macalister[1] and Pokorny[2] still hold this view, but the tendency among most philologists to-day is to treat the Picts as Keltic; many will admit a connection with the Pictones of Gaul who have given their name to the district of Poitou. But at this point agreement ceases altogether. Diack[3] regards the Picts as Goidelic, rather more numerous voices designate them Brythons.[4] Watson[5] denies the existence of Picts in Ireland; the weight of opinion, ancient and modern, admits[6] the identity of the Picts with the Irish Cruithni. But Cruithni is merely the Goidelic form of a word which in Brythonic would have appeared as Pretani (modern Welsh, Pryden). This is just the name of the people who gave their name to the British Isles which are called the Pretanic islands by Greek authors[7] as early as the fourth century B.C. Whether Cruithni represents a Goidelic translation of an original Pretani or whether the latter name is itself a translation of an original Qretani by Brythonic invaders of Britain or even Gaulish neighbours is not thereby determined.[8]

The Picts, who in English, Irish, and Norse sources appear as the leading people in North Britain, are, however, mentioned by Roman writers first in A.D. 297. Allied with the Irish Scots they appear thereafter as pirates from the north, "swarming from their coracles". Ammianus in the middle of the fourth century mentions two main groups of Picts—the Verturiones whose name survives in Fortrenn, and the Dicalydones. The latter may incorporate the Caledonii, who in the second and early third centuries were the leading nation north of the Forth. But even these are not mentioned explicitly by Tacitus to whom Galgacus' followers are just Britanni.

---

[1] *Ireland in Pre-Celtic Times*, p. 253.

[2] *History of Ireland*, p. 16.

[3] *Revue celtique*, xxxviii, p. 119; Fraser, *SGS.*, ii, p. 200, adopts a sceptical attitude.

[4] Cf. Hubert, *The Celts*, pp. 203 ff.

[5] *Celtic Place-names*, p. 11; cf. Fraser, *SGS.*, ii, p. 176, n. 1.

[6] So MacNeil (*Phases of Irish History*), Hubert, Loth, Macalister, Pokorny, etc.

[7] Pytheas (of Marseilles); his work is only known through later writers. Spellings vary between Πρετανικαί and Πρεττανικαί.

[8] Loth, *Rev. celt.*, xxxviii, p. 281.

The tribal and place-names recorded by Ptolemy can mostly be explained satisfactorily as Brythonic.[1] But a few, notably Bodotria (the Forth) and Ebudæ (the Hebrides) might be pre-Keltic. And Diack [2] maintains that Devana (the Don) and other names from Pictavia must always have been Goidelic, and have not been Gaelicized from older Brythonic forms. On the other hand, Watson adduces many instances of the translations of originally Brythonic names into Goidelic by the Scots. When experts differ so completely, the archæologist must walk warily. But fortunately in some crucial cases there is less uncertainty.

Epidion Akron, the Mull of Kintyre, is unambiguously a Brythonic word.[3] And the Epidii who gave their name to the cape must be a branch of our castle-builders. The Cornavii, who occupied part of the castle-province in Caithness or Suther-land, are a branch of the British Cornavii, established in or about the modern Cheshire. (Incidentally the latter lived not so far from the Yorkshire caves which produced relics of our castle culture, and a weaving comb was picked up on the coast of Cheshire itself.) So the Dumnonii of Ayrshire must be related to those of Devon. These were Brythonic, and archæologically their territory falls well within the Iron Age B or Glastonbury province. The Keltic character of the castle-builders is thus far established, and it is probable that all were Brythonic.

Watson [4] has drawn attention to an indication of the presence of Kelts in the castle area at a still earlier date. The name of the Orkney Islands, Orcades, is undoubtedly Keltic. In Irish literature the islands are called Inse Orc, Isles of the Orcs, i.e. Boars, while Inse Cat, Isles of the Cats—Shetland or Caithness—are also mentioned. Both names recur in Ireland [5] as clan or tribal appellations. Watson accordingly concludes that the Orcs were just the totemic boar clan, presumably of the Picts. Now the name appears to go back to Pytheas, a Massiliote who travelled in the West shortly before 300 B.C. If that be true and if the name Orcas be really Keltic, there must have been Kelts in Orkney by the fourth century B.C.

[1] Watson, pp. 15 ff.
[2] *Rev. celt.*, xxxviii, p. 119; Fraser, *SGS.*, ii, p. 187, criticizes Diack's interpretation.
[3] But it might be a translation of a Goidelic name by Ptolemy's informant, not what the actual inhabitants used.
[4] *Place-names*, pp. 6, 60 ff.
[5] Macalister, *IPCT.*, p. 250.

Watson [1] then proposes to identify the Picts with the broch-builders. Restricted in the first two centuries of our era to the far north, they would subsequently have spread southward. The Lowland brochs would be memorials of this descent of the Picts. Watson's thesis is hard to reconcile with the archæological data. The broch culture was already in decay by the time the Picts begin to figure in literature; the Roman relics from Torwoodlee broch in the Lowlands imply its foundation before A.D. 100,[2] two centuries too early for the theory; but no broch need be older than 100 B.C. Hence the Kelts responsible for the name Orkney in the fourth century B.C. can only have been the " Late Bronze Age invaders " who were in occupation of Jarlshof down to the coming of the broch-builders.

Now a good case could be made out for identifying such Late Bronze Age invaders with the Picts if there were Picts in Ireland, i.e. provided the equation of Picts with Cruithni hold good. For the " invaders " occupied Aberdeenshire, which county was quite as Pictish in historical times as the far north. The same people are recognizable in Ireland both by pottery and the Earth-houses.[3] And finally, Earth-houses are commoner in the territory of the Pictones than in any other part of Gaul. So that, wherever Picts or their relatives are attested historically, we find archæologically our Late Bronze Age invaders, the Jarlshof complex. The two terms of the proposition could with a little ingenuity be made to coincide completely by the inclusion of Cornwall, the remaining region where Earth-houses are numerous. Pretani is the equivalent of Cruithni, i.e. Picts. But it is notorious that a country is often called after a tribe inhabiting an important part of it. But to the Greek and Gaulish traders of the fourth century B.C., the most important part of the Pretanic Islands would have been Cornwall, the source of tin. Hence there would have been Pretani, i.e. Picts, in Cornwall too.

Moreover, we had to admit both at Jarlshof and Old Keig an intermixture between the Late Bronze Age invaders and the earlier inhabitants of collectivist tradition and " Iberian " affinities. The peculiar relations between these and the " invaders ", implied by Old Keig where the " foreign " chief is buried in a monument of the aboriginal cult,[4] would be most

[1] *Op. cit.*, pp. 56 ff.
[2] Above, p. 205.
[3] Above, p. 188.
[4] Above, p. 176.

easily explained by the sort of matriarchy and exogamy attested for the historical Picts.

It seems, then, virtually certain that the Late Bronze Age invaders, both in Shetland and Aberdeenshire, were Kelts, either Brythonic or Goidelic. Now English and Irish prehistorians are anxious to derive the ancestors of the Irish Goidels from the Continent via Britain. Peake [1] and Mahr,[2] in particular, identify the " sword-bearers " who first introduced the socketed axe and slashing sword into England with the Goidels. Apart from the Late Bronze Age invaders of the North no such intruders have yet been recognized in Scotland. Still, the first settlers on Traprain Law might have been descendants of the Yorkshire branch of such a group, did it exist. And Elgee [3] has adduced ingenious, but not altogether convincing, arguments for regarding the Brigantes as Goidelic. In that case, since our Lowlanders are not easily distinguishable from Brigantes archæologically, a Goidelic element might be admitted in Southern Scotland also ; Goidelic names of persons and places occur in the Lowlands in pre-Scottic times.[4] The Brythonic names would then have to be attributed to the sprinkling of La Tène heroes from the Arras group and the folk movements of the Roman period. The Arras charioteers can be identified safely with the Parisii who were unquestionably Brythonic.

This argument presupposes that the Picts were Goidelic as Diack maintains. It is not yet demonstrable archæologically. Indeed, it requires a rather closer relationship between the first townsmen of Traprain and the people of Old Keig and Jarlshof than would have been inferred from the relics alone. But the only alternative, if pre-Scottic Goidels must be found in North Britain, would be to identify them with the Beaker-folk, as was done by Abercromby,[5] whom Loth and Hubert [6] still follow. That is, indeed, a desperate expedient since in Ireland, the Goidelic land *par excellence*, the Beaker-folk never established a footing.

The positive results of the foregoing investigation might then be summarized as follows. Scotland was first colonized in Atlantic times by small bands of fishers and hunters, who arrived by sea from the south-west and from the Baltic respectively,

---

[1] *The Bronze Age and the Celtic World.*
[2] Article " Archæology ". [3] *North-East Yorkshire*, p. 225.
[4] Personal names of fifth century, *SGS.*, ii, p. 228 ; but they may belong to missionaries.
[5] *BAP.*, ii, p. 99. [6] *Op. cit.*, p. 171.

and led a sort of strand-looper existence along the beaches of the west coast and the Forth estuary. Rather later, tiny groups of hunters using pigmy flints filtered in through the forests from Northern England.

A regular colonizing movement also by sea began perhaps as early as 2000 B.C., but certainly before 1500 B.C.[1] " Neolithic " peasants of the English Windmill Hill culture spread all along the western coasts and round Cape Wrath. They were led by chieftains of southern, Iberic, origin, endowed with supernatural powers, who were interred in monumental tombs. The little groups would be organized in exogamous clans such as survived into historical times among the Picts. Though devoted to a primitive agriculture, they created a maritime civilization which embraced Ireland and even touched Shetland and Scandinavia. The peasants occupied every patch of land on the west coast which was not too heavily wooded nor too swampy, as well as the more open, wind-swept tracts of the Hebrides, Orkney, Caithness, and Sutherland. They spread inland from the west coasts to the Cheviots, the Lammermuirs, and across to the Tay basin; while from their bases in the north they crossed the Moray Firth to the mouths of the Nairn and Ness and the coasts of Aberdeenshire.

But during the same centuries Beaker-folk, coasting up from England or crossing the North Sea from the Low Countries, were settling along our eastern seaboard. These round-headed invaders were more pastoral and more warlike than the " Neolithic " peasants and perhaps more worldly, more ready to appreciate metal when it arrived. Though related to the Battle-axe people of the Continent, whom some authorities regard as Indo-European,[2] they can hardly be termed Kelts, and had better remain nameless. From the coasts they spread inland, occupying the whole of Aberdeenshire where they retained their identity till the Late Bronze Age; some may have crossed from the Lothians to the west coasts. In any case, other colonists of the same group followed the route of the Neolithic settlers up the west coasts even to Skye and the Hebrides. Owing to the matriarchal exogamous organization of the " Neolithic " communities of the west and north, Beaker-folk replaced the old " Iberic " chiefs and

---

[1] The higher dating advocated by the author in *Antiquity*, 1932 (p. 185, table) seems less probable in view of revisions of Ægean chronology proposed by Åberg (*Bronzezeitliche und früheisenzeitliche Chronologie*, iv) and Reinecke (*Germania*, 1929–1930, p. 59). The Scottish evidence is all in favour of minimum datings.

[2] Childe, *The Aryans*, p. 195.

obtained admission to the communal tombs. But in the Hebrides
and Orkney and in the Nairn–Ness valley, the old traditions
maintained their dominance. From the last-named region the
Neolithic cultivators spread into the Spey valley and eventually
into Aberdeenshire, preserving their predominantly agricultural
economy and many of the old rites till late in the Bronze Age.[1]

The west, though dominated now by the Beaker-folk, maintained its traditional connections with Ireland and the south-west.
Round Loch Crinan and the Forth of Clyde new immigrants
from that quarter may even have superseded the Beaker-folk
in the chieftainship. In any case, bronze tools and weapons
and then bronze-smiths found their way into Scotland from this
side, and rudimentary trade relations were established with
England as well as Ireland. Eventually, a few objects characteristic
of the Middle Bronze Age industry came into use south of the
Southern Uplands, but farther north primitive flat axes and
triangular daggers were still made and competed with Neolithic
tools till the Late Bronze Age.

Before 750 B.C. a reorganization of the metal industry throughout Europe and the reopening of old trade routes allowed new
tools and weapons, new techniques, and new craftsmen to spread
over Great Britain. But the old, predominantly pastoral, economy
persisted, and more attention was still paid to the performance
of ceremonies and the erection of sepulchral monuments than
to the development of a mundane economy.

A change was initiated by the Keltic immigration. The first
bands of Kelts were in occupation of Orkney and the north by
the fourth century B.C. Though still retaining bronze tools
and weapons of Britannico-Hibernian pattern, they probably
introduced new breeds of cattle and more intensive agriculture.
They may have come from Southern England through Ireland,
but they may also have followed an inverse route starting between
the Rhine and the Weser [2] and making the northern isles a base
for descents upon Ireland and Cornwall. In any case they easily
blended with the " Neolithic " inhabitants, thanks to the latter's
matriarchal organization, and formed the nucleus of the
historical Picts.

Other waves of Keltic invasion soon followed. By 200 B.C.

[1] Above, p. 175.
[2] Hubert's arguments for locating the cradle of the Goeidels and Picts here are
enticing ; Weser and other river-names are Keltic.

groups, probably Brythonic,[1] crossing the North Sea from Northern Gaul, had landed near the mouth of the Tay and round the head of the Moray Firth and were spreading across to the Firth of Clyde and the western coasts of Inverness and Argyll. Contingents, allied to the Brigantes of North Britain, perhaps already led by Brythonic chiefs from the Parisii, came to reinforce the older inhabitants of the Lowlands. And in the first century B.C. Brythons from the south-west spread all along the west coasts and round Cape Wrath, precisely as the Neolithic colonists had done in the second millennium B.C. Each petty chief seized upon a strip of suitable land for his retainers to cultivate, and built him a castle to overawe the former inhabitants and serve as a base for raids on the rich lands of Ireland, England, and the Scottish Lowlands. In the far north the Picts became for a time subject to these Brythonic conquerors.

The later Keltic invaders introduced regular iron working as well as new industries. With the aid of iron tools they began clearing and draining the land, rendering possible an intensification of agriculture and a rapid growth in the population. But no State emerged ; constant warfare and internecine feuds prevented the growth of any higher civilization. And into this welter of barbarism were hurled the shattered remnants of tribes, broken by the Roman Conquest. And the legions followed, impotent to establish effectively a *pax romana* in Caledonia, but destructive enough in their " punitive expeditions " and " measures of pacification ".

[1] Most La Tène Kelts were Brythonic.

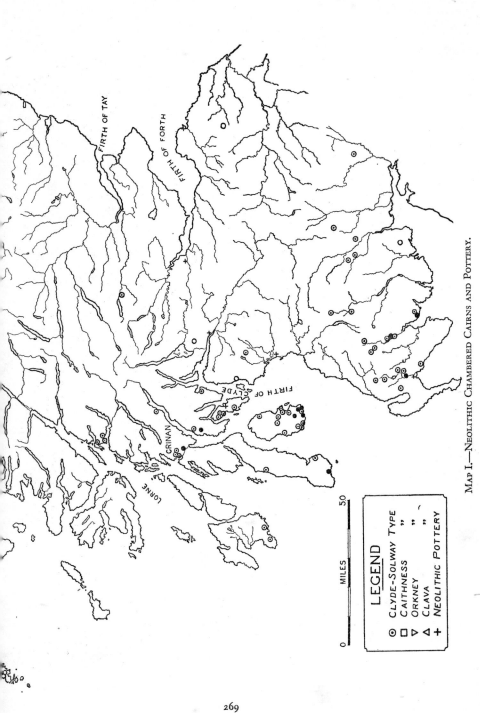

MAP I.—NEOLITHIC CHAMBERED CAIRNS AND POTTERY.

FIRTH OF TAY

FIRTH OF FORTH

FIRTH OF CLYDE

CRINAN

LORNE

MILES

0   50

LEGEND

⊙ CLYDE-SOLWAY TYPE
□ CAITHNESS   ,,
▽ ORKNEY   ,,
△ CLAVA   ,,
+ NEOLITHIC POTTERY

269

MORAY FIRTH

270

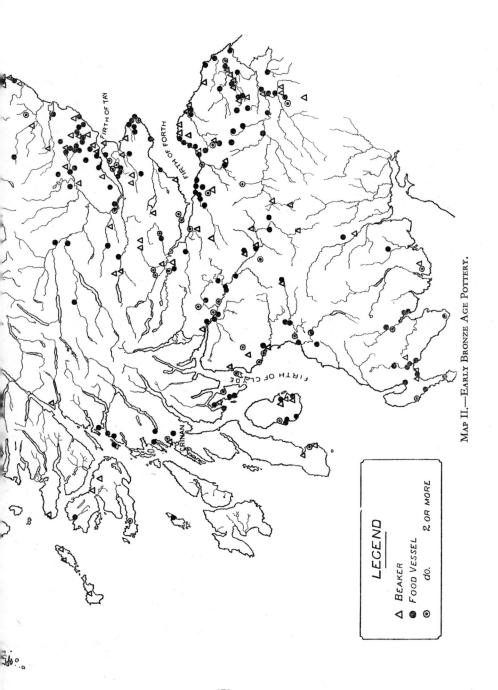

FIRTH OF TAY

FIRTH OF FORTH

FIRTH OF CLYDE

CRINAN

MAP II.—EARLY BRONZE AGE POTTERY.

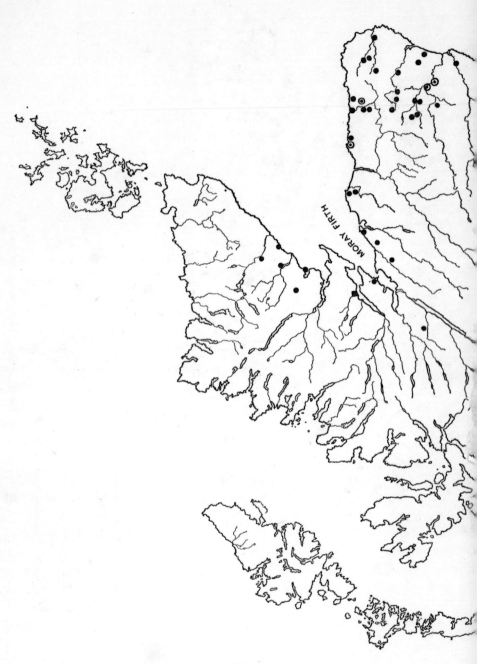

MORAY FIRTH

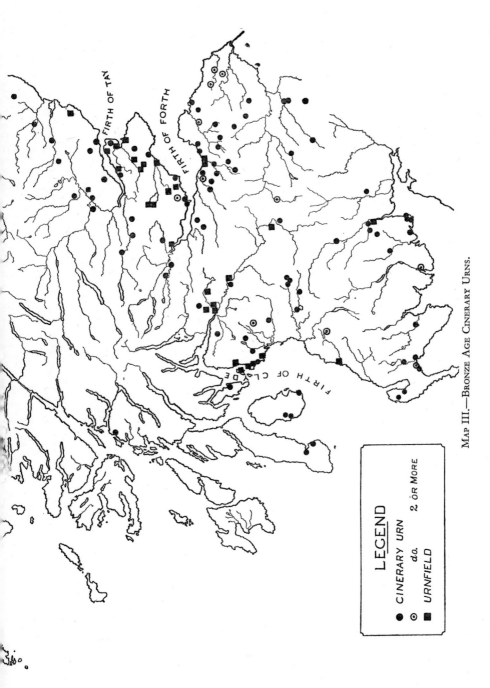

MAP III.—BRONZE AGE CINERARY URNS.

LEGEND

CINERARY URN
● do.   2 OR MORE
⊙ URNFIELD
■

FIRTH OF TAY

FIRTH OF FORTH

FIRTH OF CLYDE

MORAY FIRTH

274

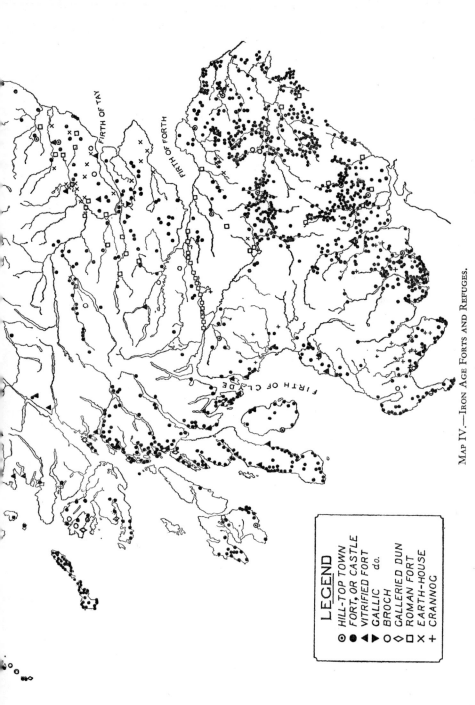

LEGEND

- ⊙ HILL-TOP TOWN
- ● FORT, OR CASTLE
- ◀ ▶ VITRIFIED FORT
- GALLIC   do.
- ○ BROCH
- ◇ GALLERIED DUN
- □ ROMAN FORT
- ✕ EARTH-HOUSE
- + CRANNOG

FIRTH OF TAY

FIRTH OF FORTH

FIRTH OF CLYDE

Map IV.—Iron Age Forts and Refuges.

INDEX

Printed in Great Britain by Stephen Austin & Sons, Ltd., Hertford.